Jason Francisco

ALIVE AND DESTROYED

A Meditation on the Holocaust in Time

Daylight

Cofounders: Taj Forer and Michael Itkoff
Creative Director: Ursula Damm
Copy Editor: Gabrielle Fastman

ISBN: 978-1-954119-02-4

Printed by Ofset Yapimevi, Turkey

Daylight Books
E-mail: info@daylightbooks.org
Web: www.daylightbooks.org

For A.F.—with love—

PROLOGUE

In advance of the book itself, it is the Yiddish poet Arn Tsaytlin (Aaron Zeitlin) who comes to mind, and a poem of his titled "Six Lines." It is a poem I find crushing and personal—two qualities without which, to paraphrase my friend Alexander Nemerov, a poem has no need for being.

The first three lines speak from and also of a particular artistic self-consciousness: solitary, alone, forsaken, deeply creative, tasked with futile work. These lines then give themselves to a line in which nothing is written, a line of withdrawnness, retraction of speech—from which comes the poem's second half, three weighty and enigmatic statements, or proclamations, or enunciations.

I cannot help but see the middle emptiness as an essential part of the poem's meaning, a silent seventh line in a six-line poem, and for this reason, I am moved to translate it seven times. Seven: for the six days of creation and for one of ceasing, and for the annihilation, the creation's counterpoint in history, one line for each of the six million, the middle for the difference between aliveness and destroyedness.

Zeks Shures

Kh'veys: keyner darf mikh nisht af ot dem oylem,
Mikh, verter-betler af dem yidish beys-oylem.
Ver darf a lid—un nokh dertsu af yidish?

Nor bloyz dos hofnongloze af der erd iz sheyn
Un getlekh iz nor dos nos muz fargeyn.
Un nor hakhnoeh iz meridesh.

זעקס שורותֿ

כ'ווייס: קיינער דאַרף מיך נישט אויף אָט דעם עולם:
מיך, ווערטער-בעטלער אויף דעם ייִדישן בית-עולם.
ווער דאַרף אַ ליד – און נאָך דערצו אויף ייִדיש?

נאָר בלויז דאָס האָפֿנונגסלאָזע אויף דער ערד איז שיין,
און געטלעך איז נאָר דאָס, וואָס מוז פֿאַרגיין,
און נאָר הכנעה איז מרידהיש.

1.

i know: no one needs me in this world,
me: a word-scavenger in the jewish graveyard.
who needs a poem anyway—especially in yiddish?

but only the hopeless things of the earth are beautiful,
and only the fugitive things are holy,
and only humility rebels.

2.

i know: no need for me in this world.
me: a word-beggar for eternity.
who needs a poem—even a yiddish one?

but on this earth, beauty comes only when hope departs,
and holiness appears only in its own passing,
and only meekness musters rebellion.

3.

this is what i know: the others are enough, no need for me.
me: a word-beggar where the jewish is dead and buried.
who needs a song—of yiddish?

but here, only what no longer longs is beautiful,
and only what dims and ceases finds god,
and only what bows down rises up.

4.

what i know: even eternity doesn't need me.
me: the one scavenging songs in the jewish burying ground.
who needs any poem—much less a jewish one?

but here, only what lives without hope is beautiful.
and only what goes missing is of-god.
and only in gentleness, defiance.

5.

what i know of myself: there's no place for me where the rest of them meet.
me: pleading for words in the boneyard of yiddish.
who needs a poem—to say nothing of a jewish poem?

but only the lorn things of this earth are beautiful,
and only what flees stays with god,
and only the meek break free.

6.

i know: no one needs me on this earth or on that one.
me, the one gone begging for poems in the jewish infinity.
who needs a poem anyway—let alone from yiddish?

but in this world, only what outlasts hope is beautiful,
and only what lasts in transience is holy,
and only the humbled revolt.

7.

what i know: no one needs me in this world.
me: the one pleading for words from the jewish cemetery.
who needs a poem at all—yiddish aside?

but only the hopeless of the earth are beautiful,
and only the disappeared are holy,
and only the broken resist.

"Earth! Do not cover my
blood, and let there be no
resting place for my cry!"

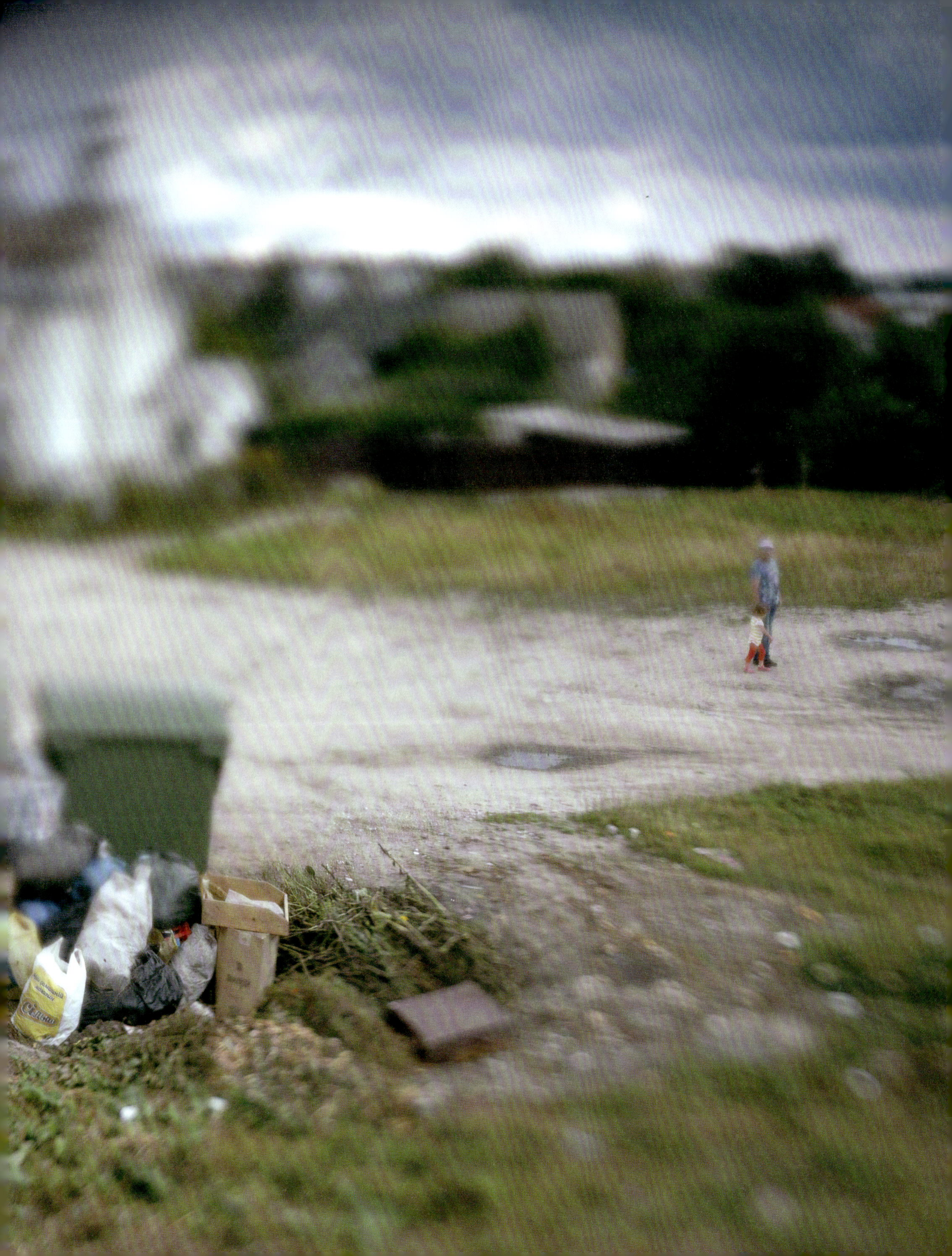

Plate 2

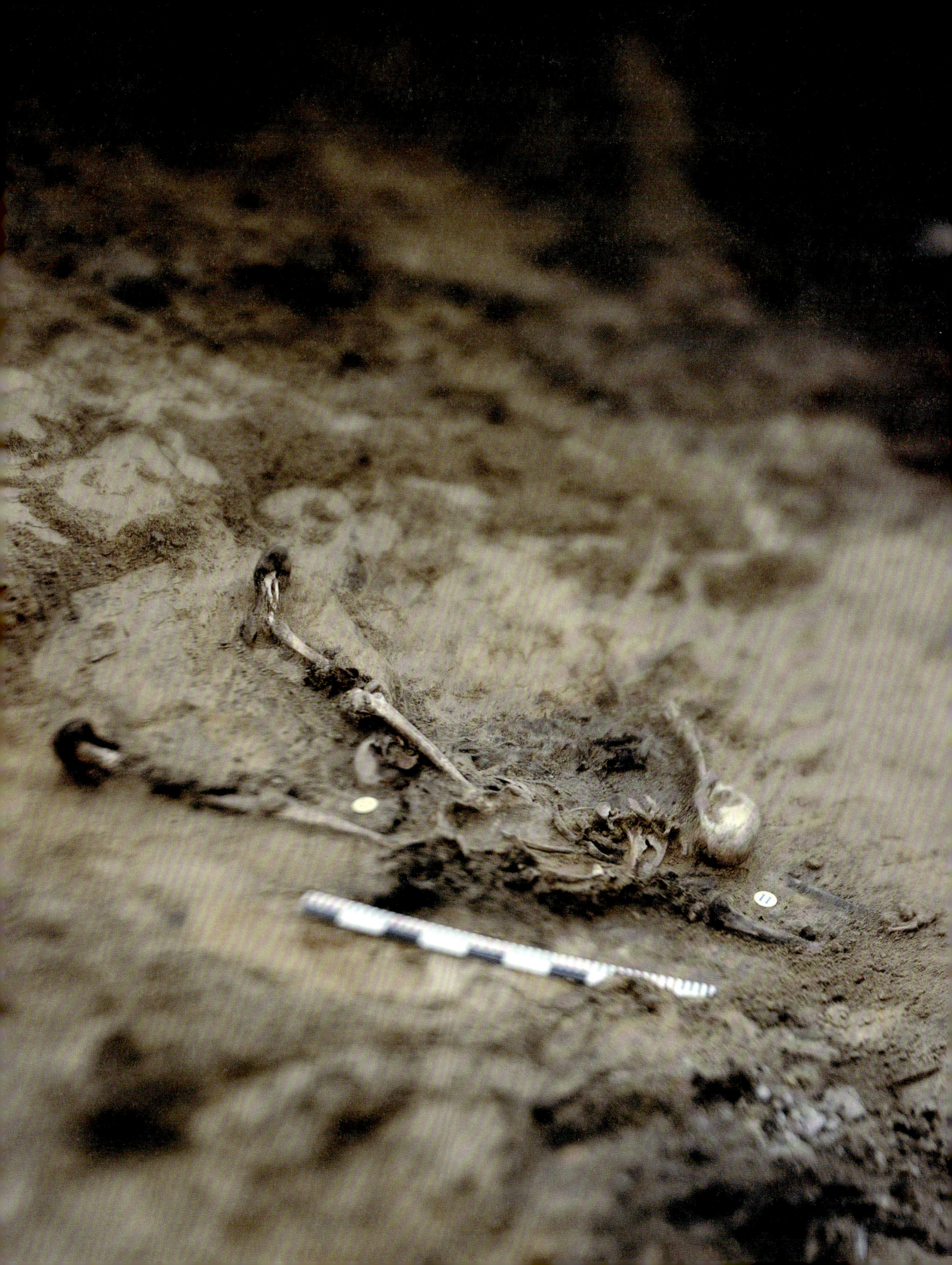

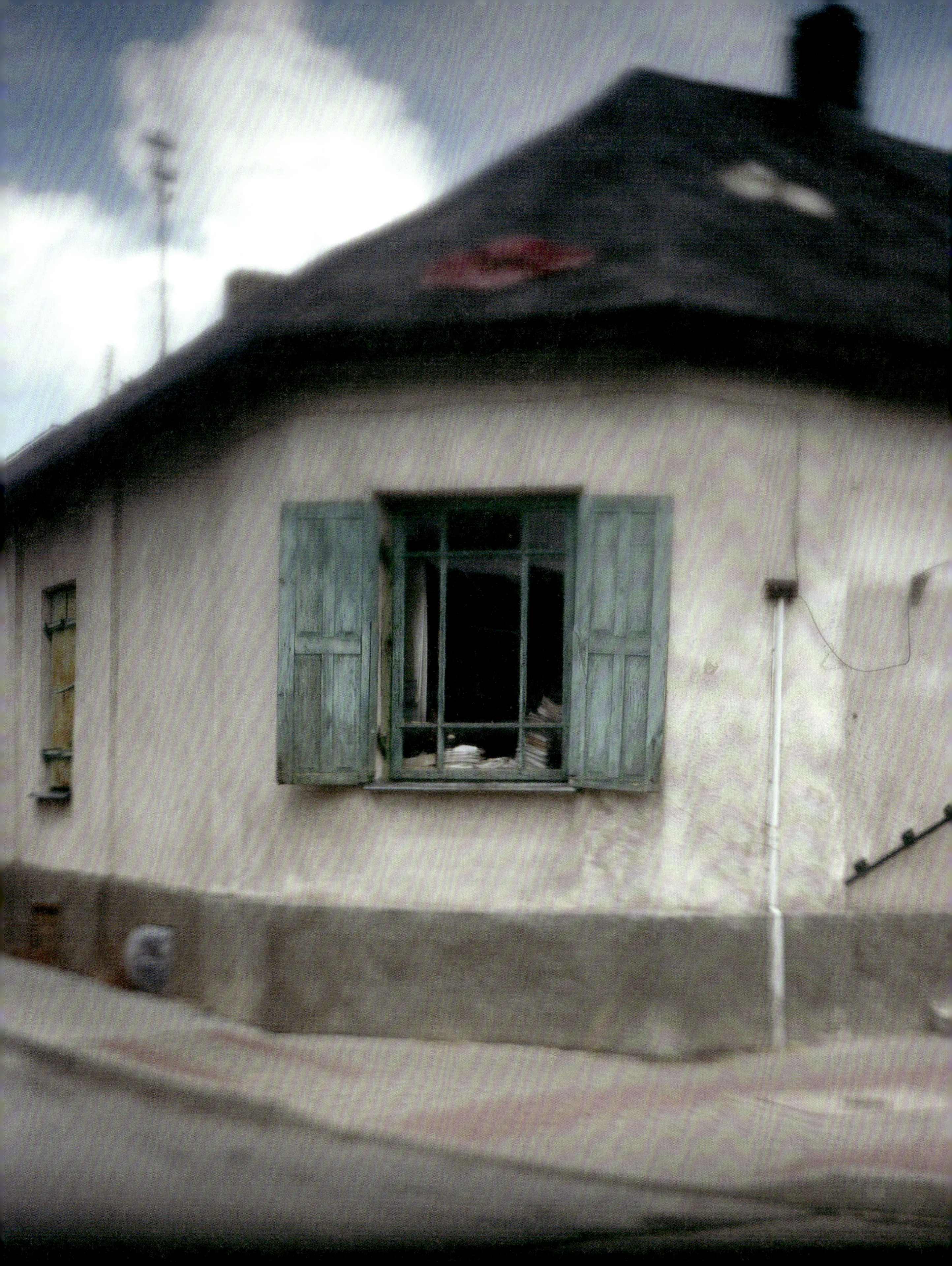

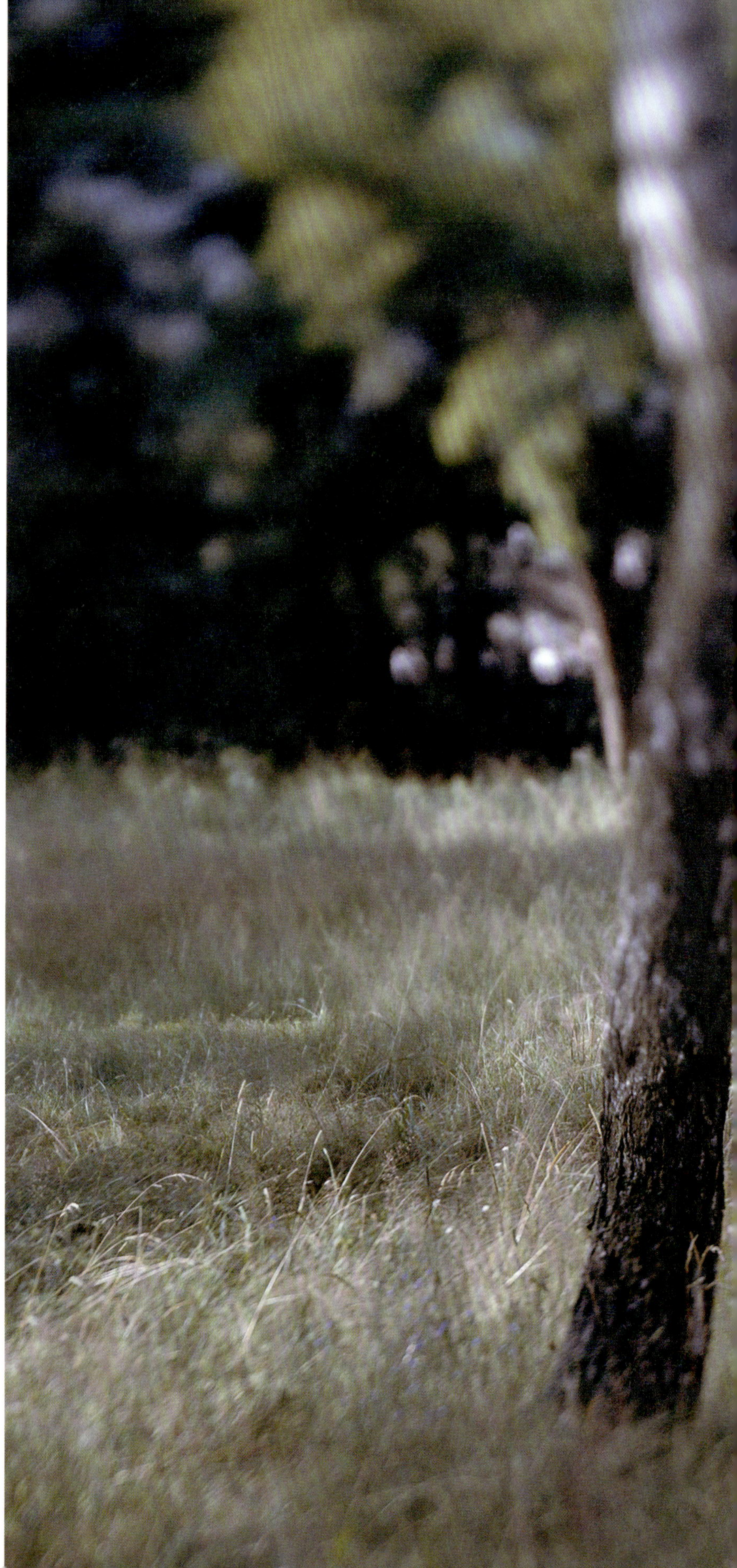

Plate 4

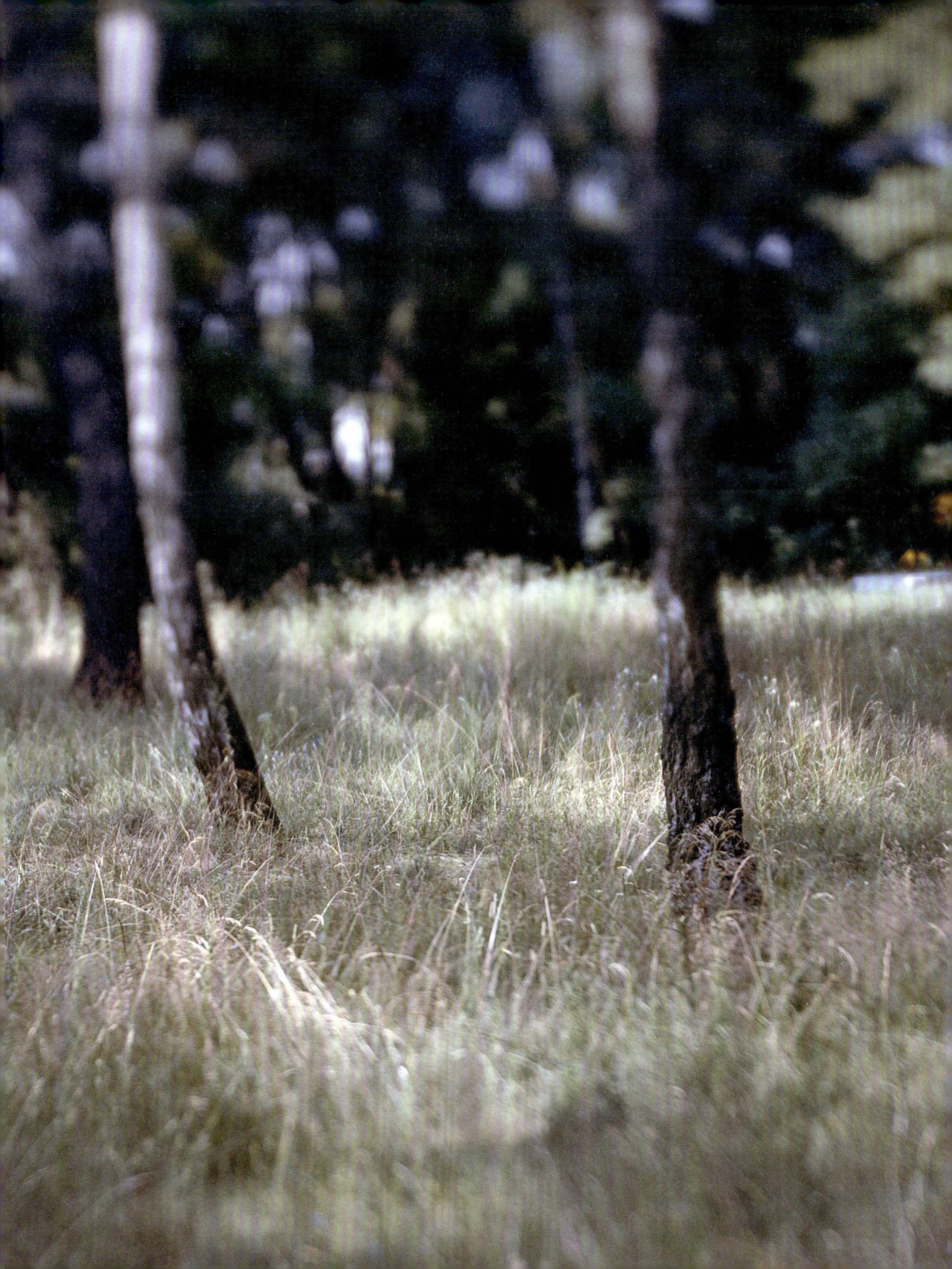

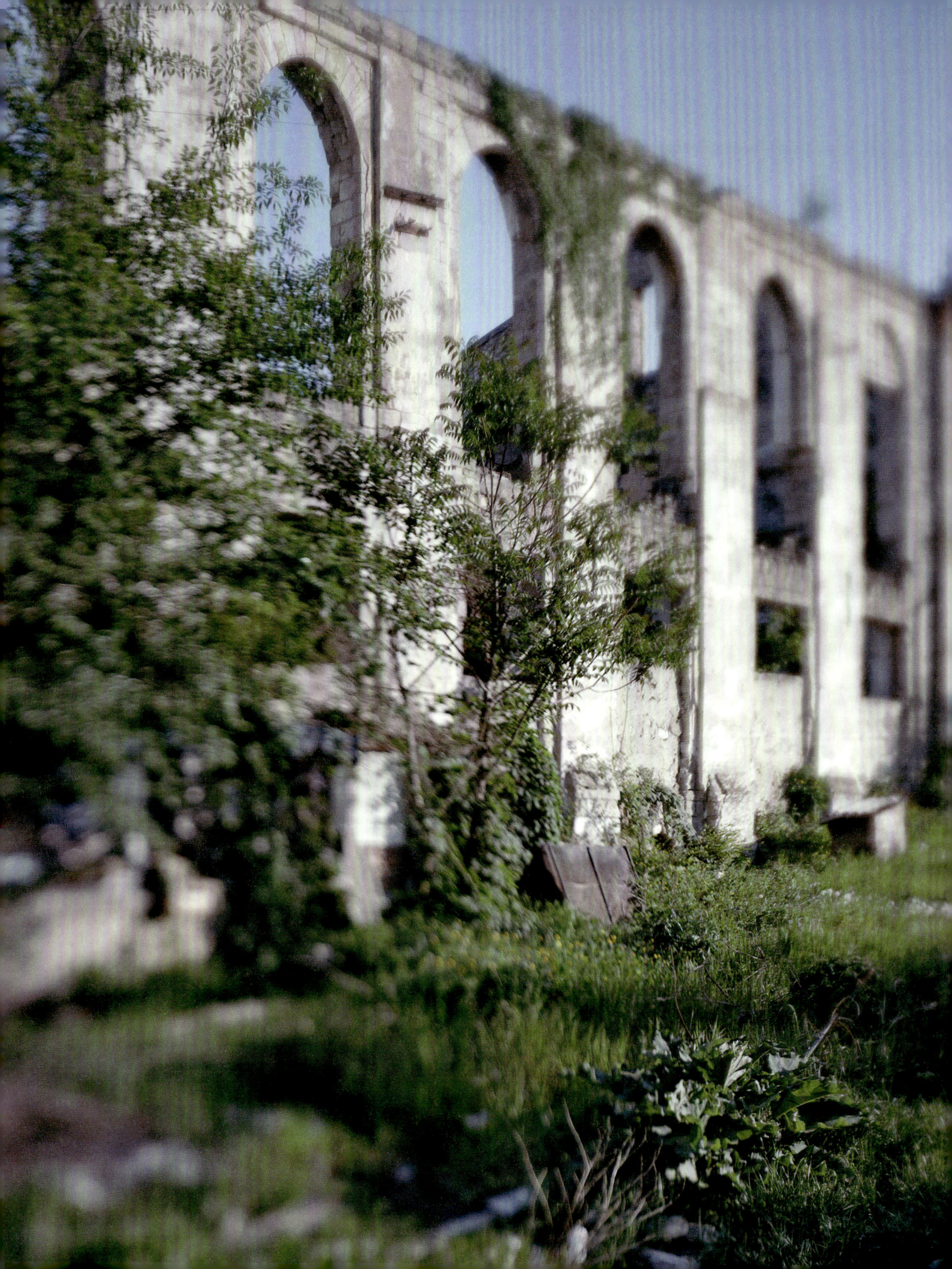

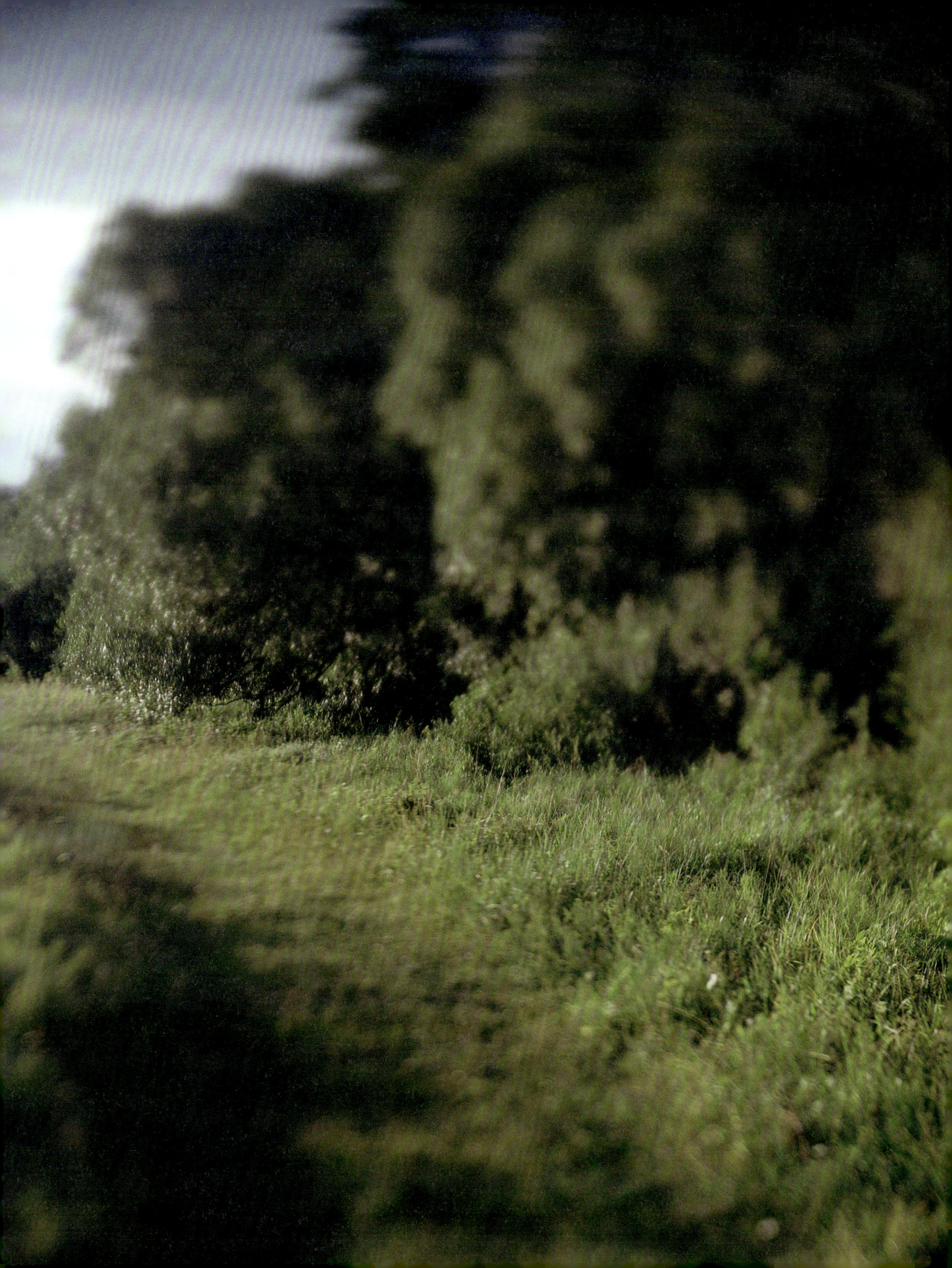

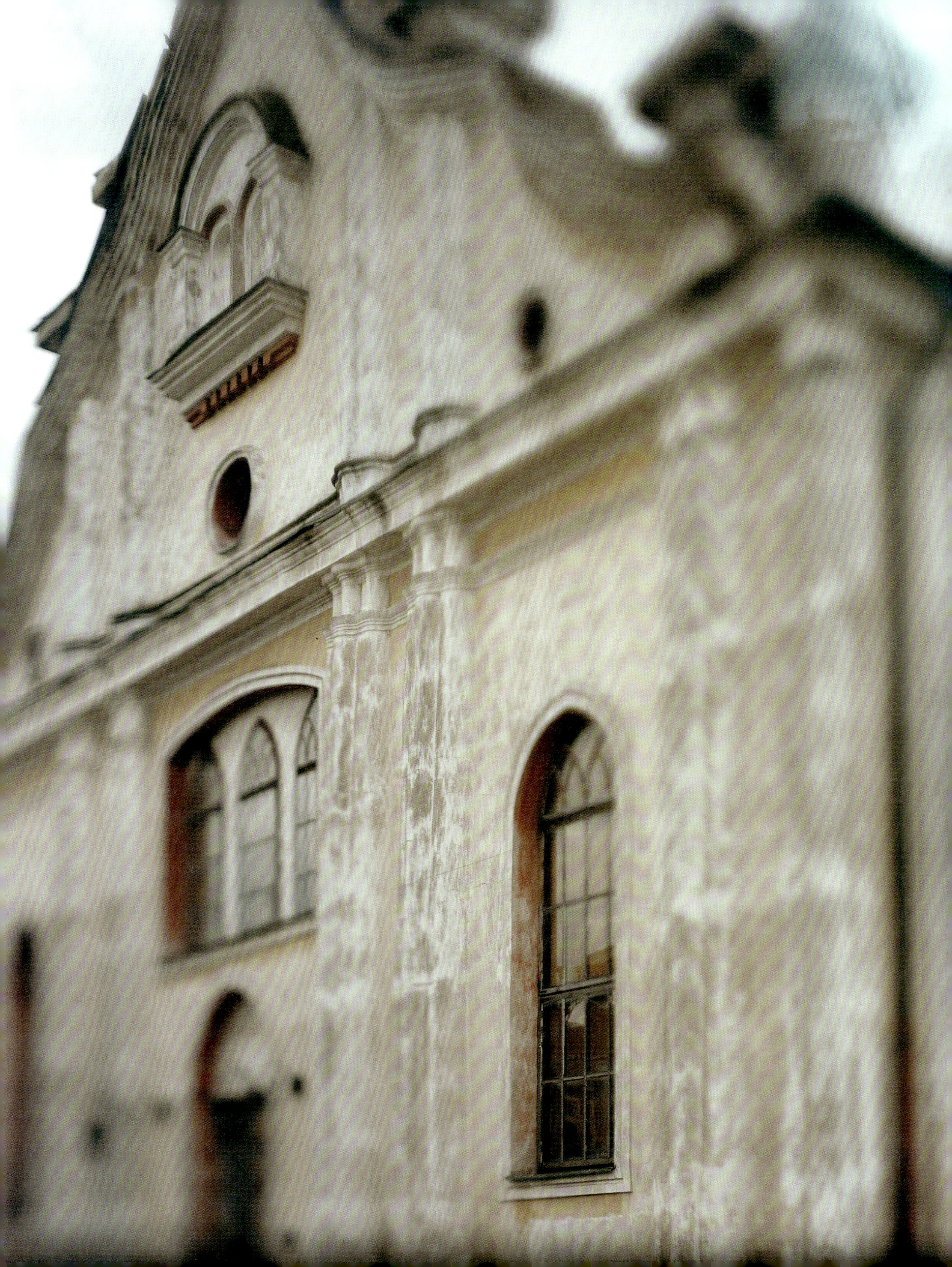

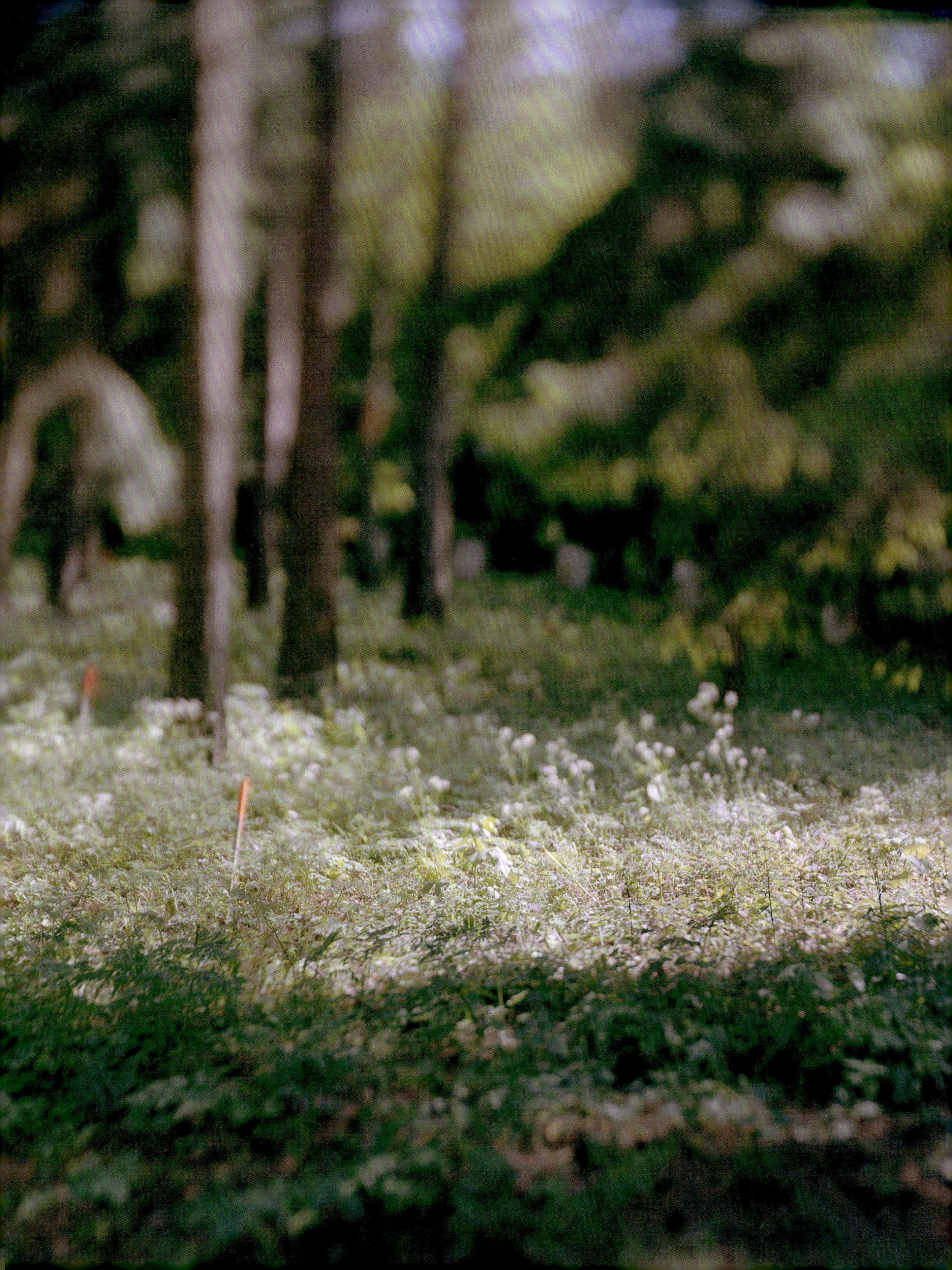

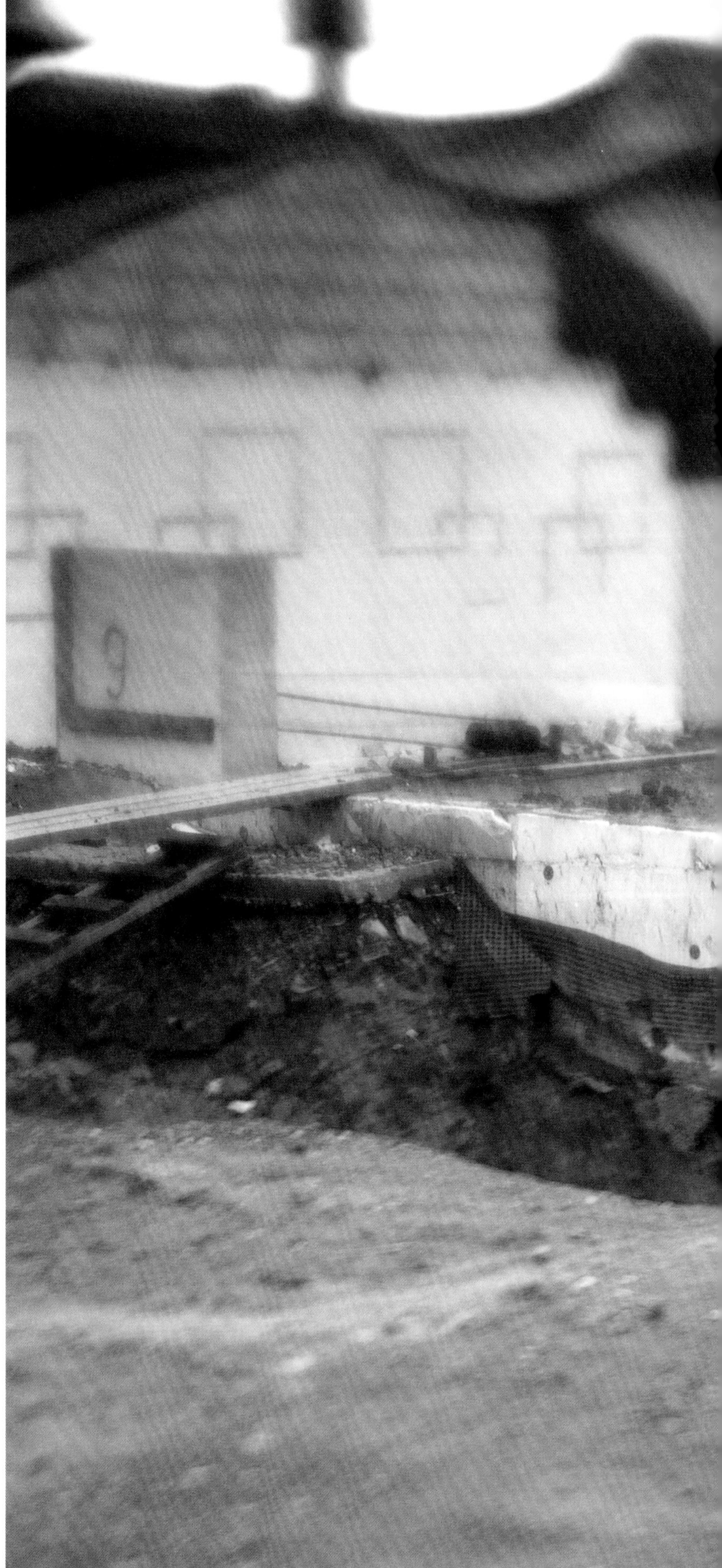

Plate 9

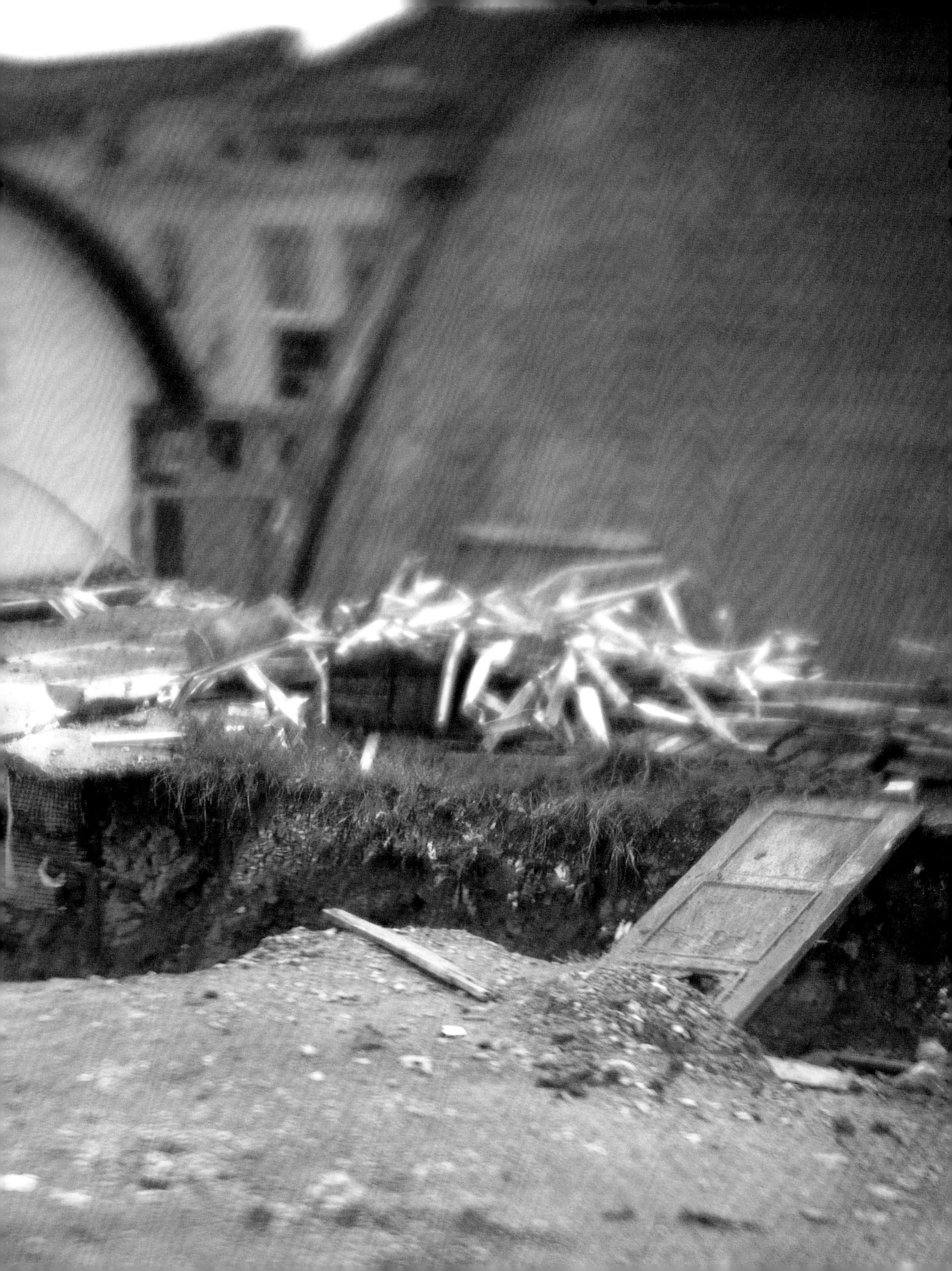

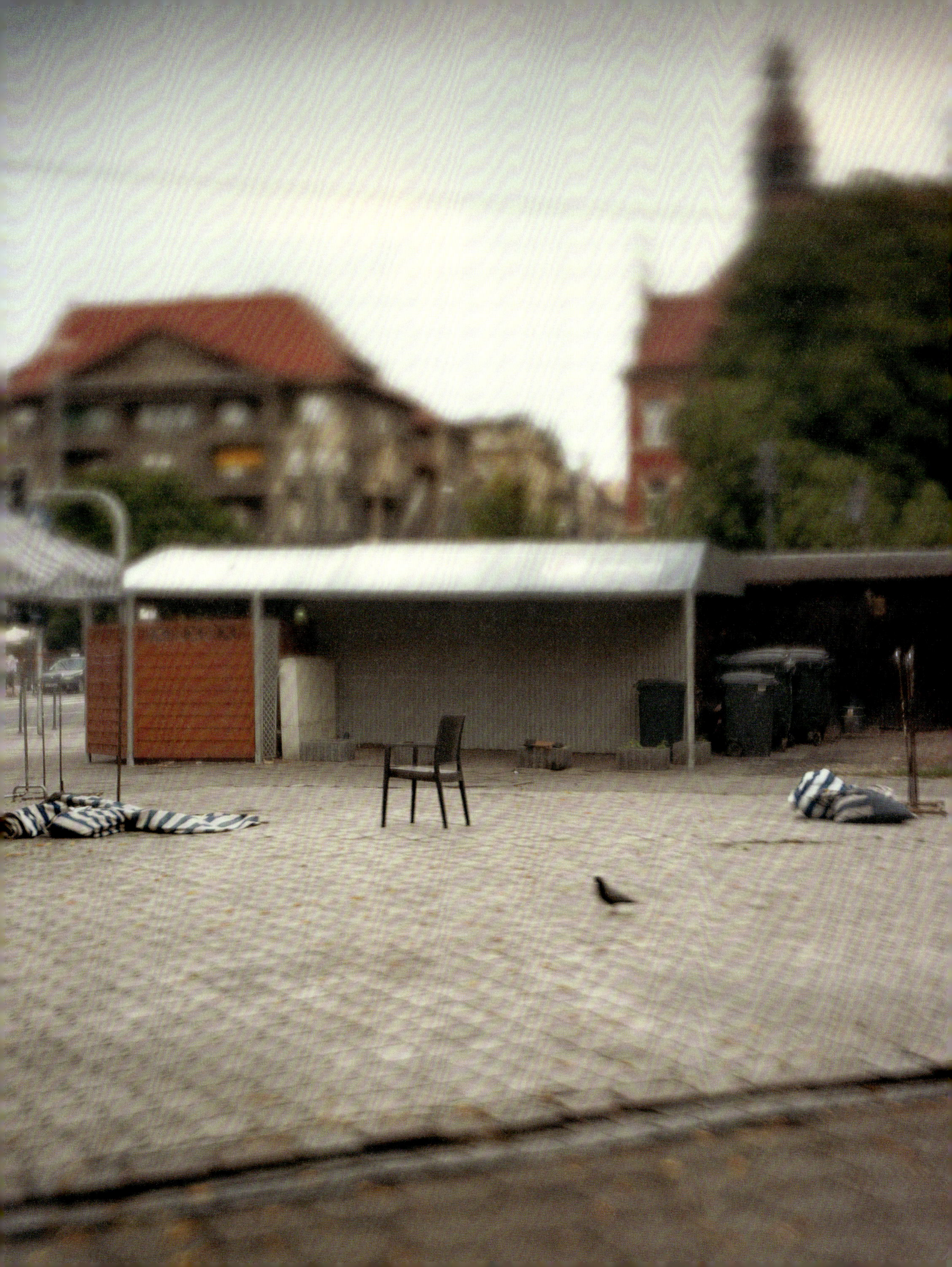

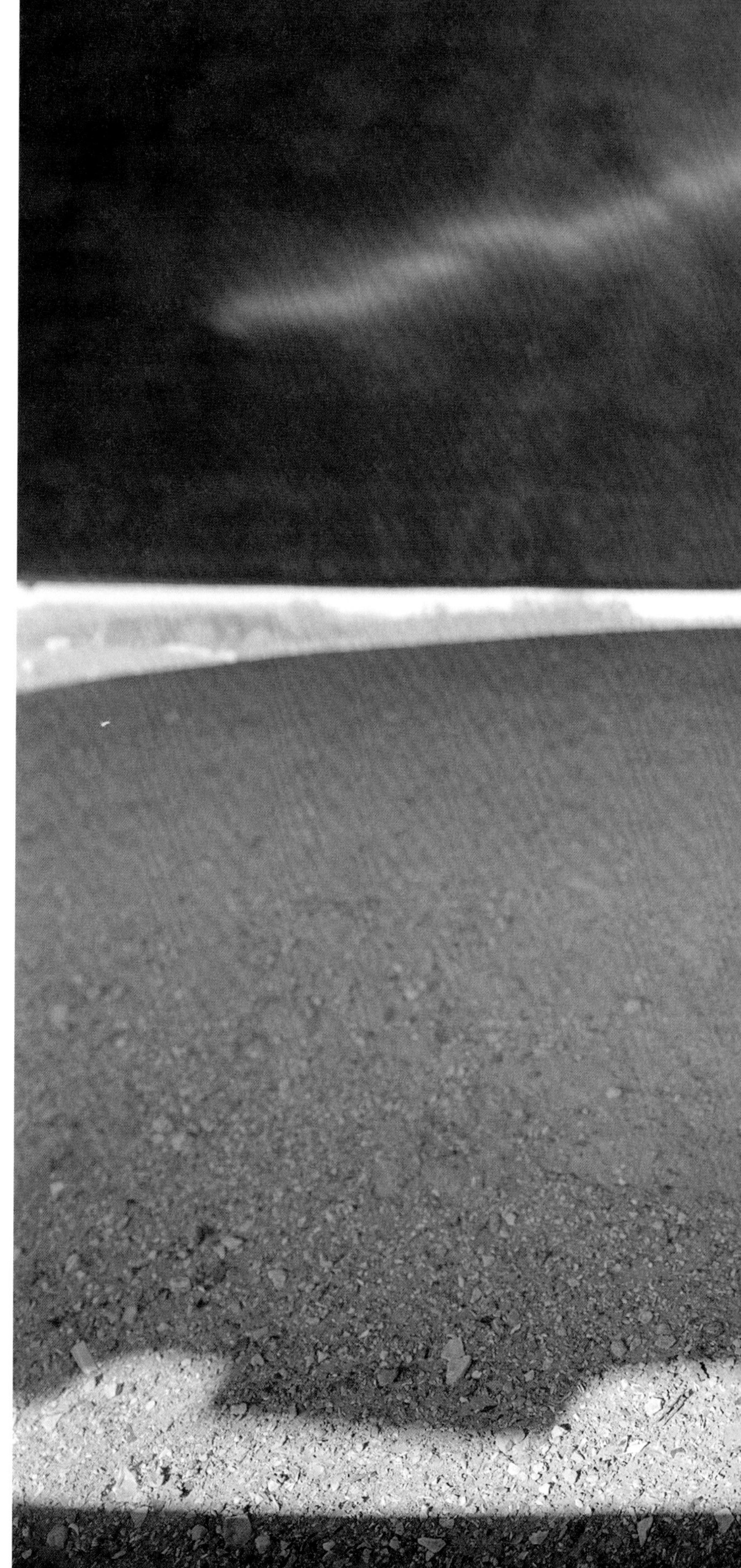

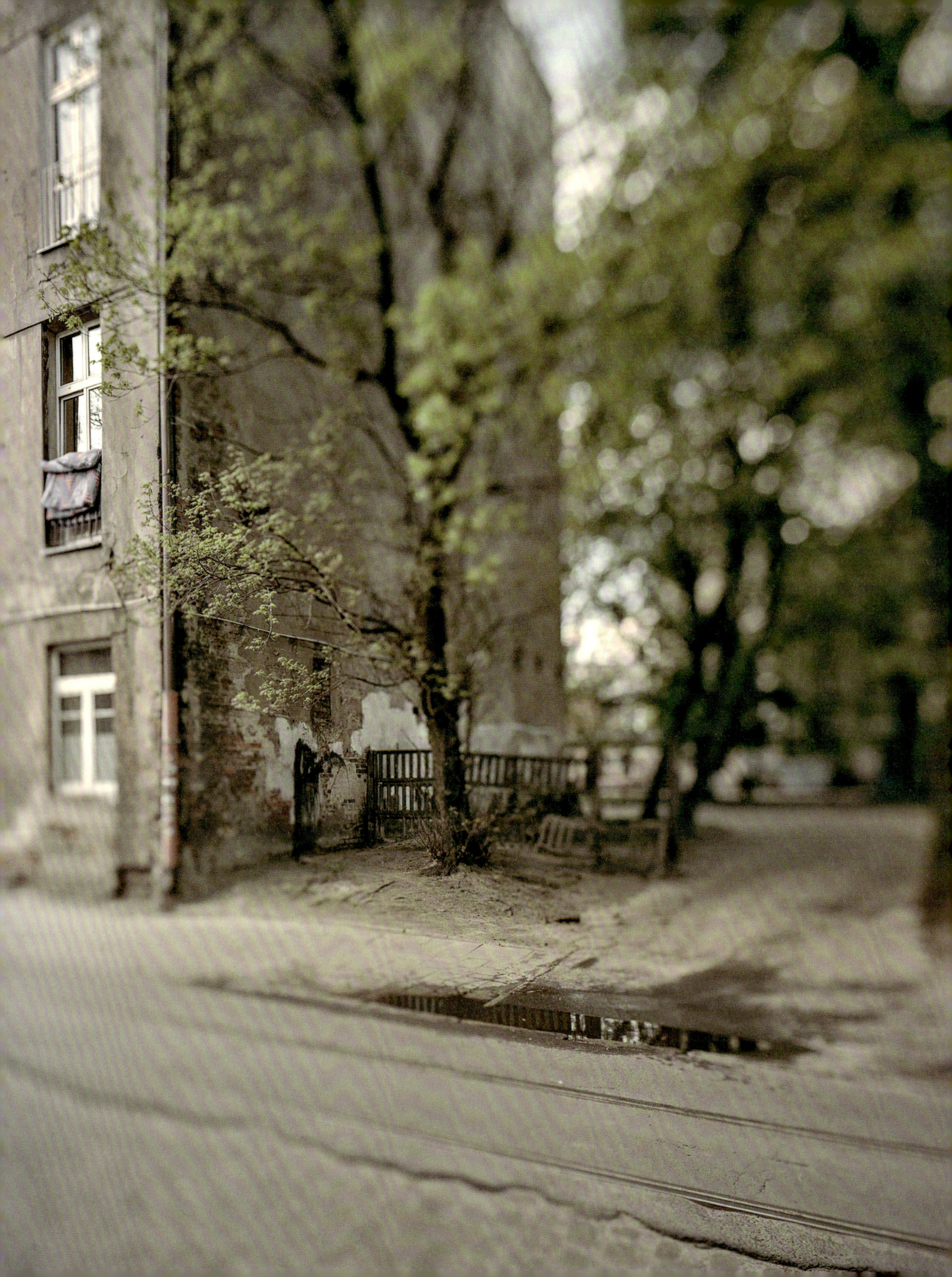

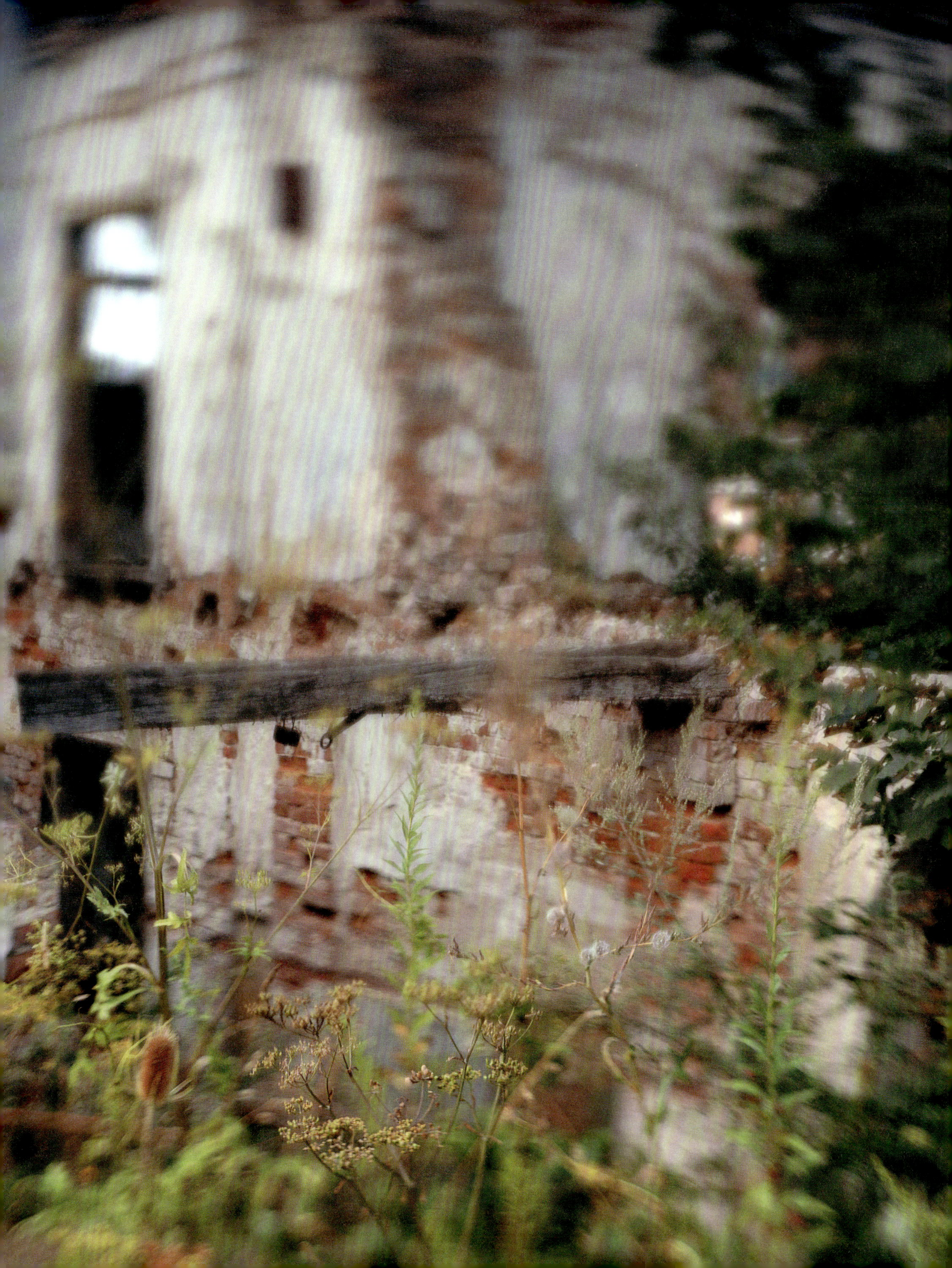

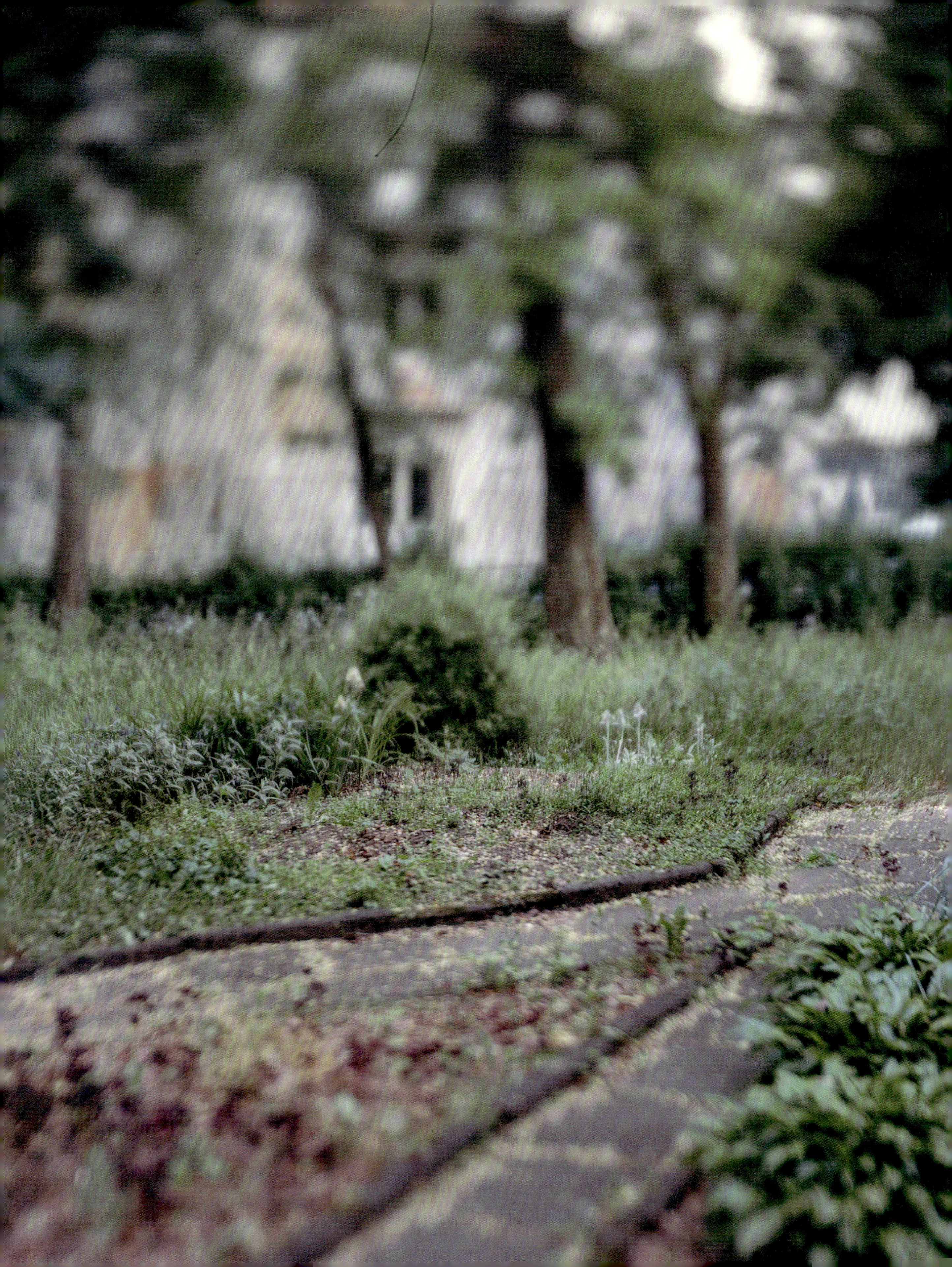

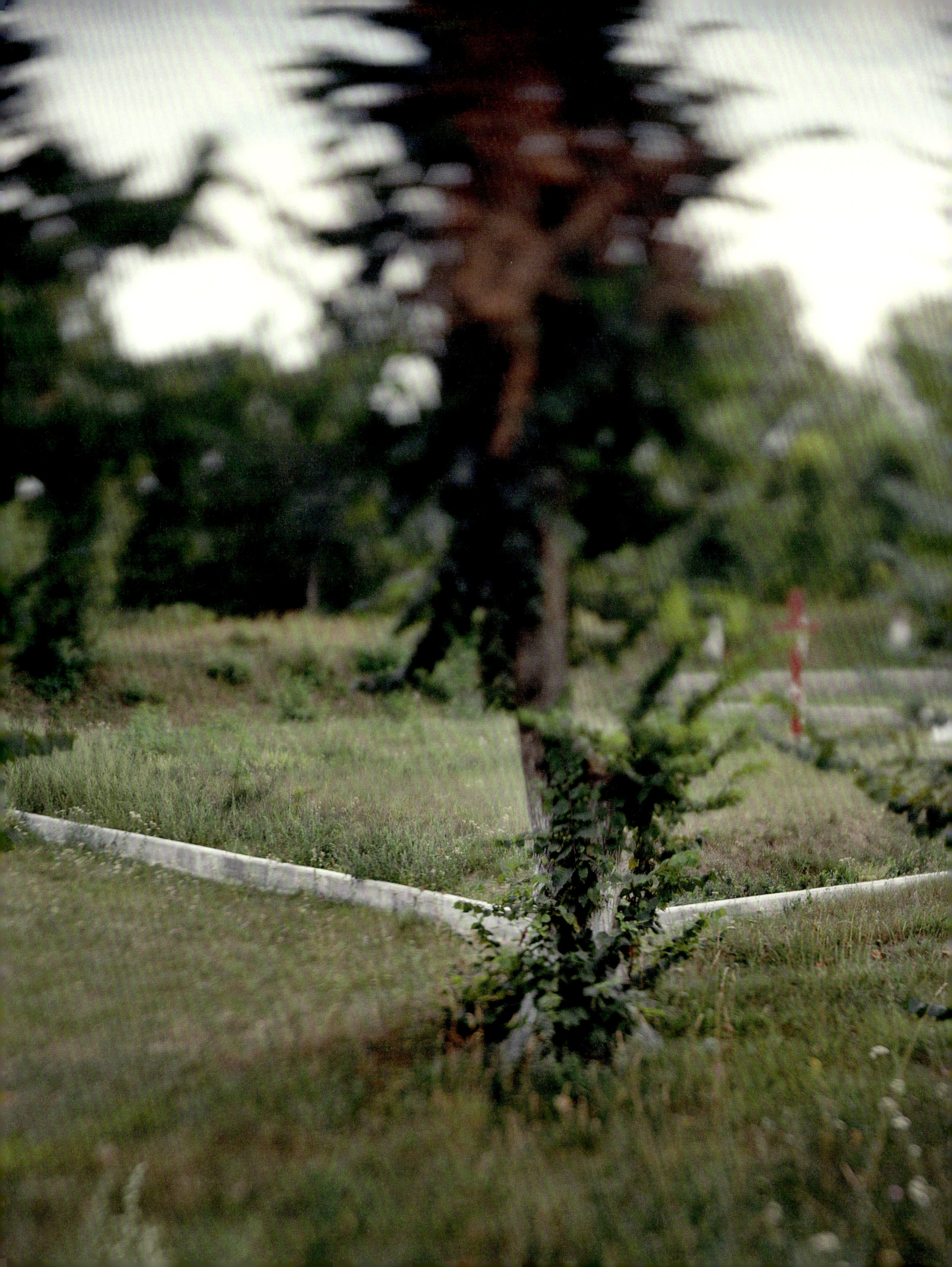

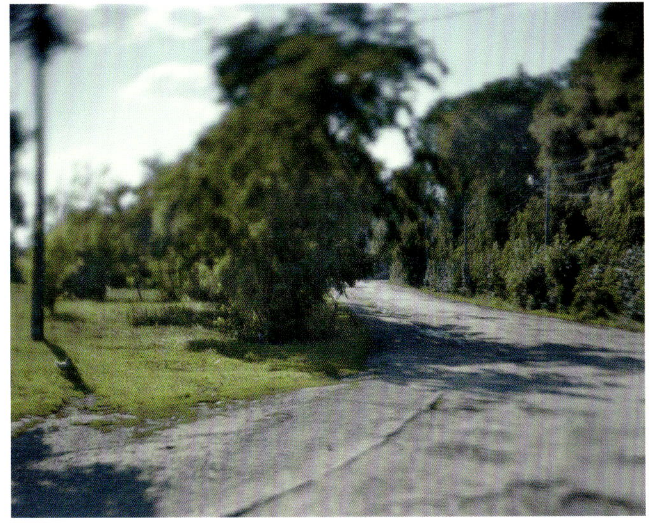
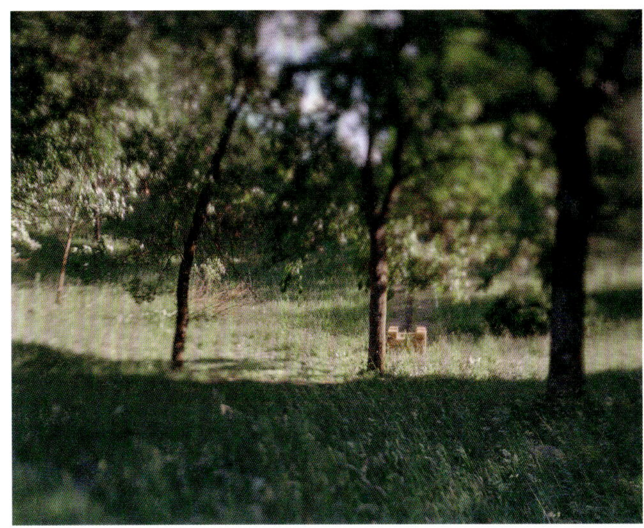
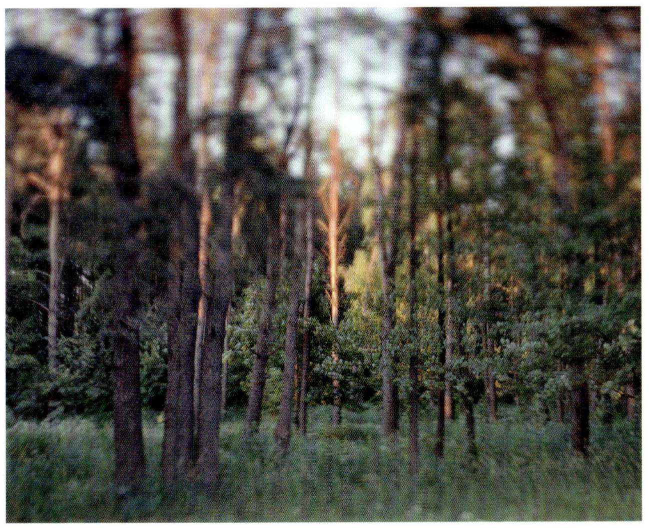
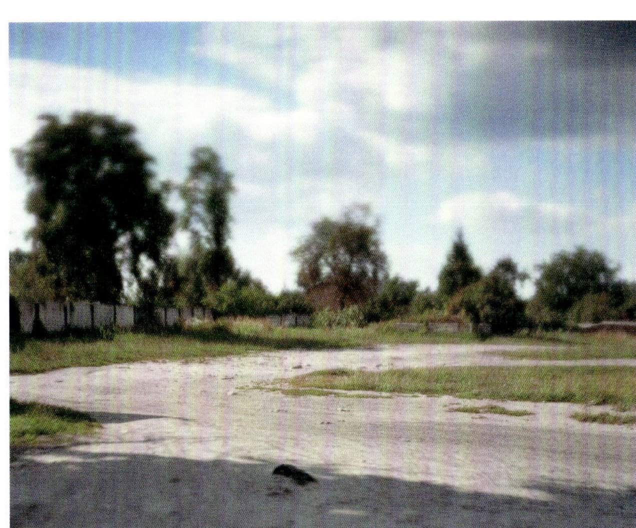
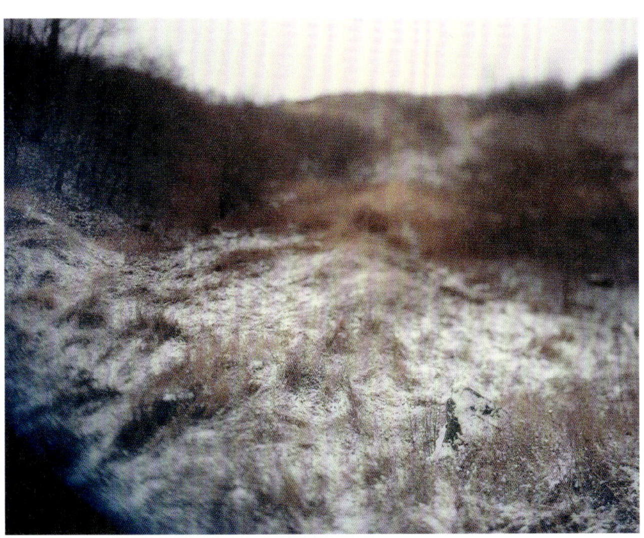
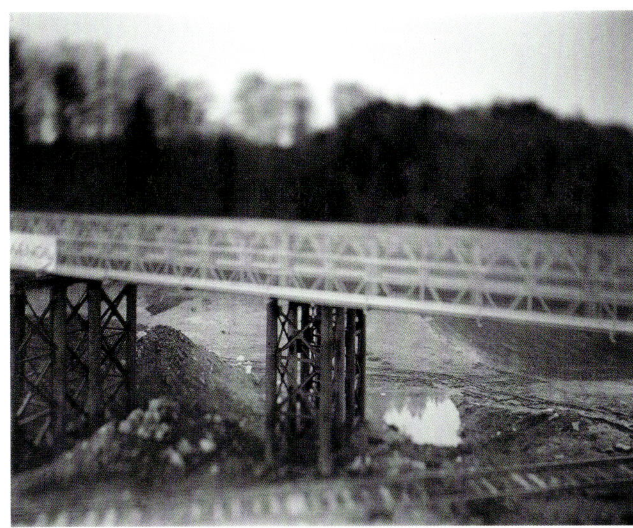

Left: Plate 15 / Right:Plate 16

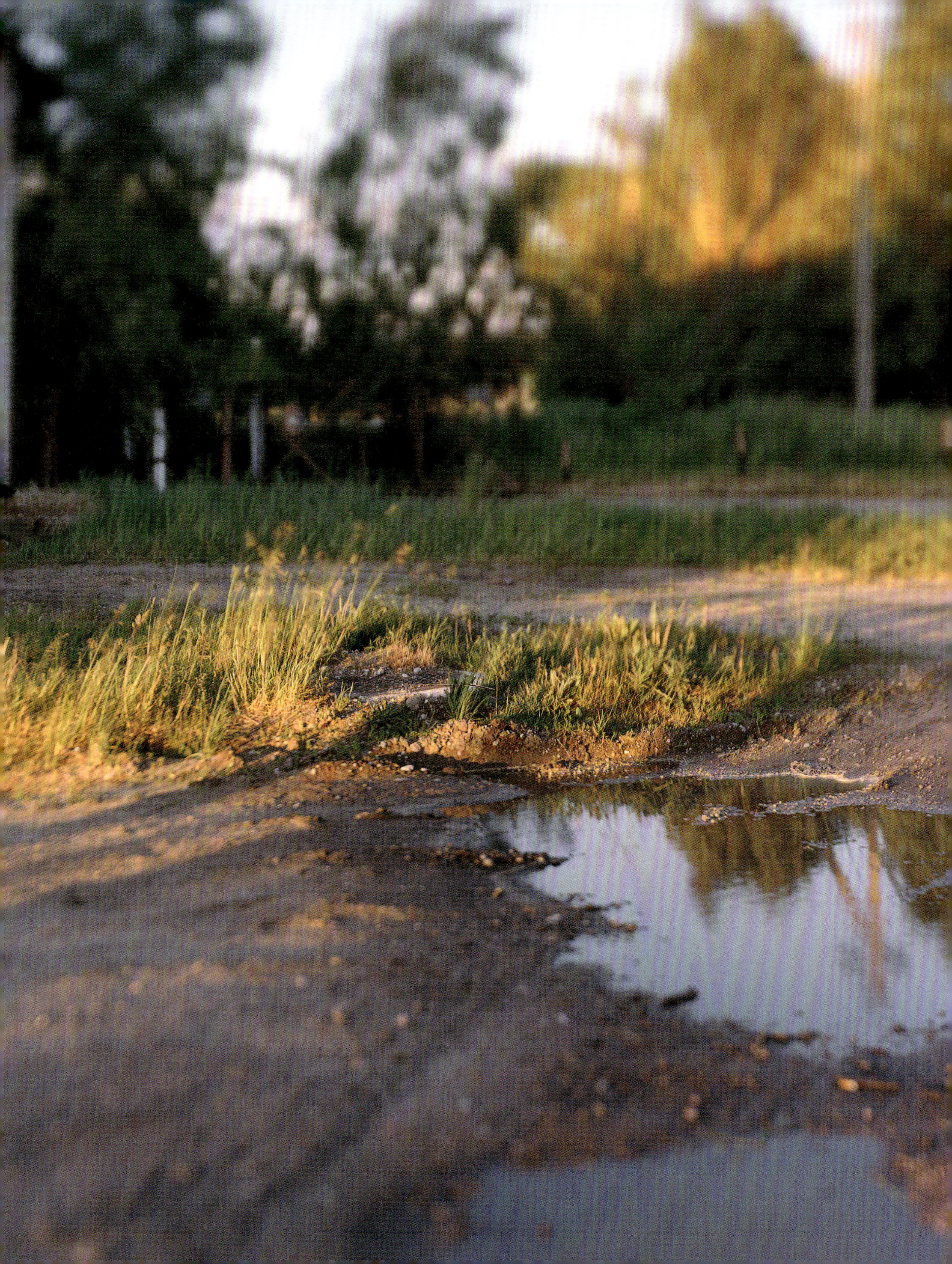

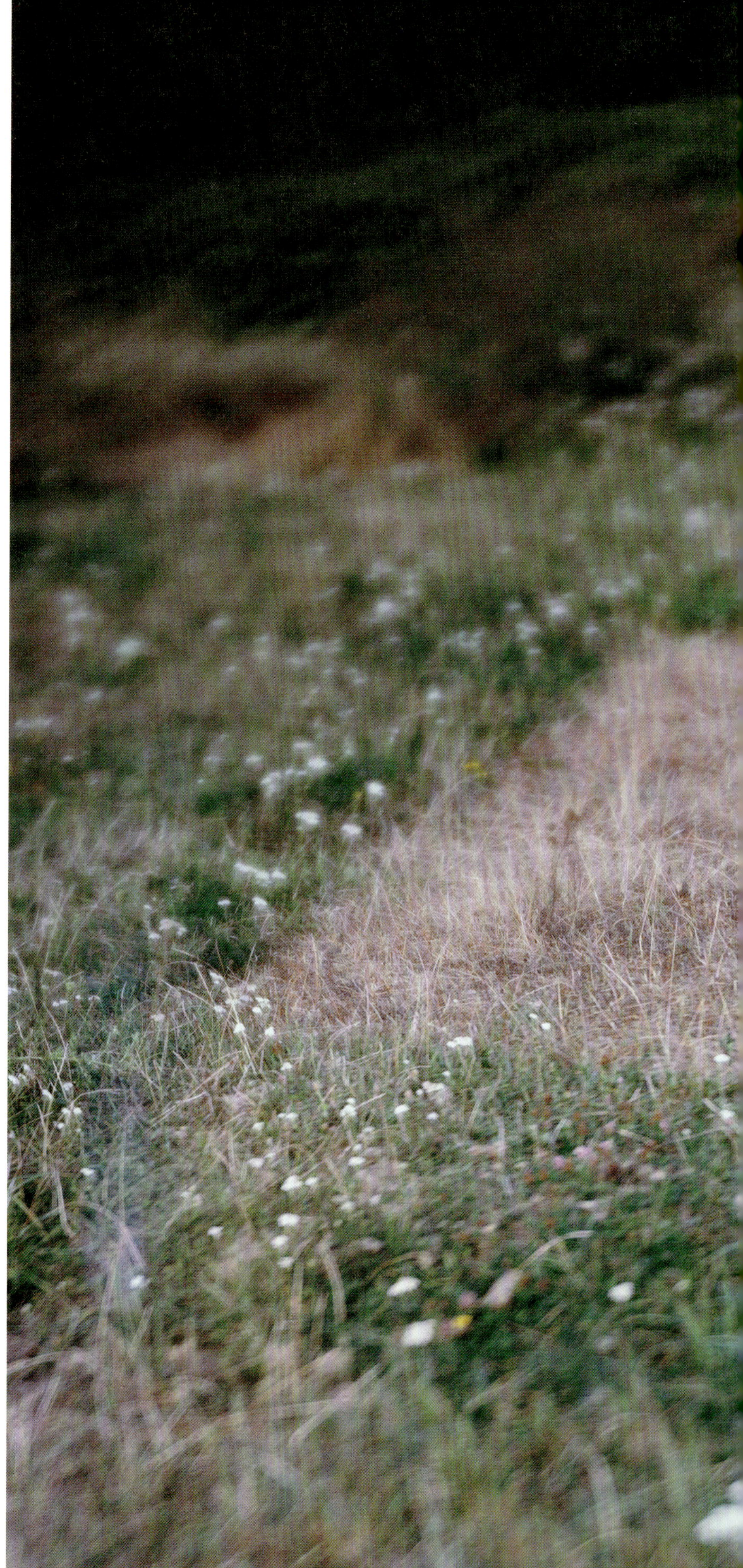

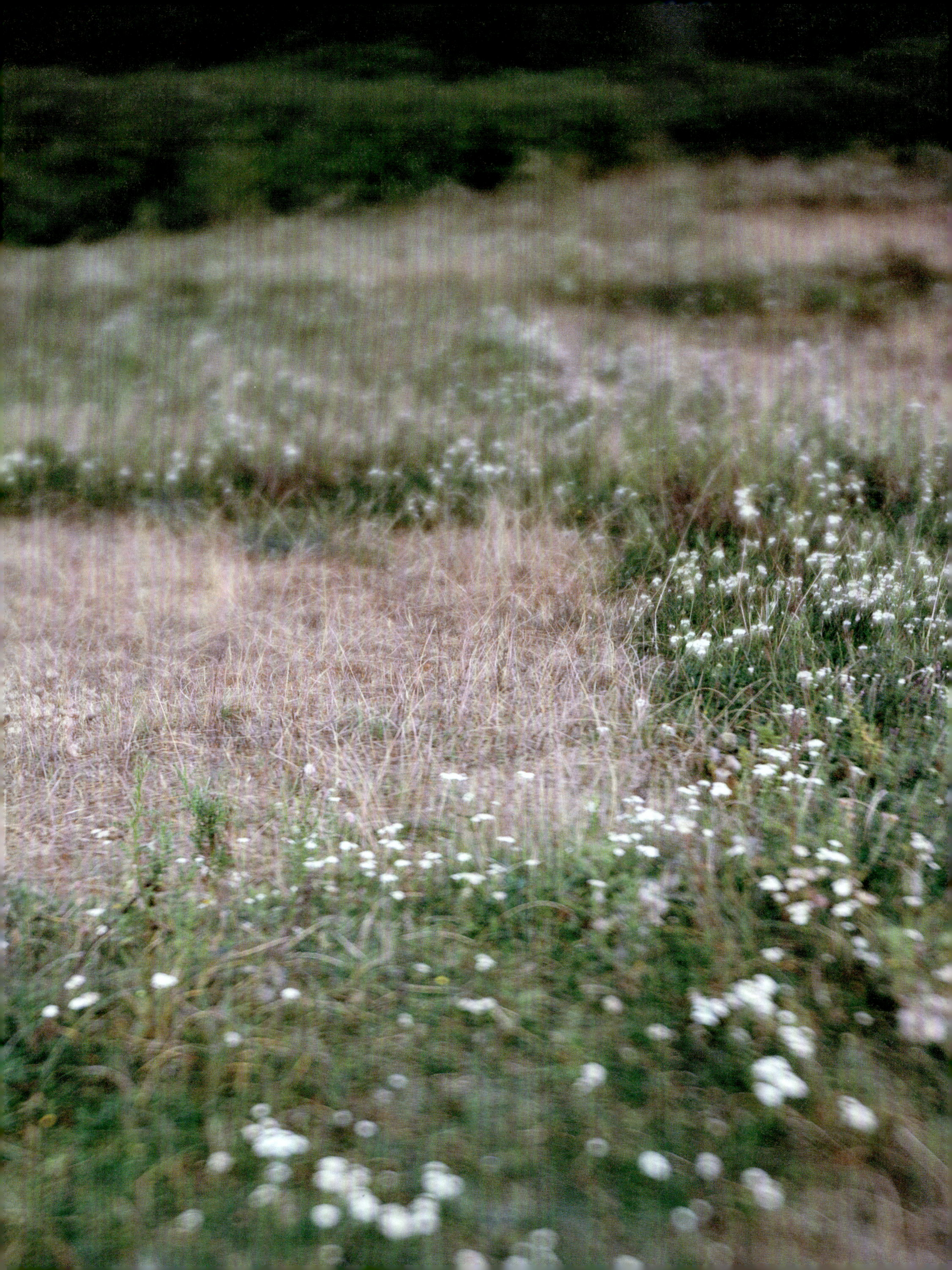

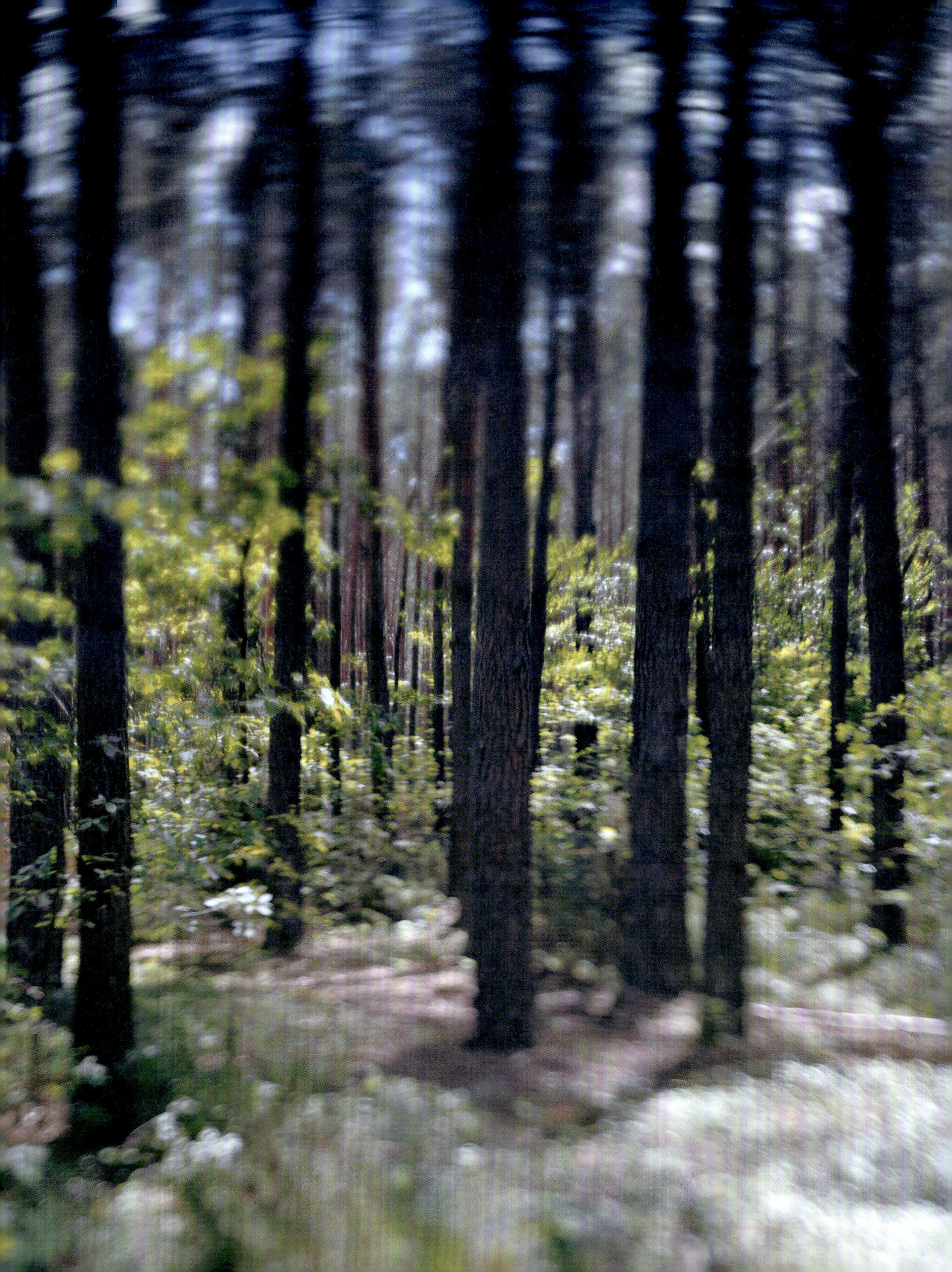

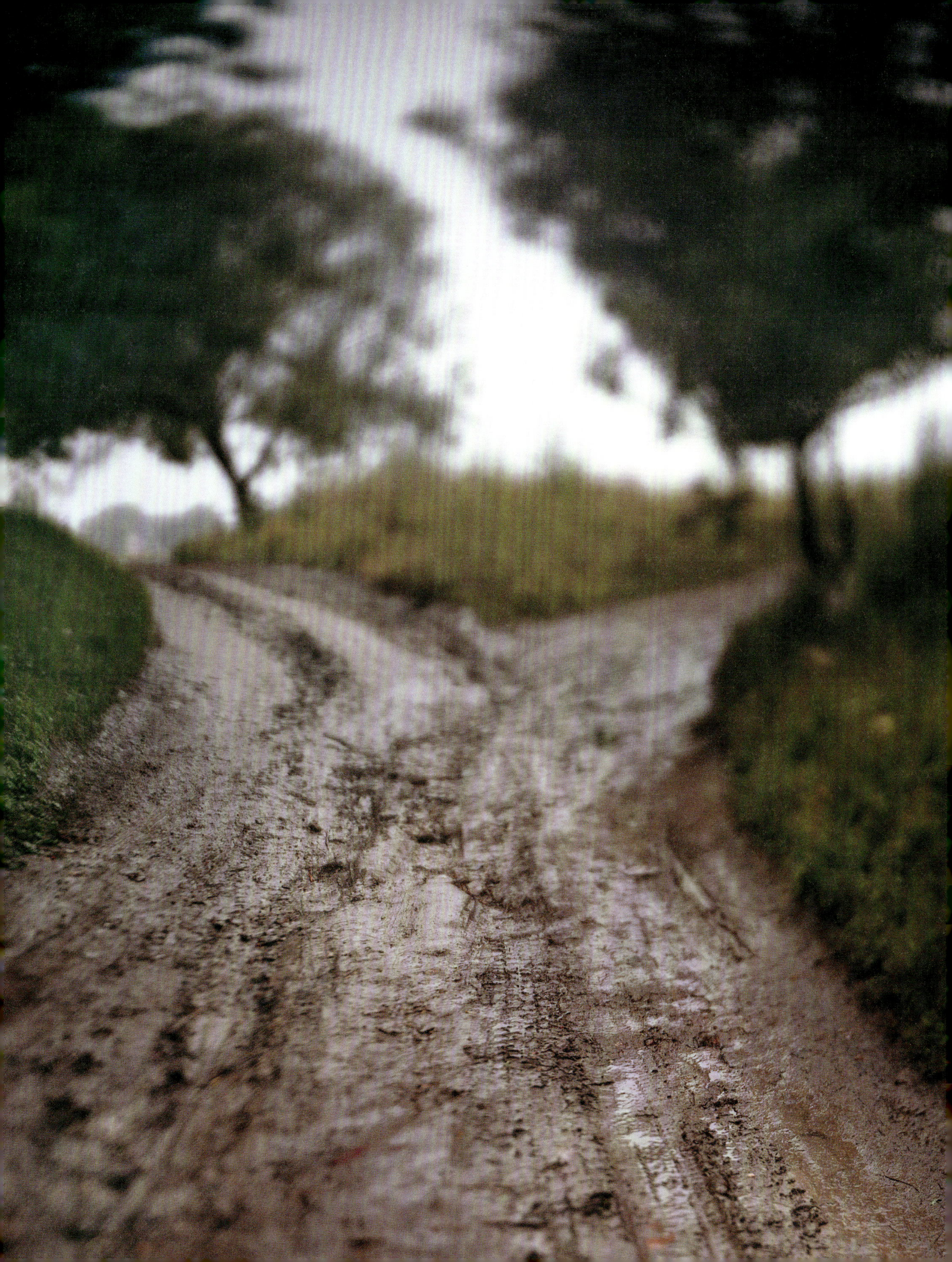

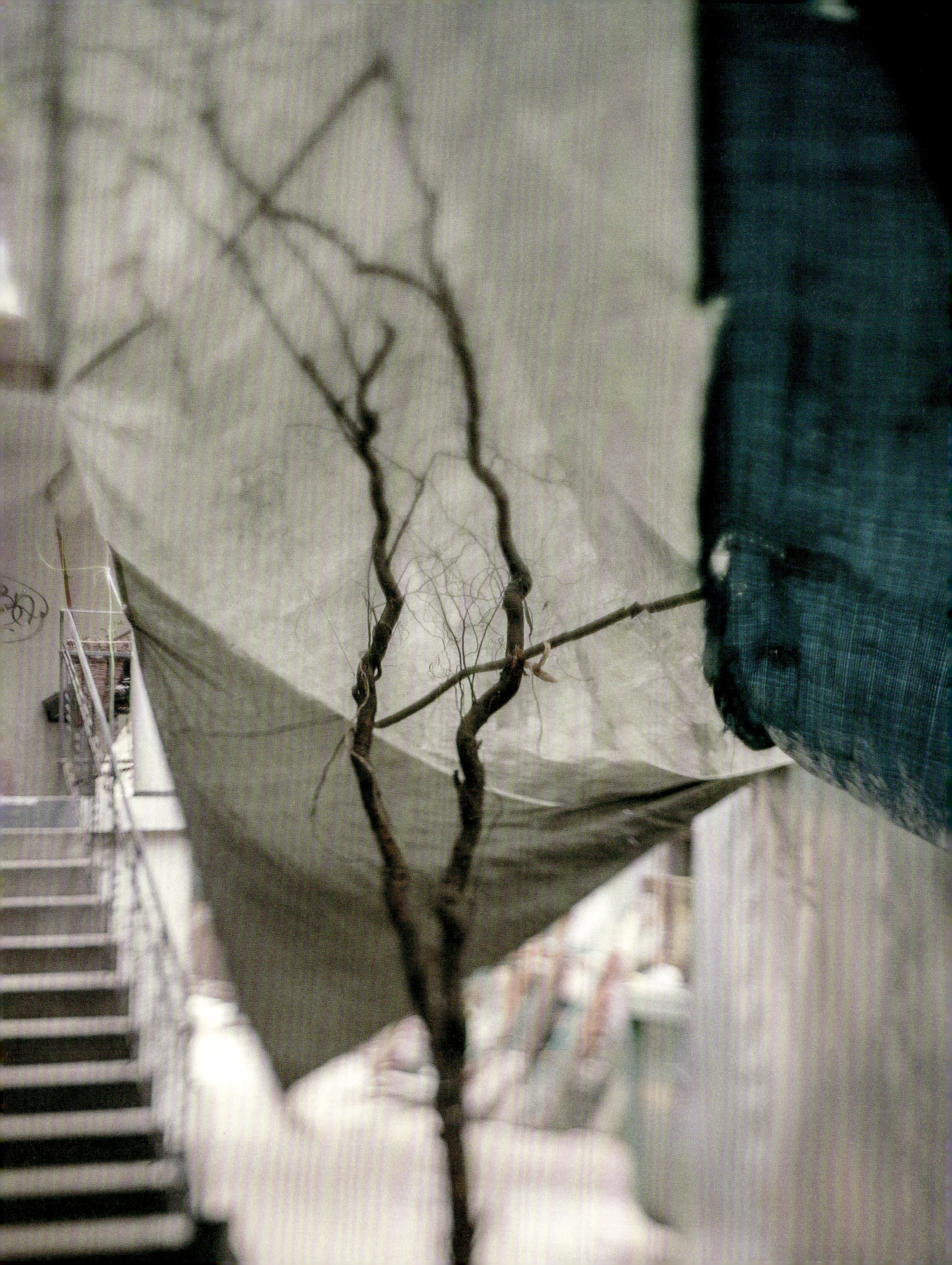

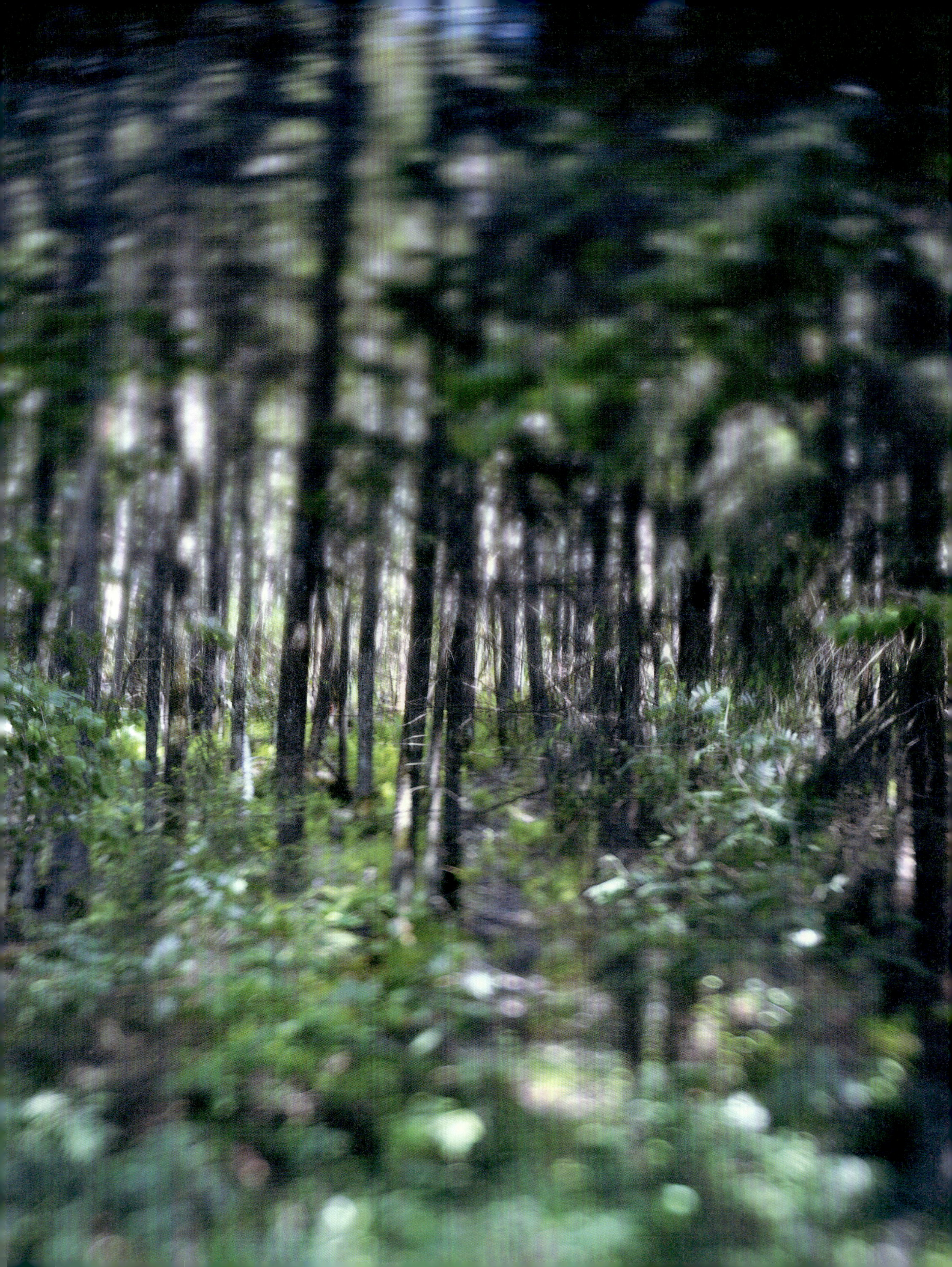

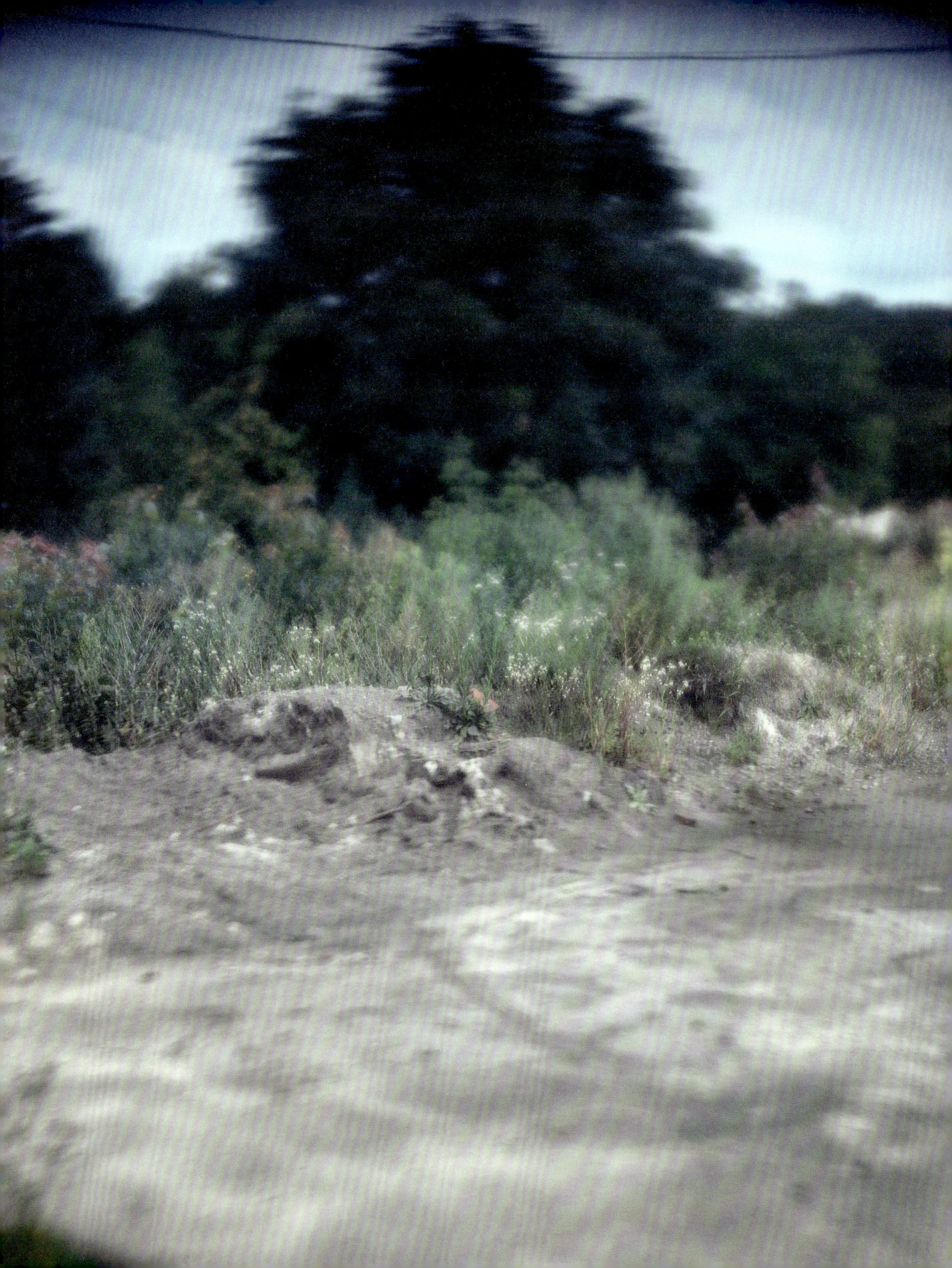

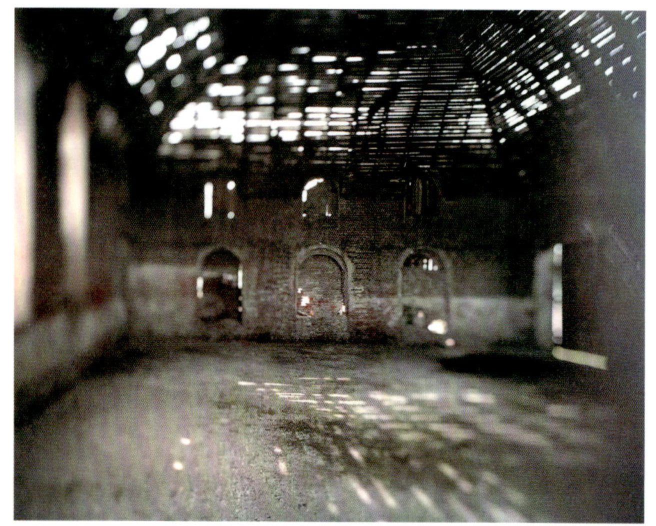
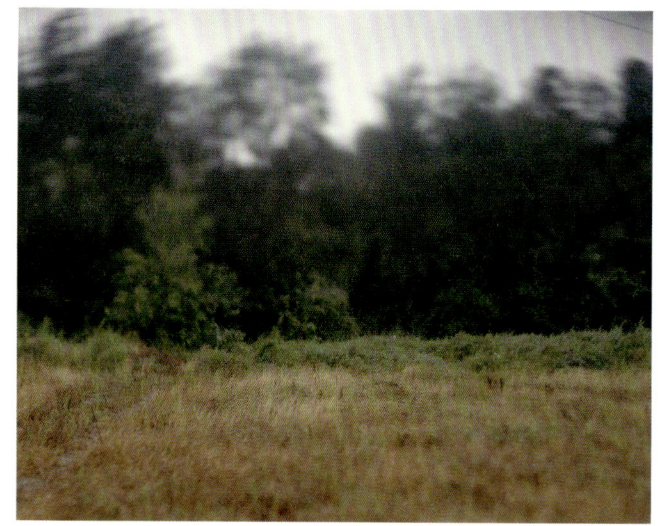
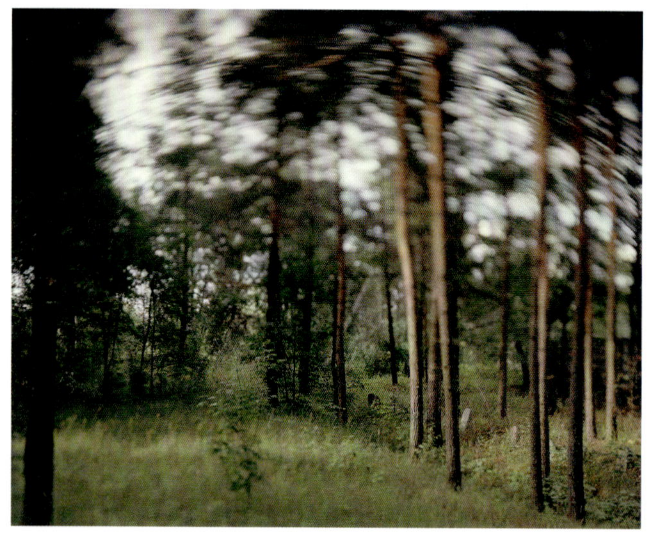
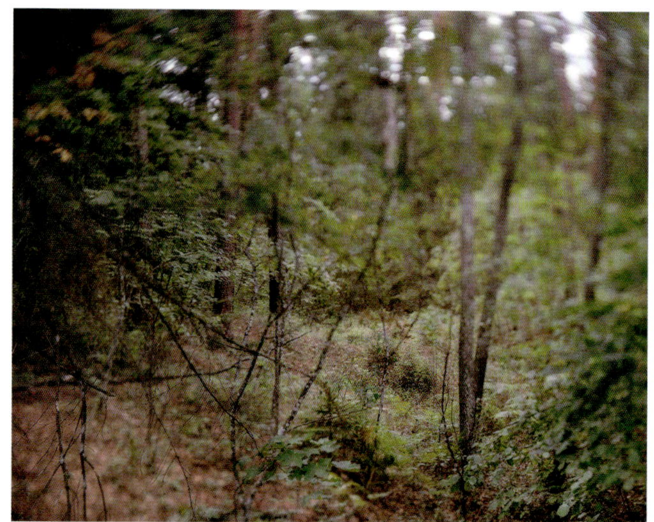
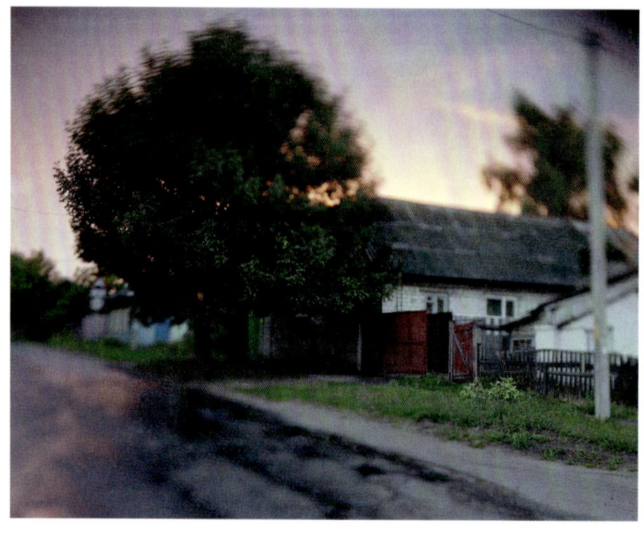
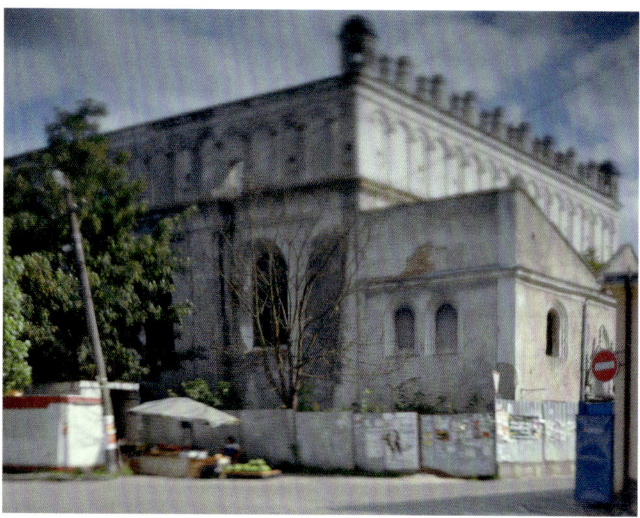

Plate 24

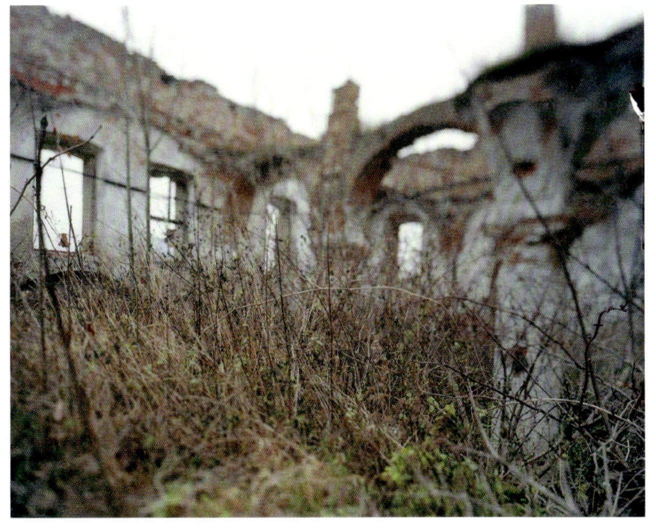
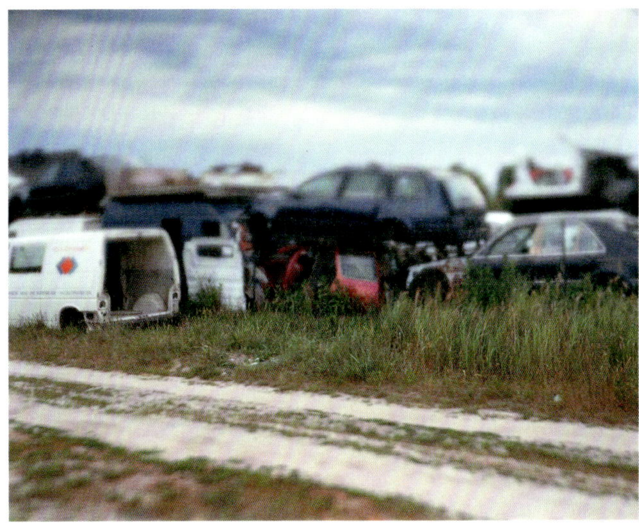
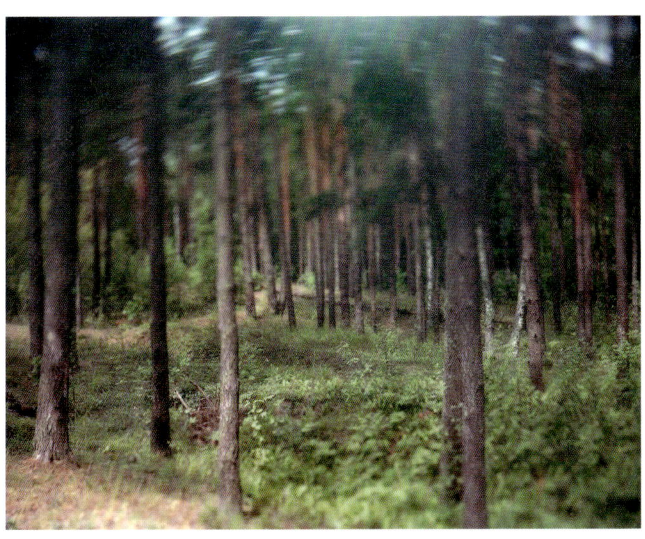
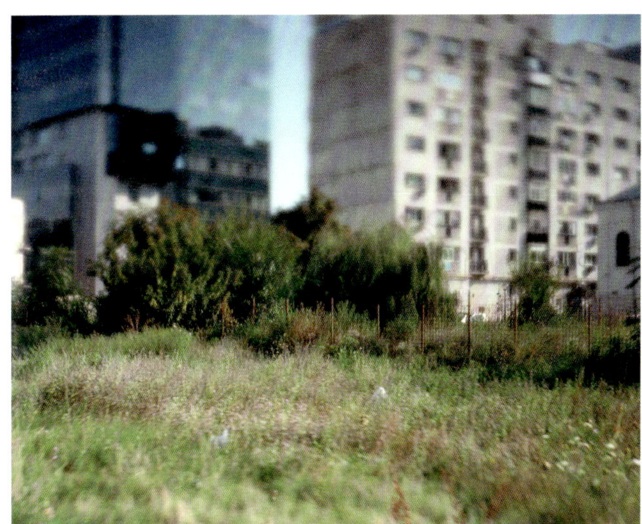
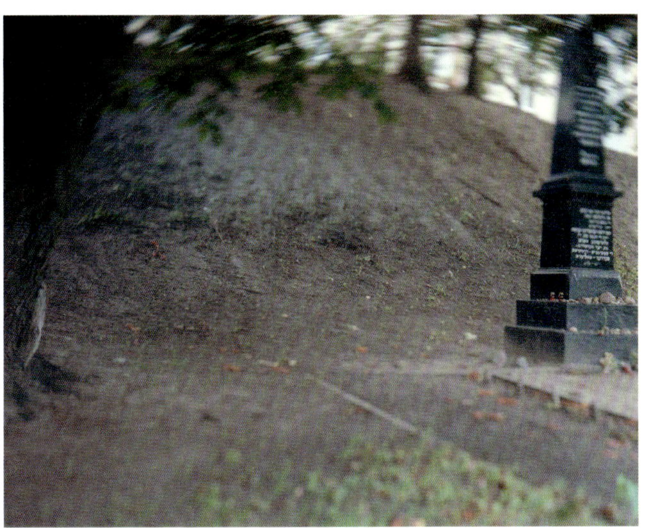
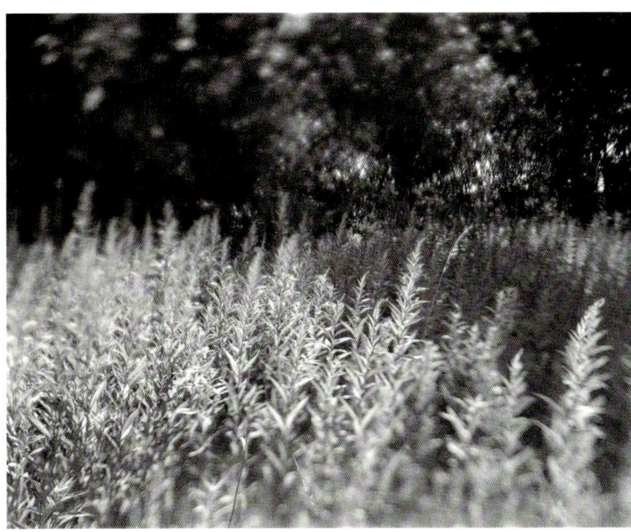

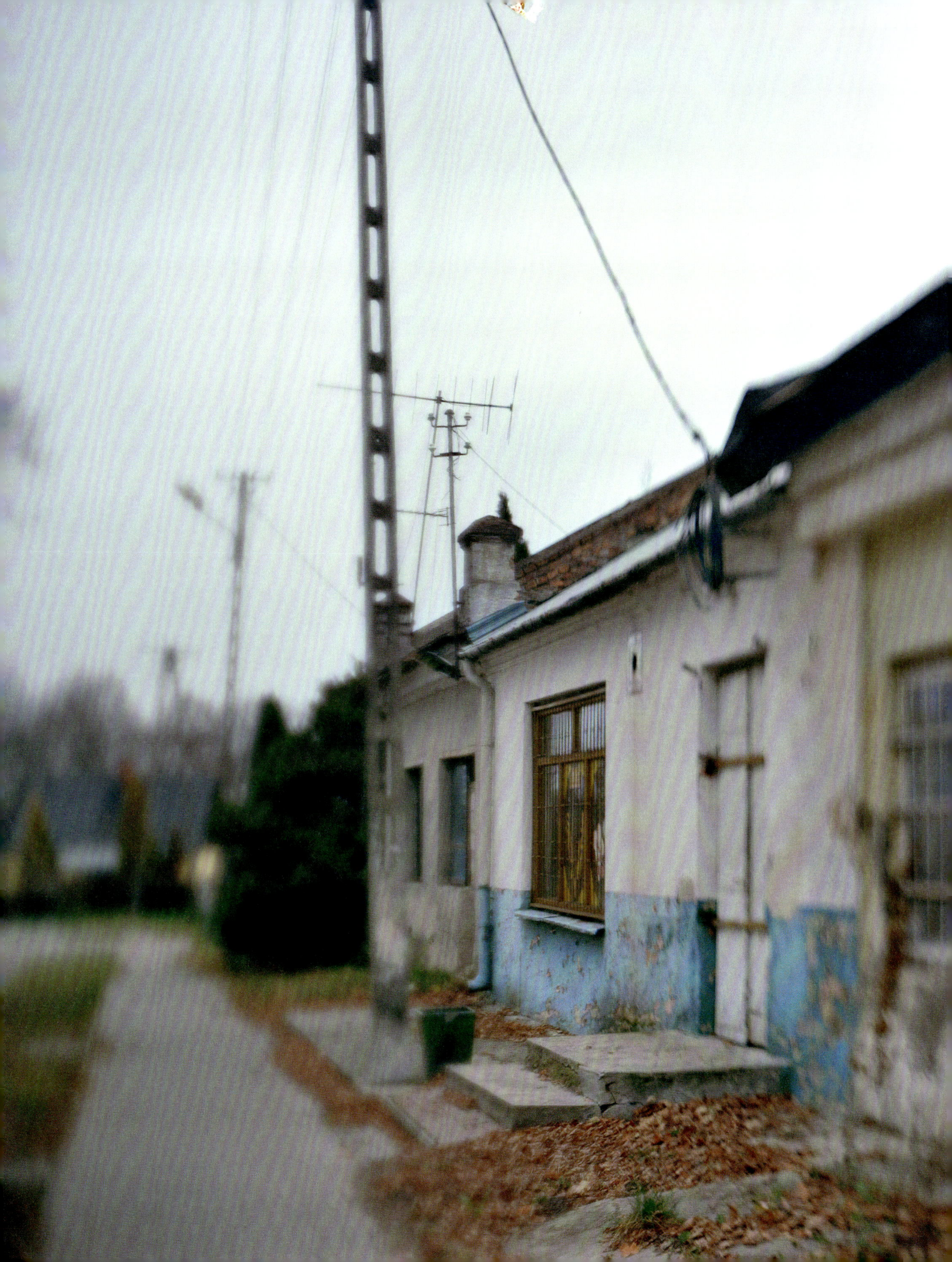

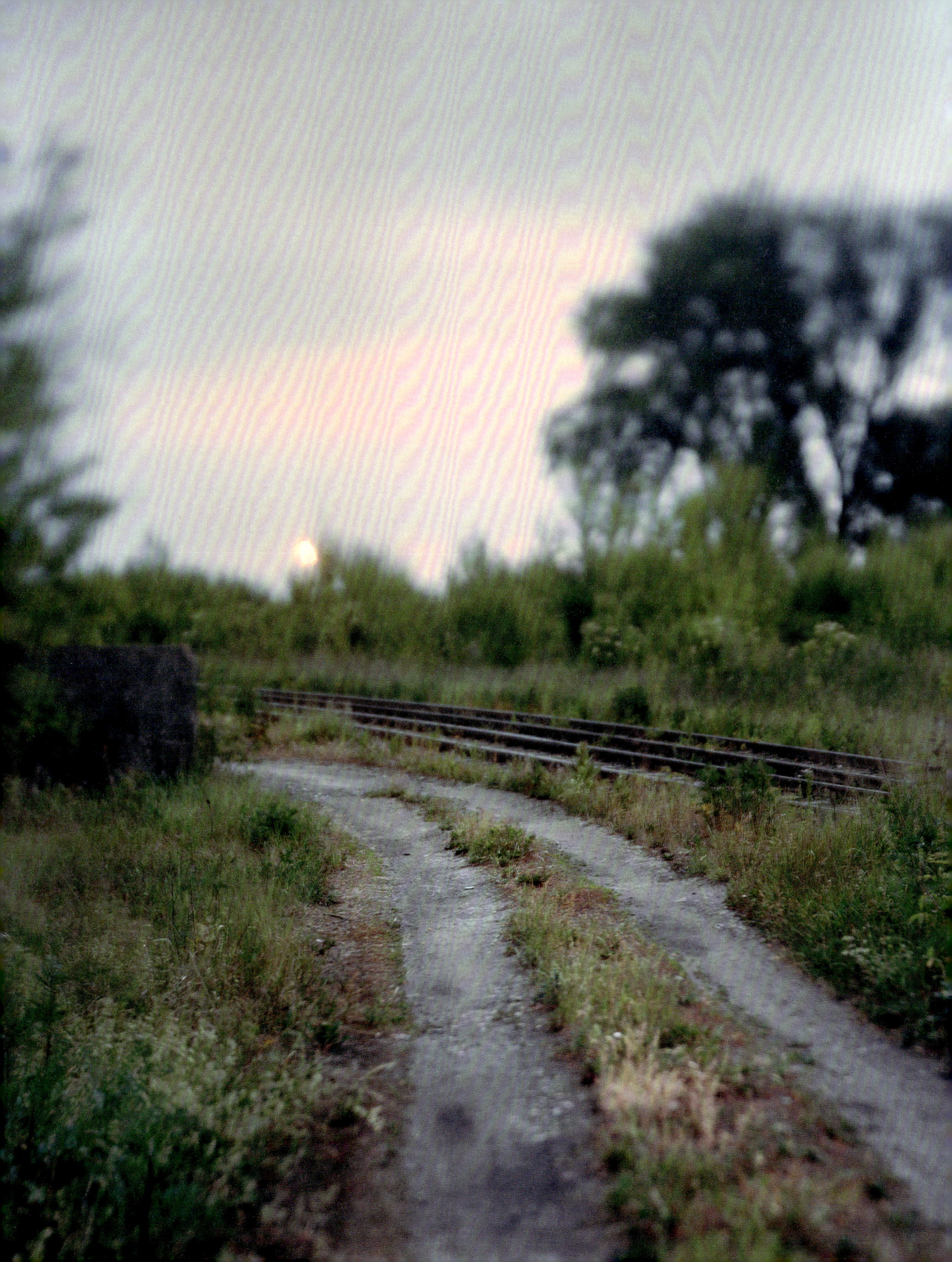

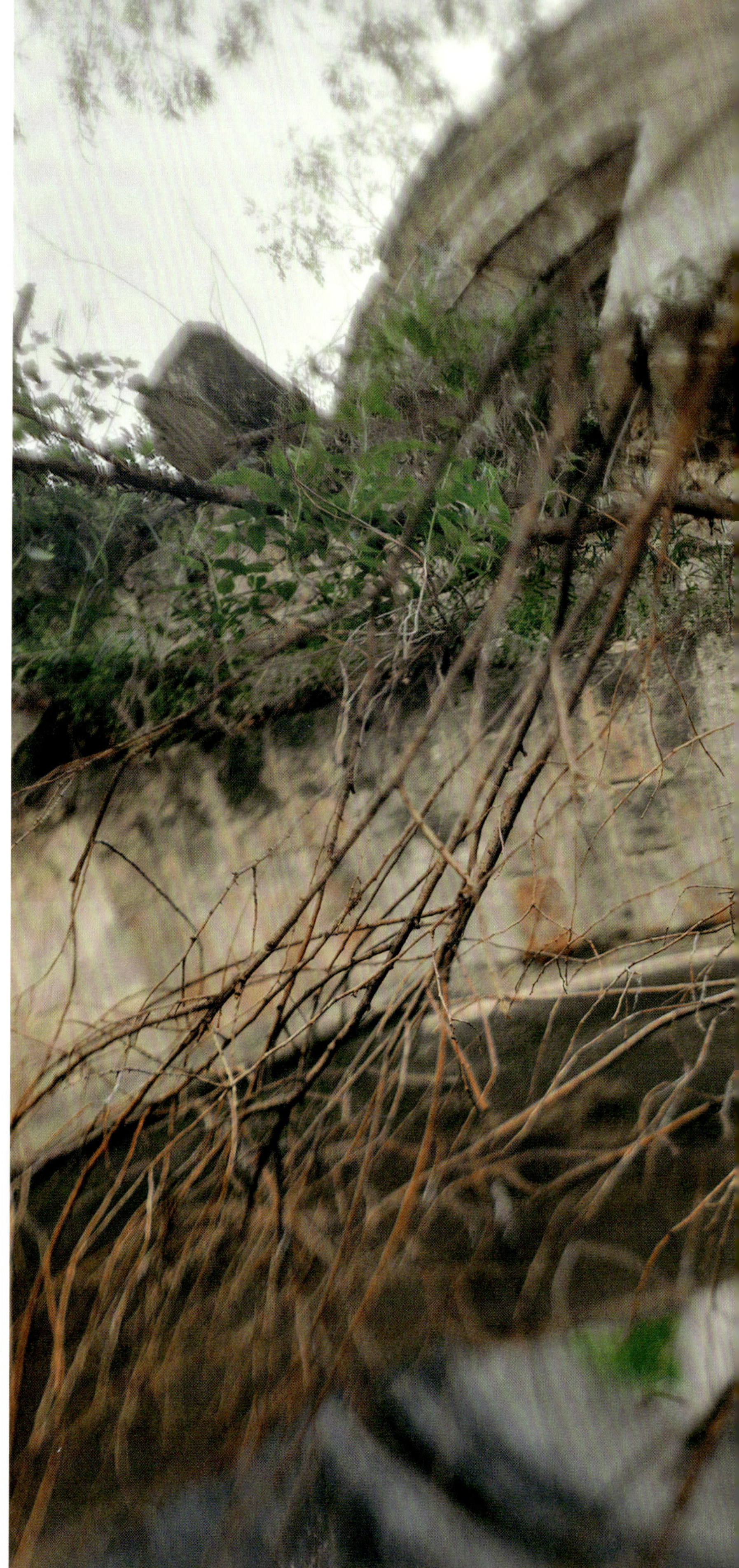

Plate 28

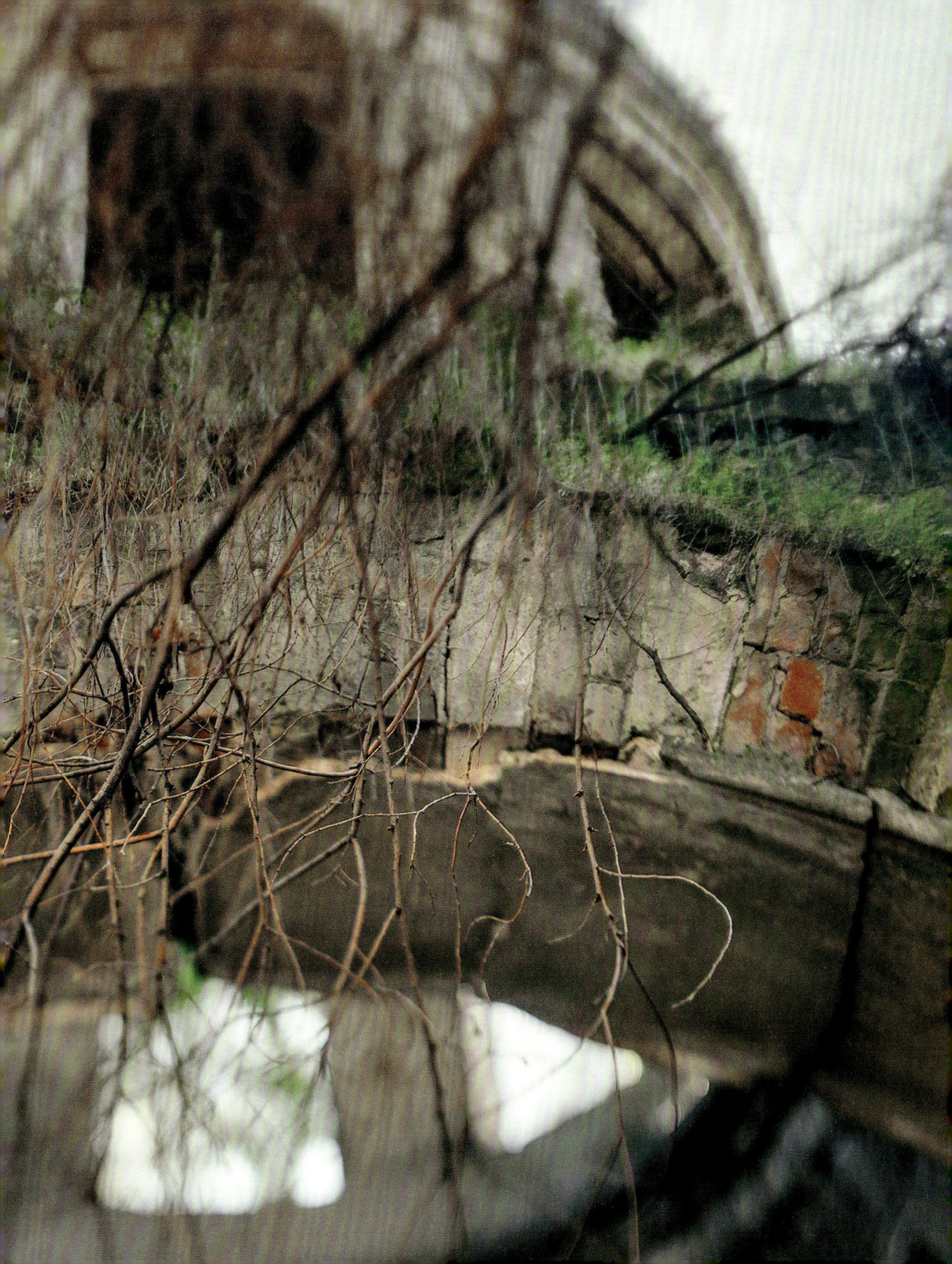

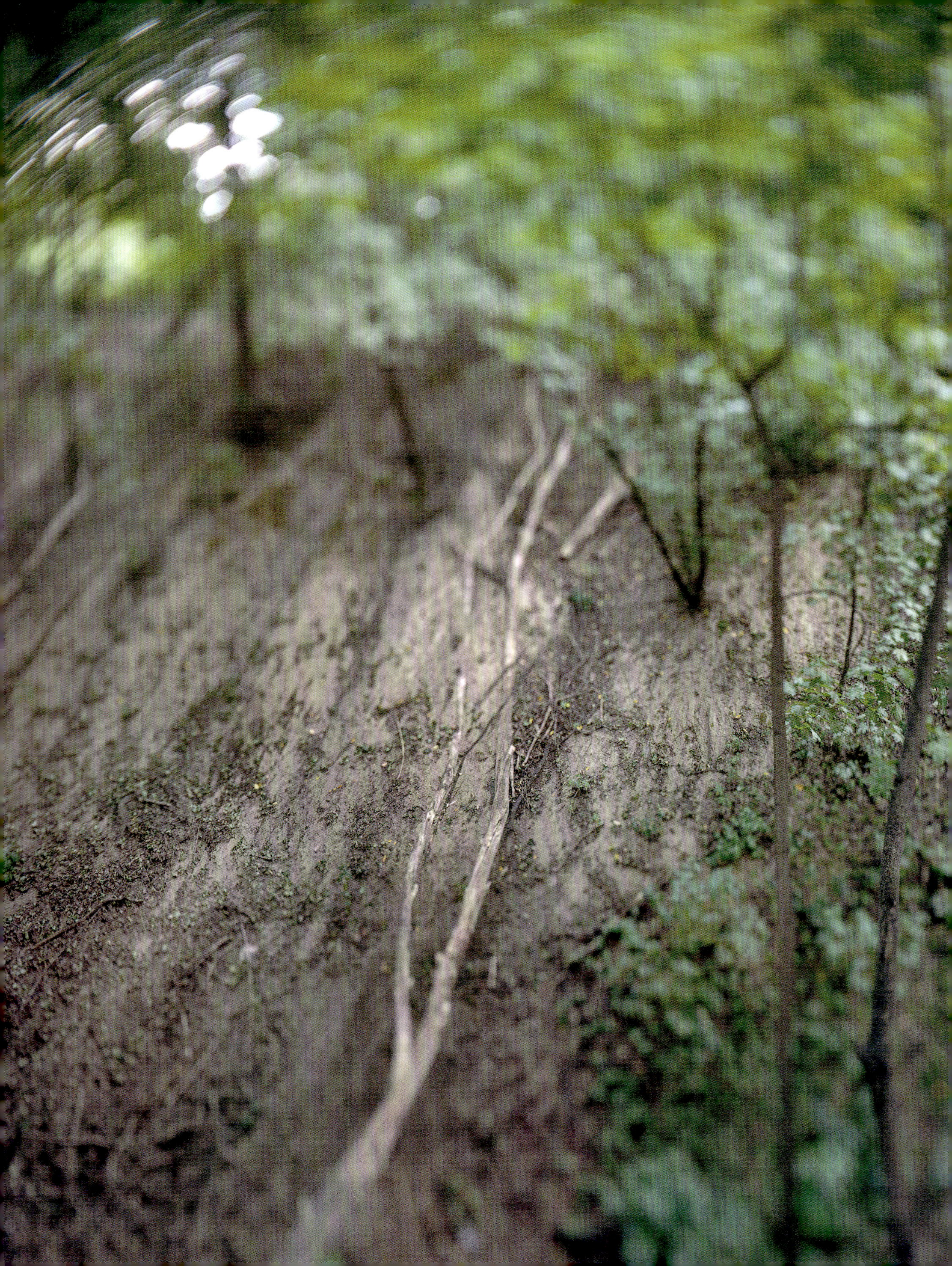

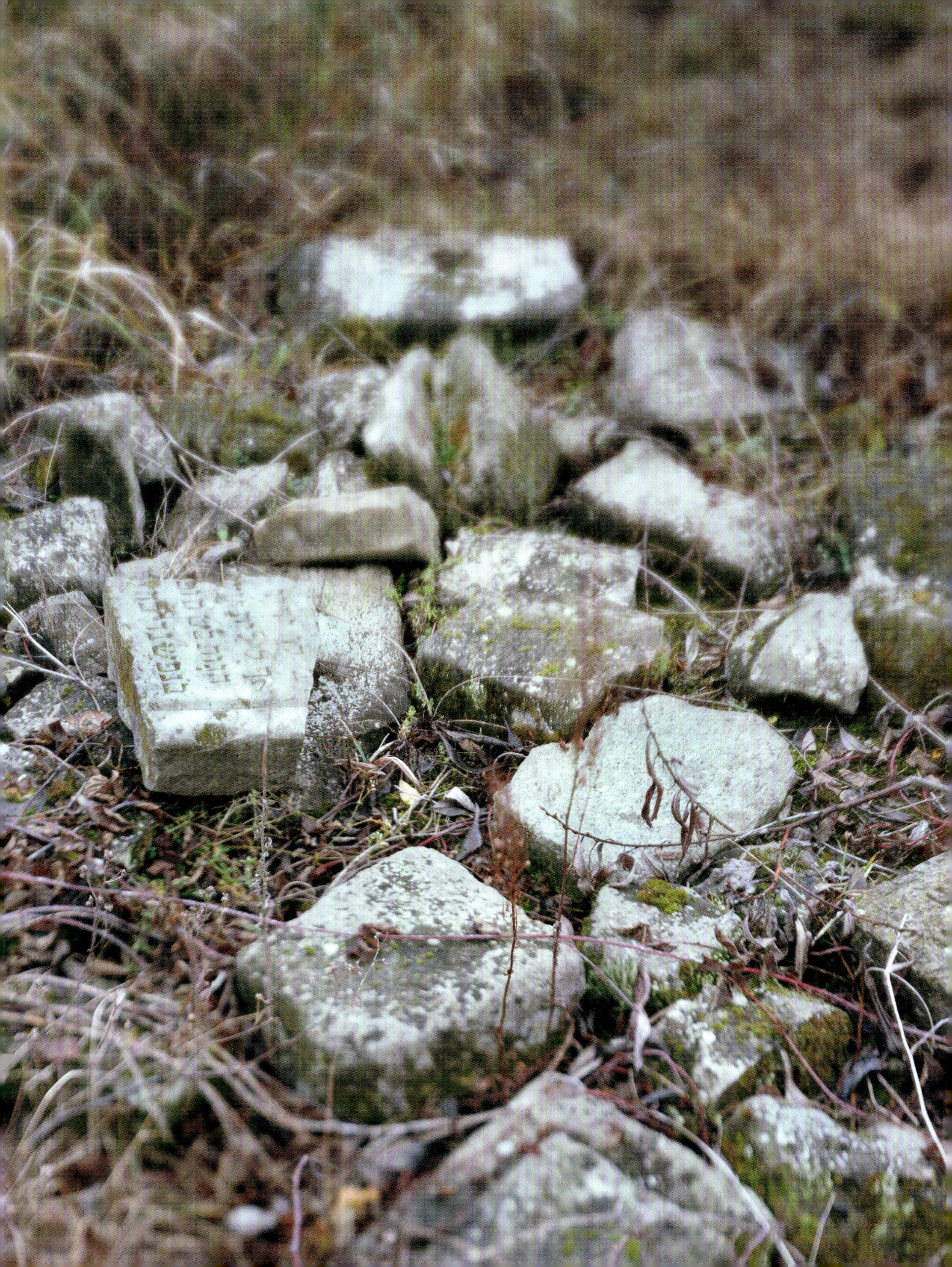

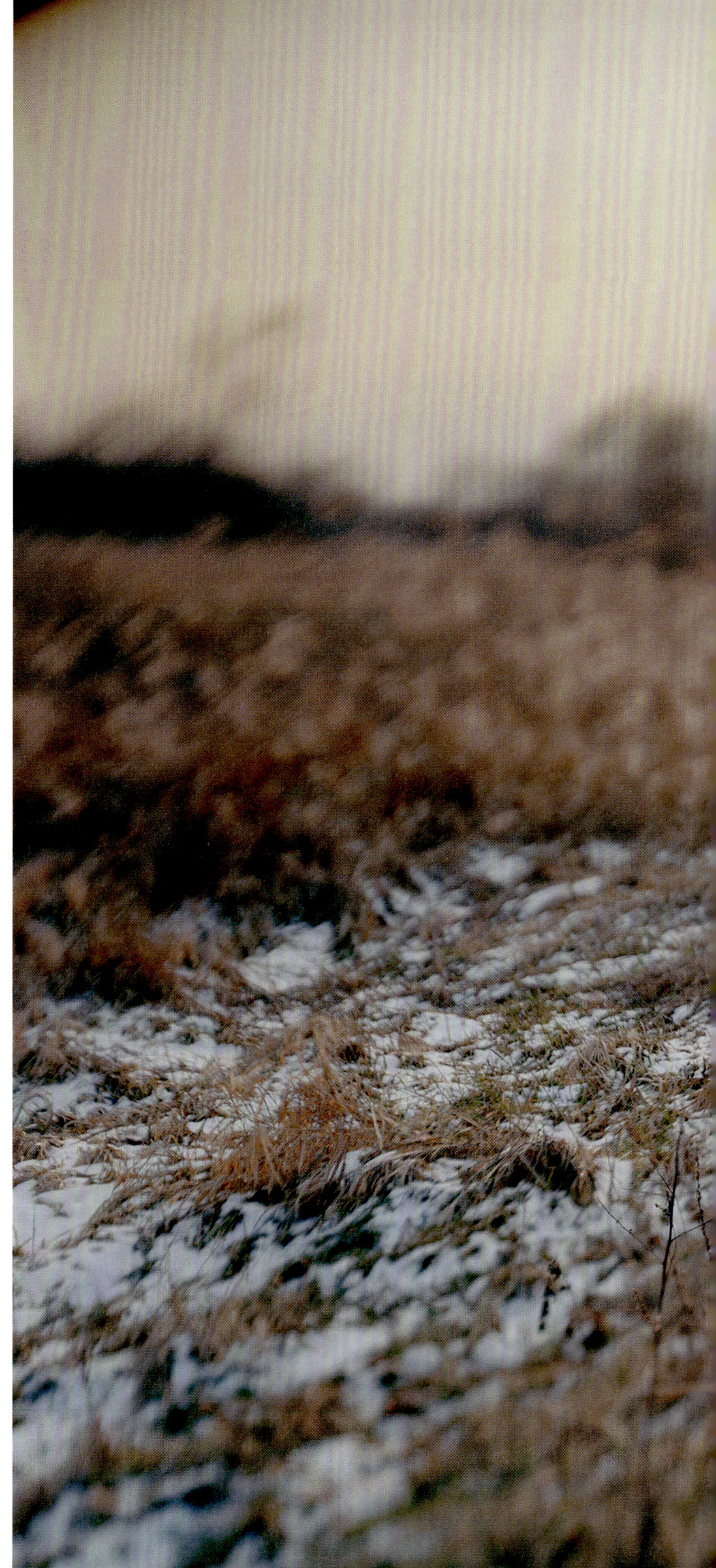

Plate 32

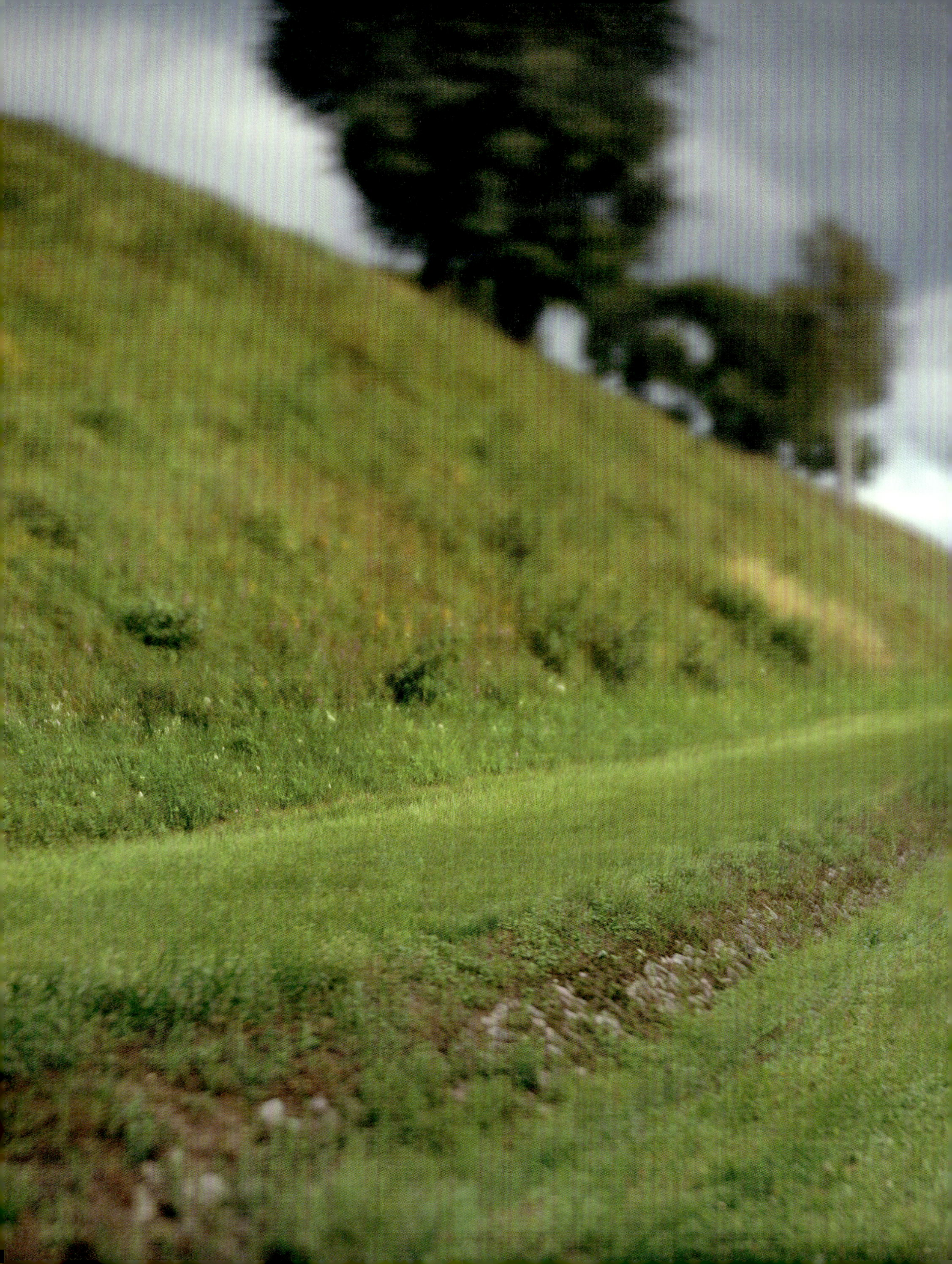

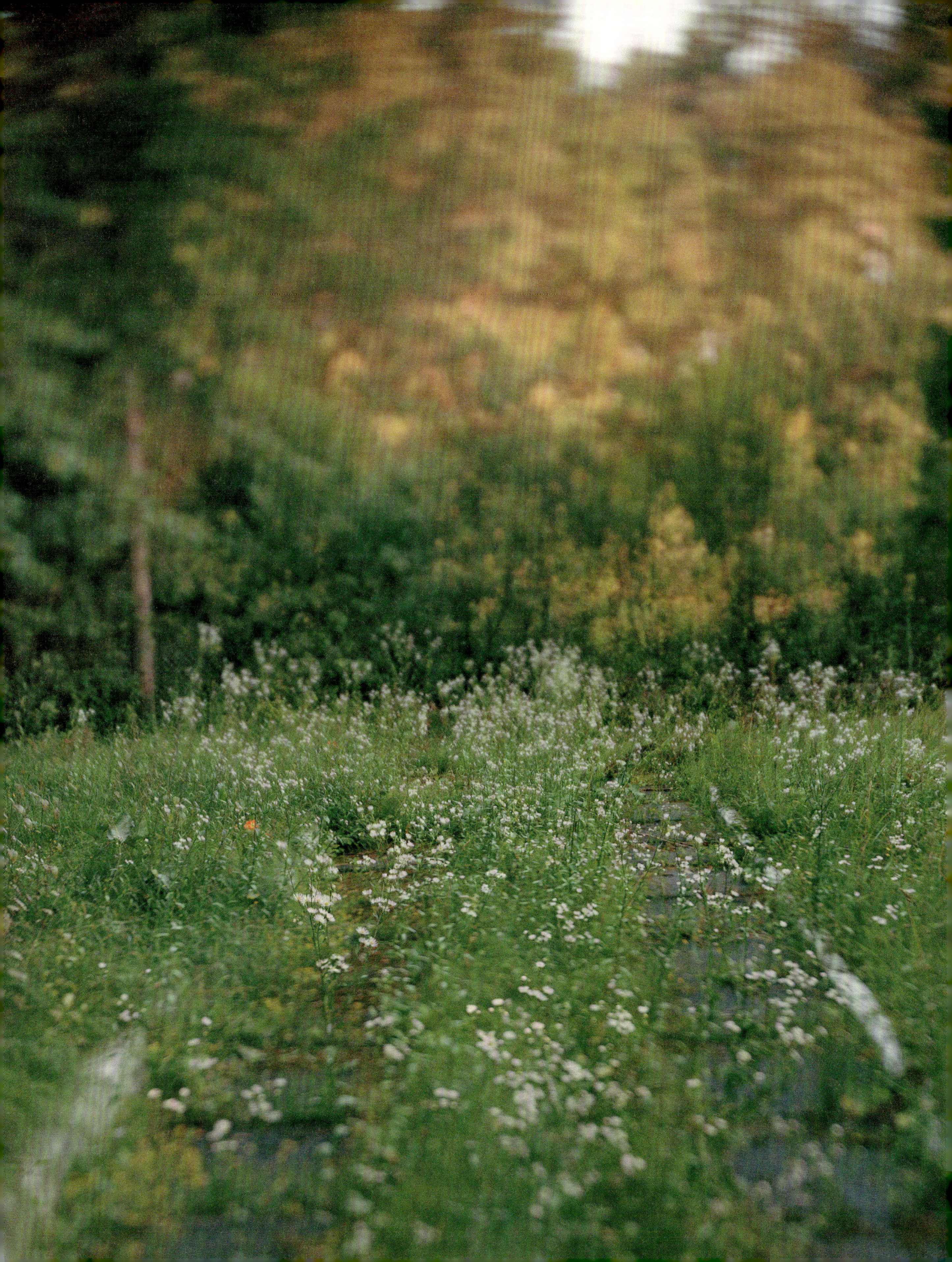

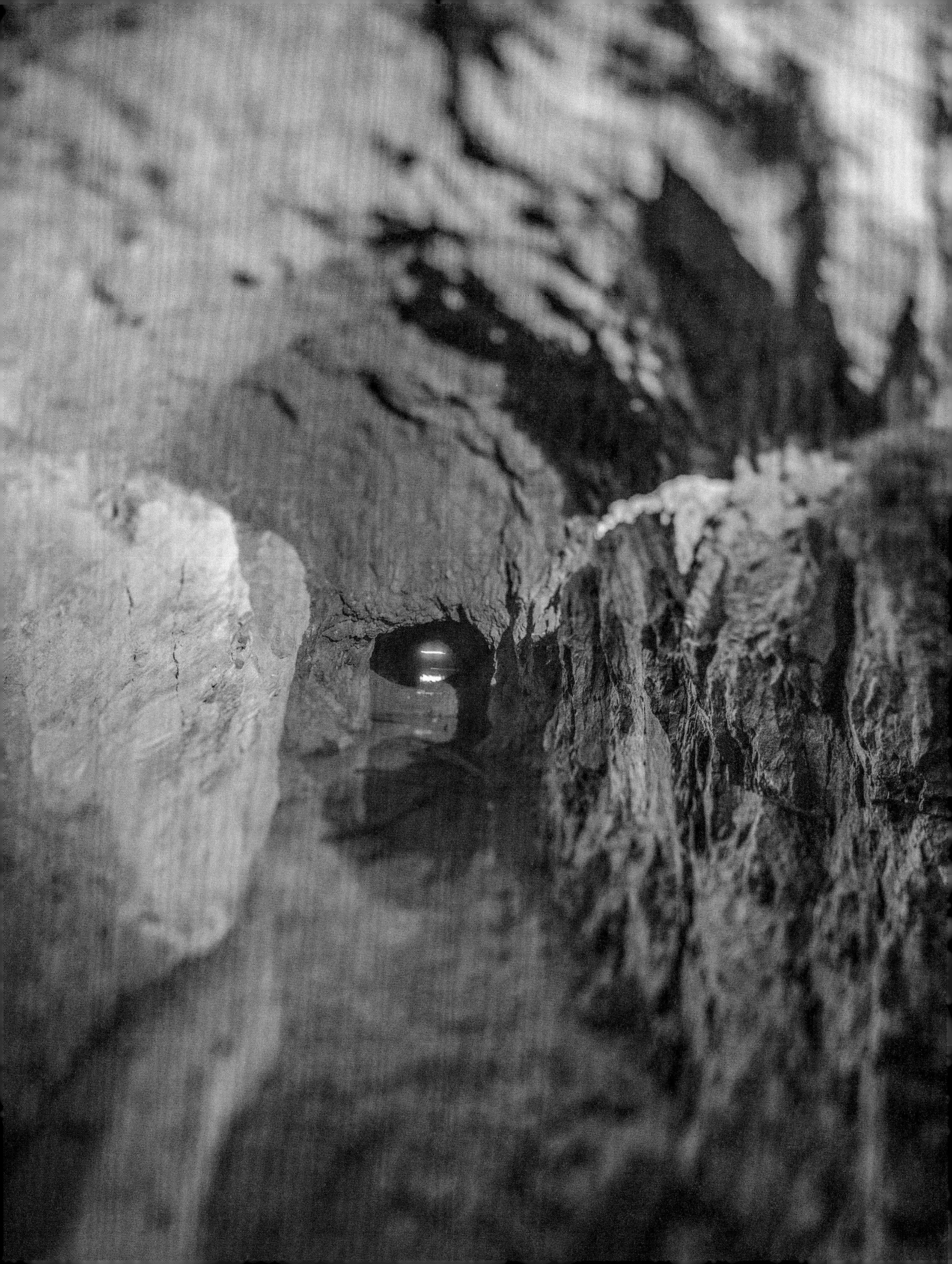

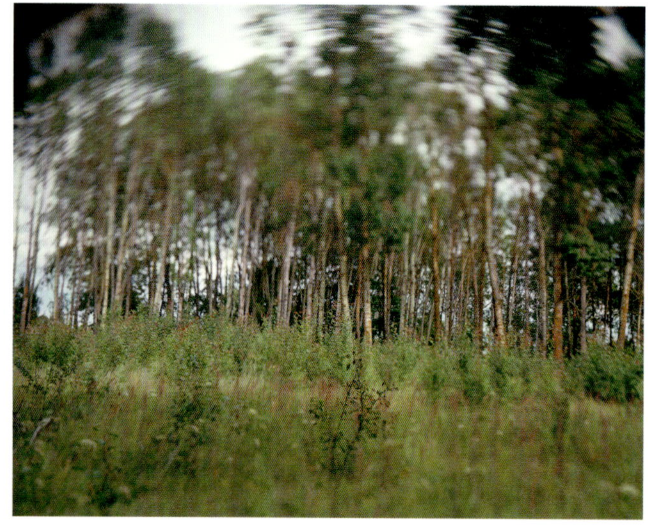
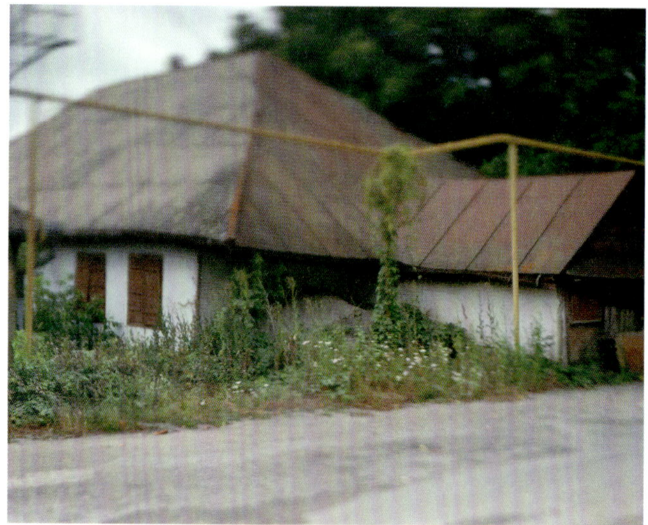
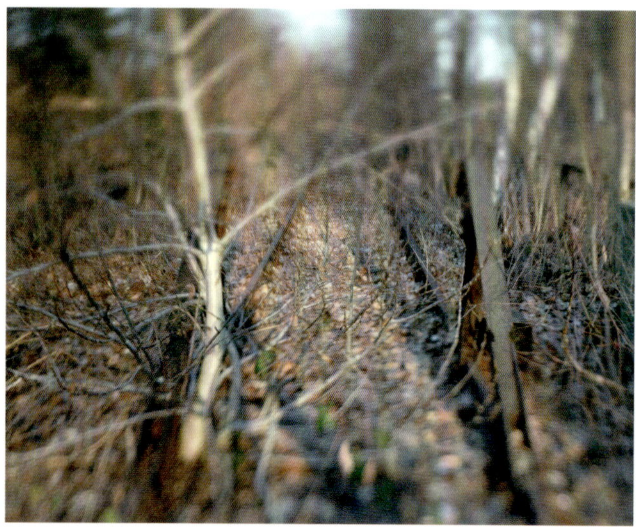
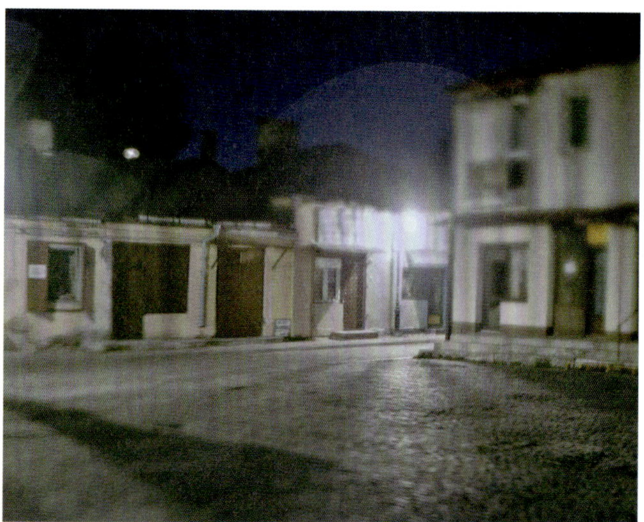
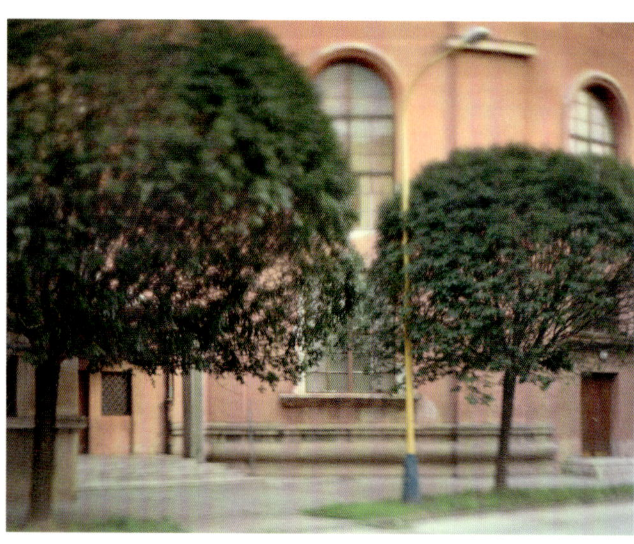
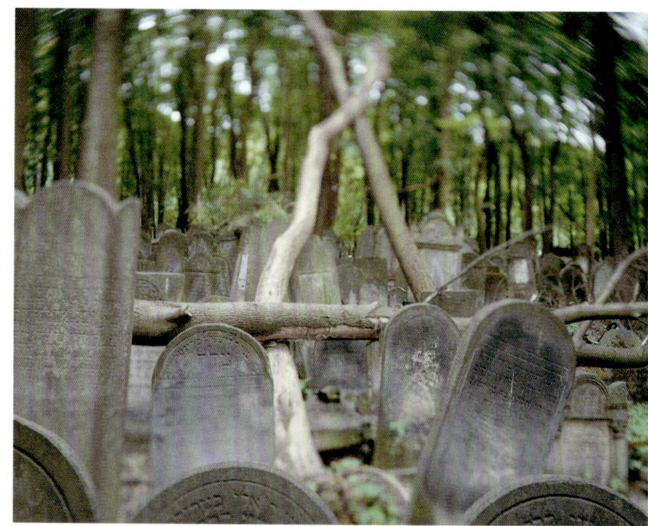

Plate 36

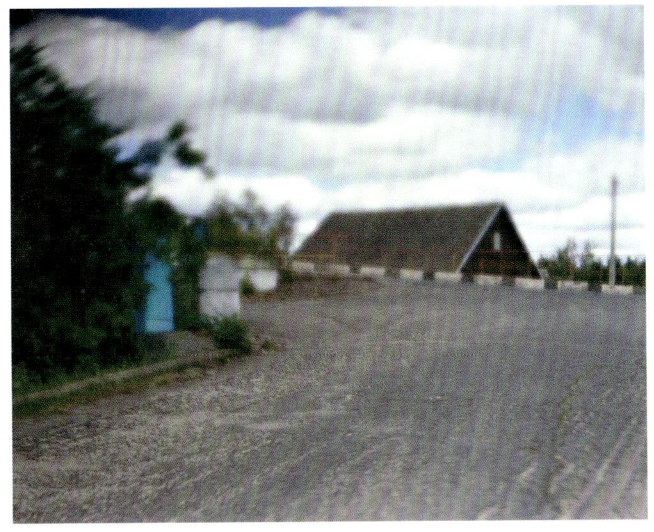
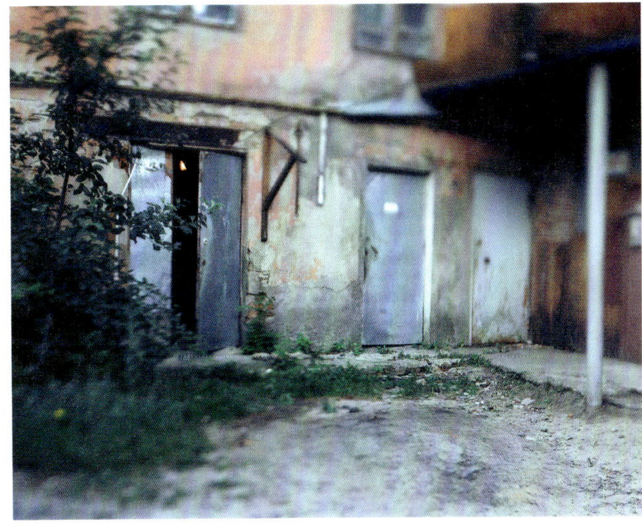

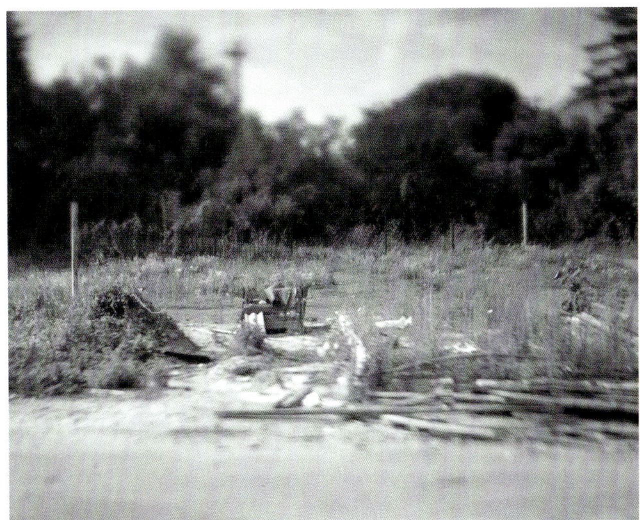
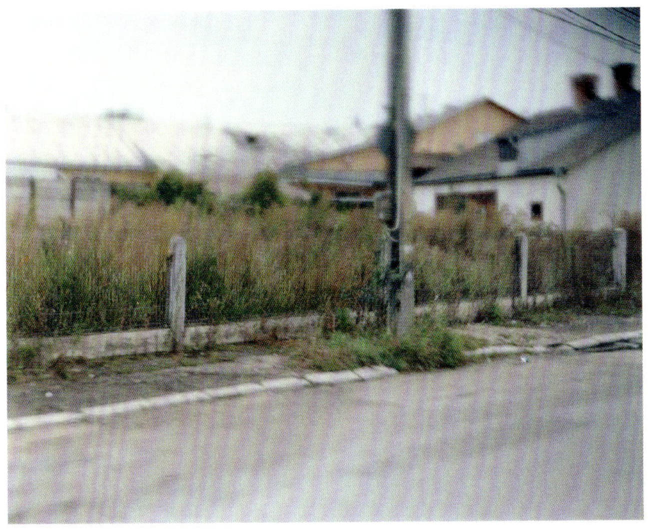
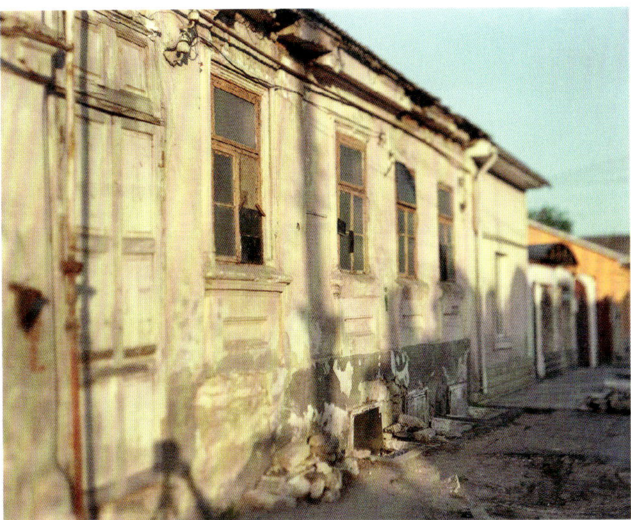

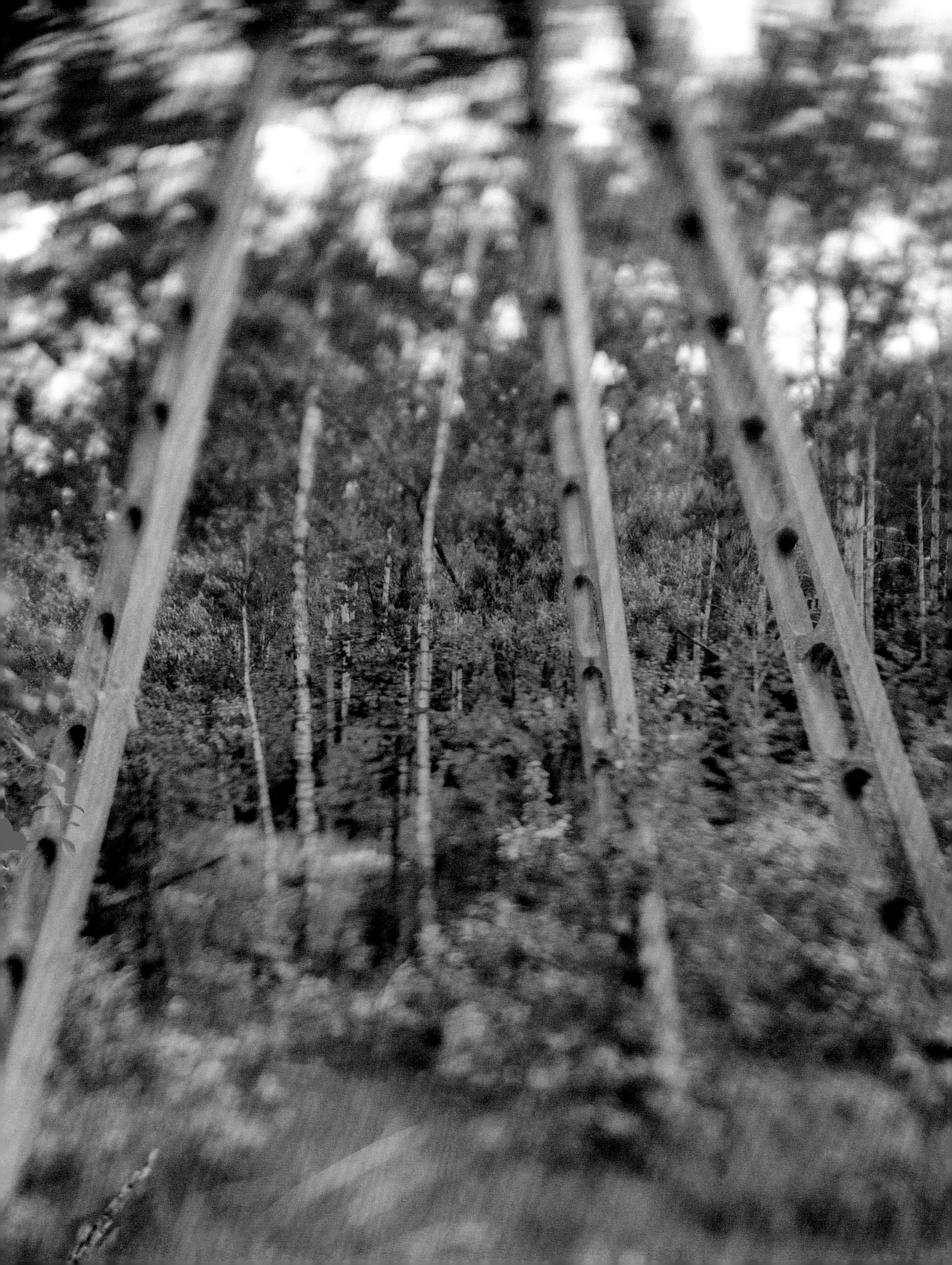

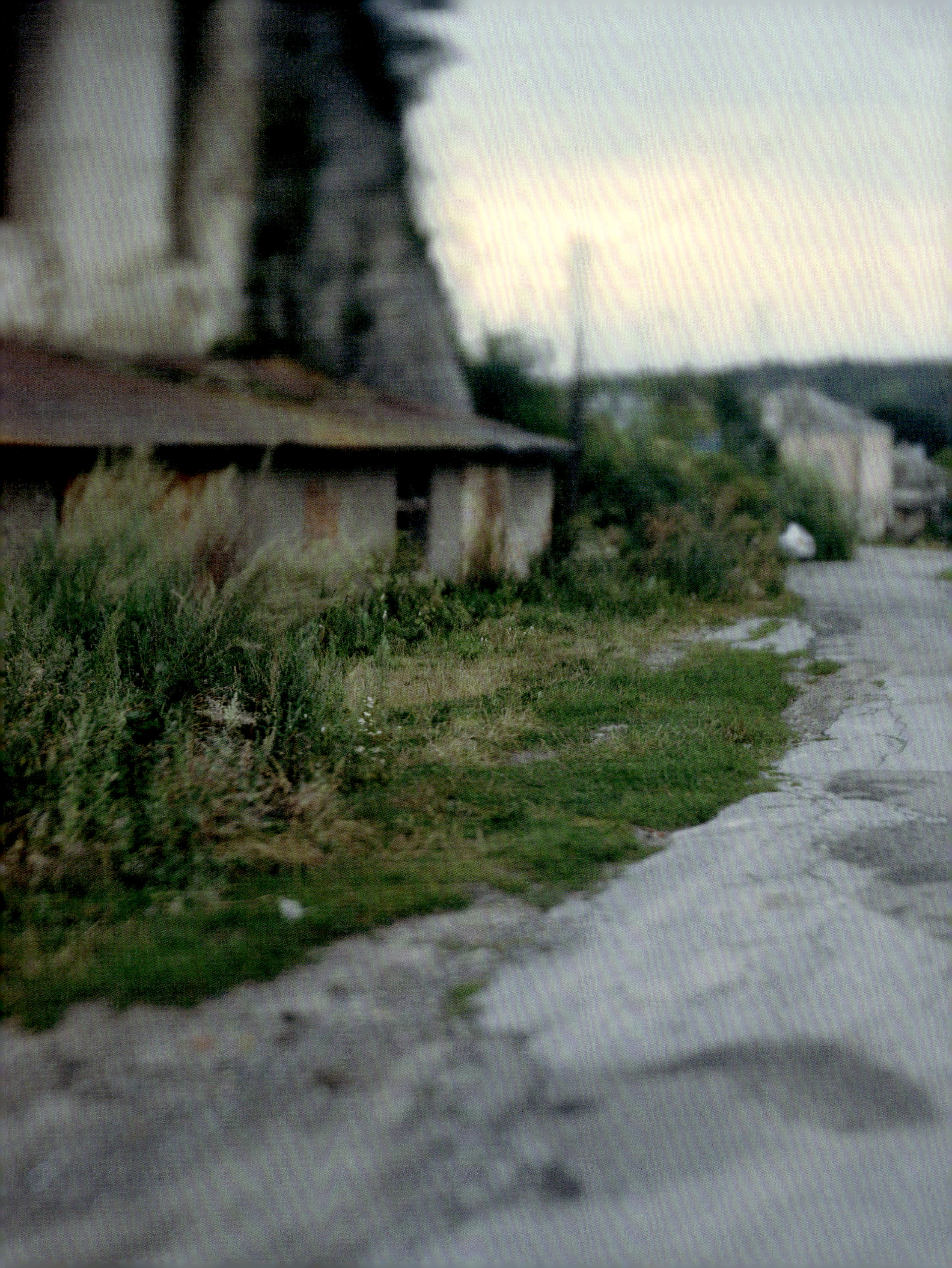

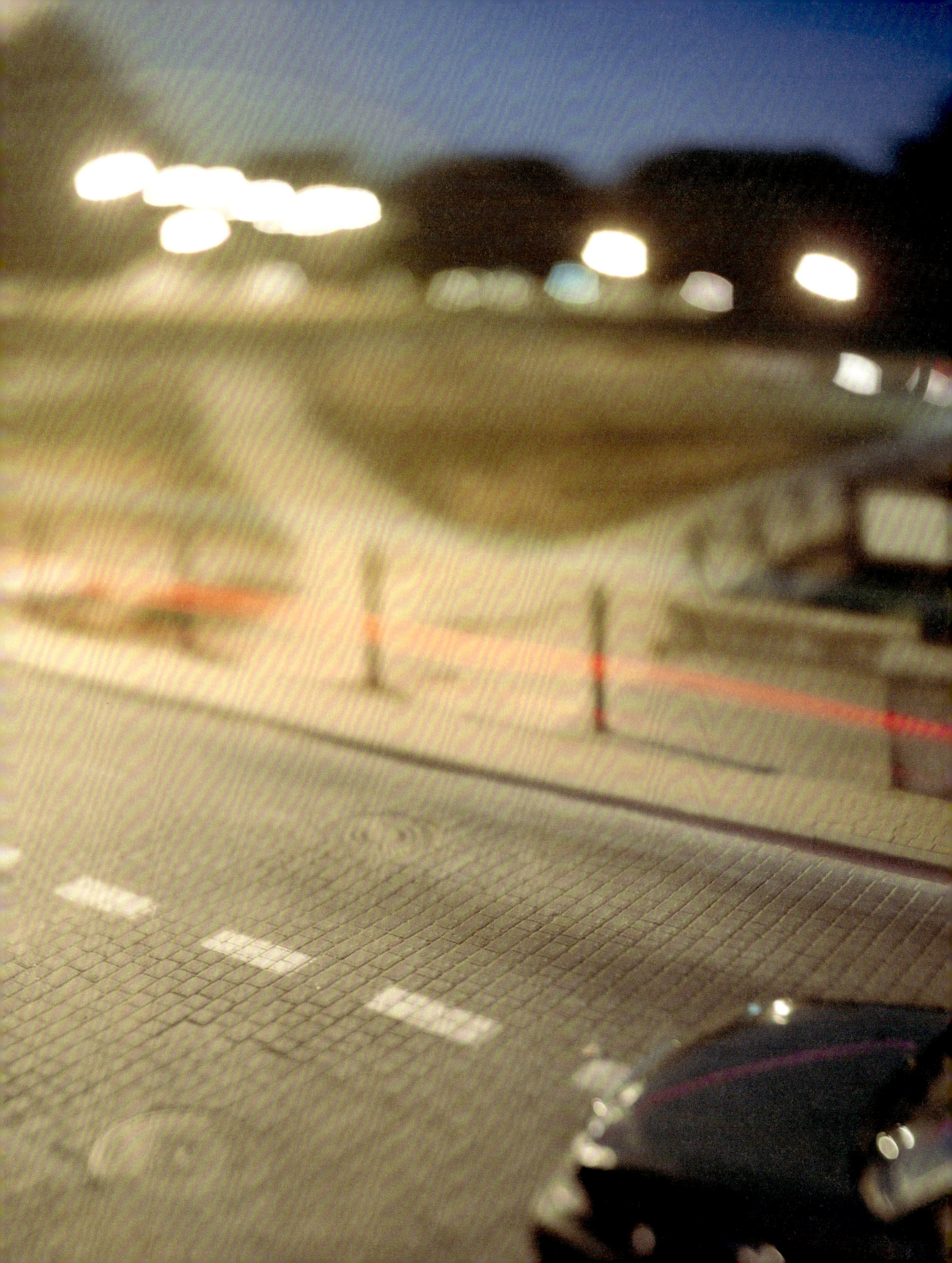

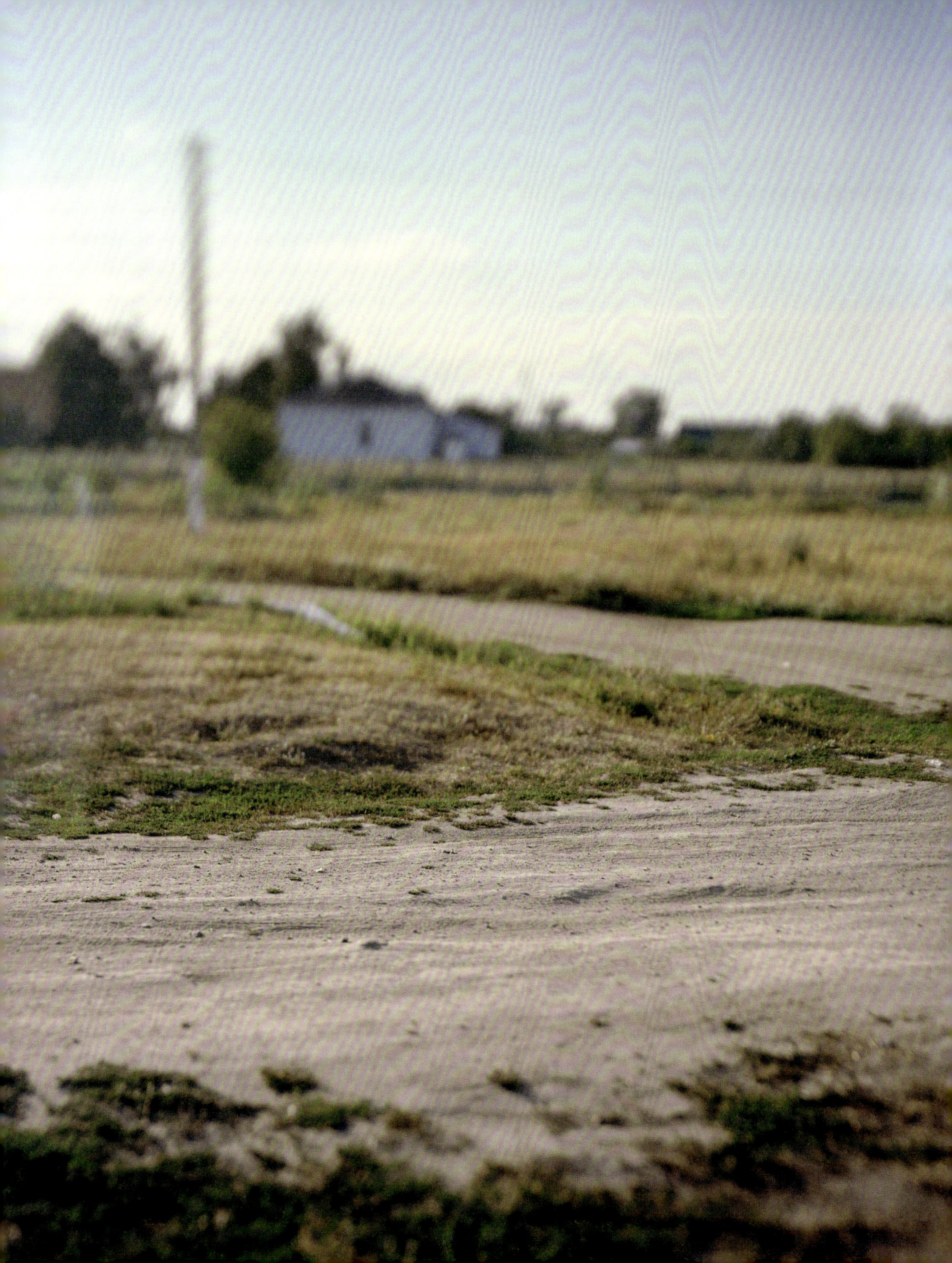

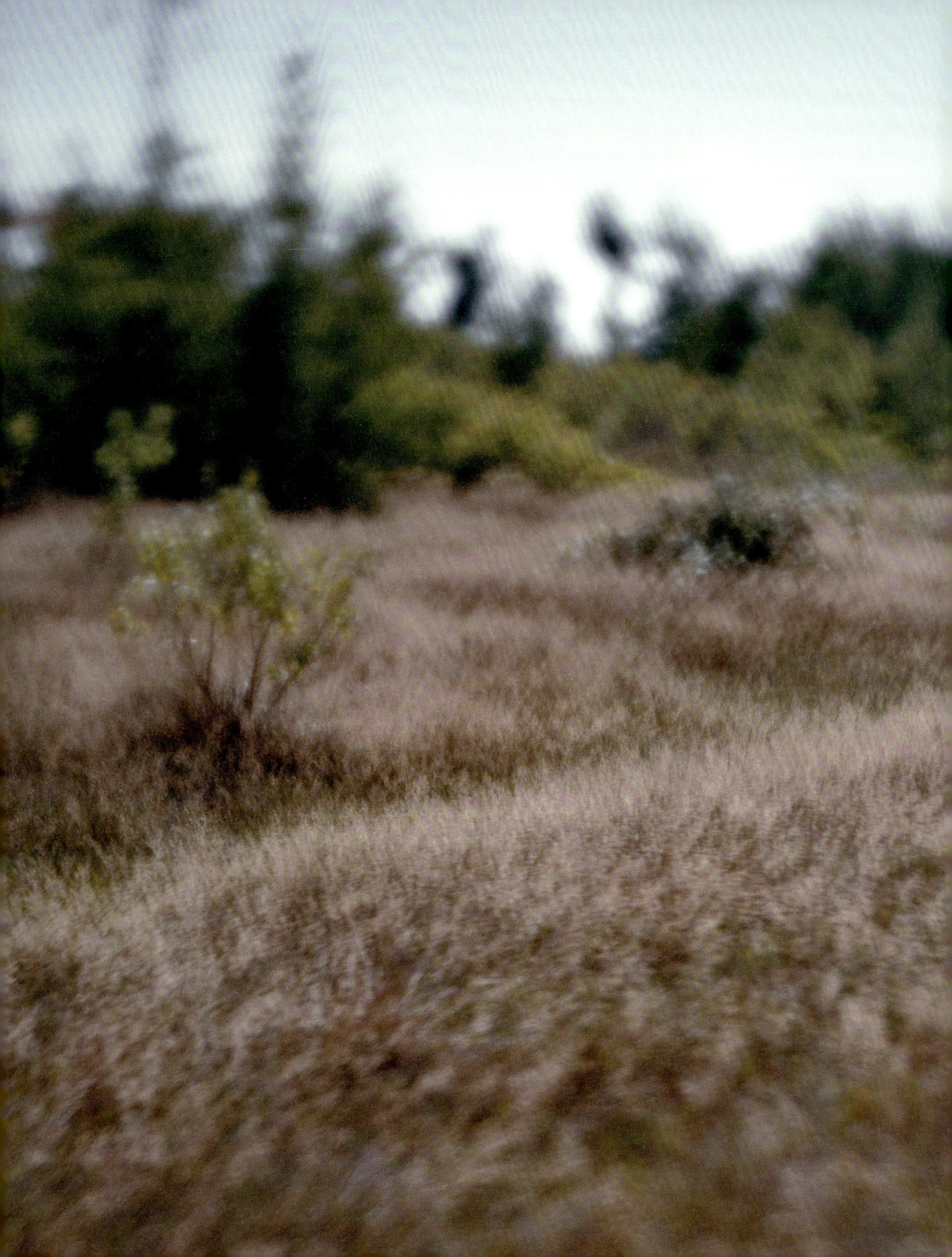

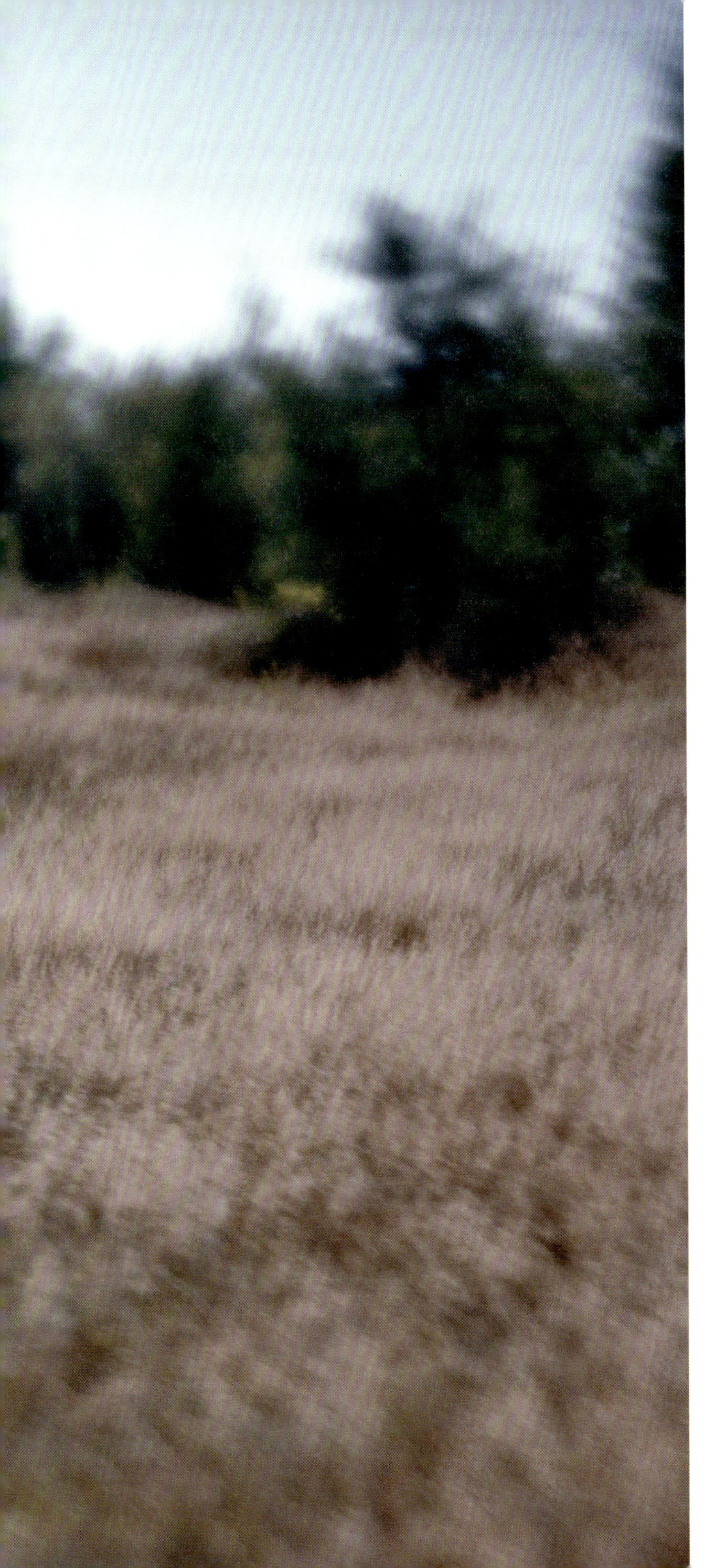

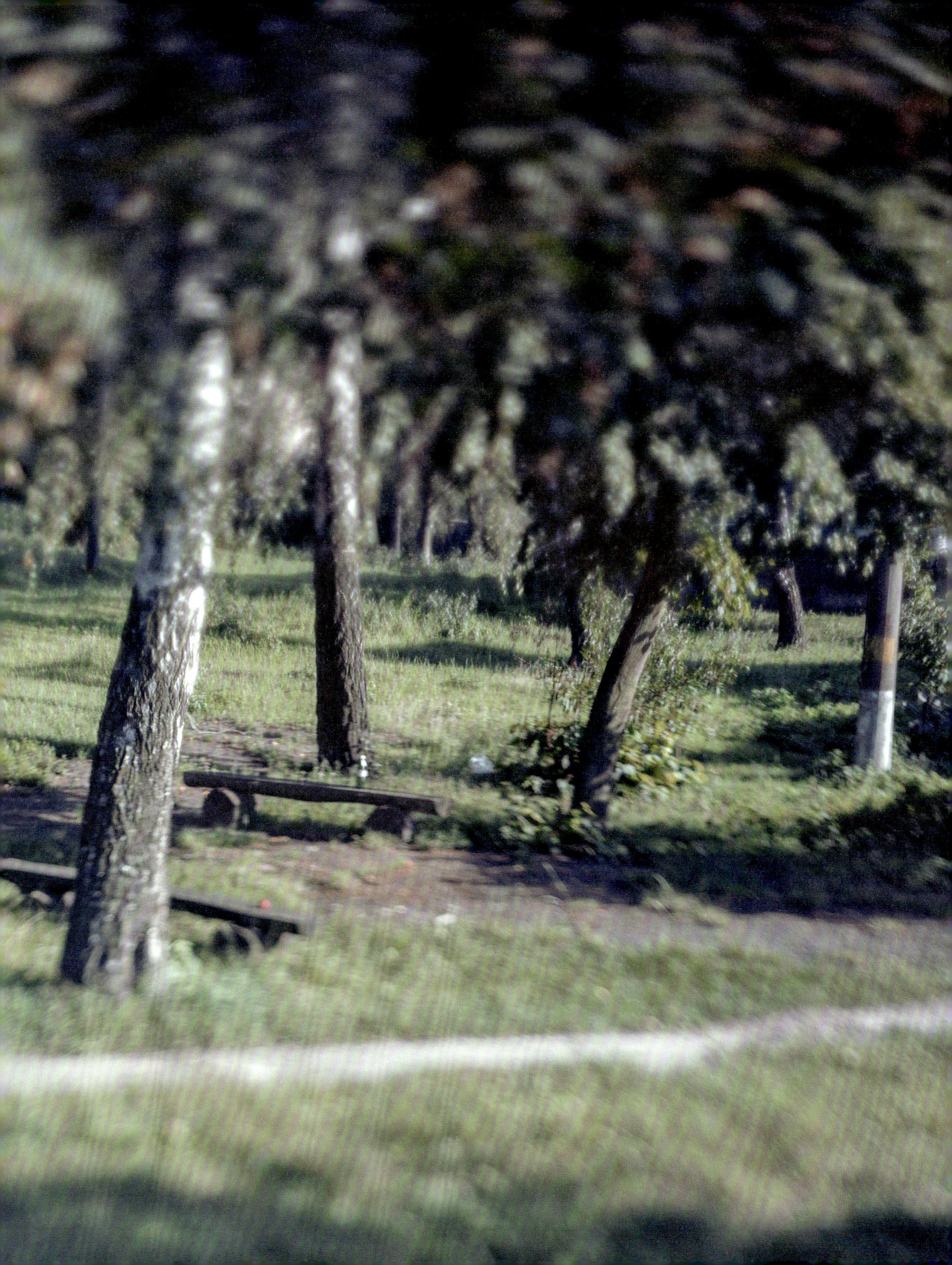

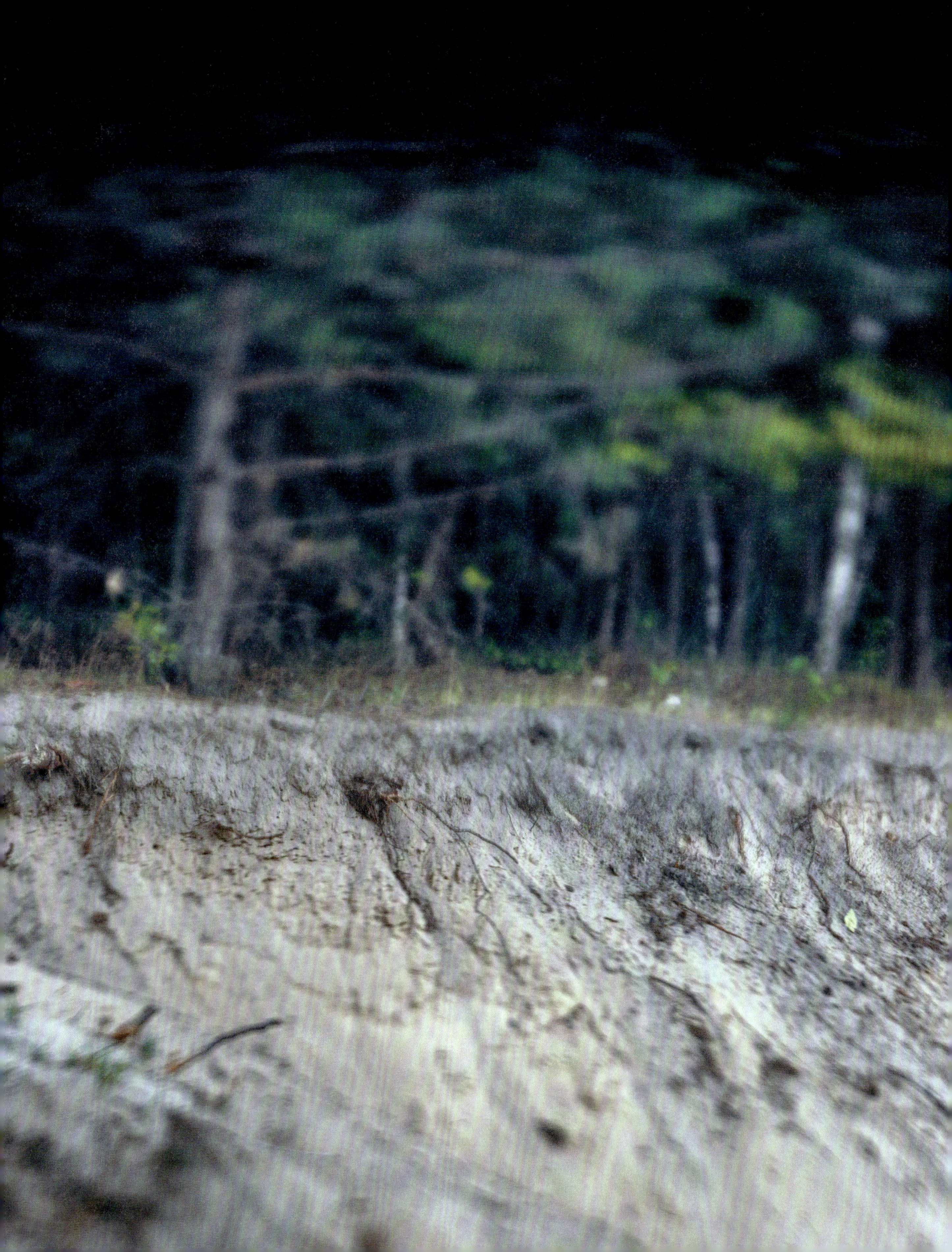

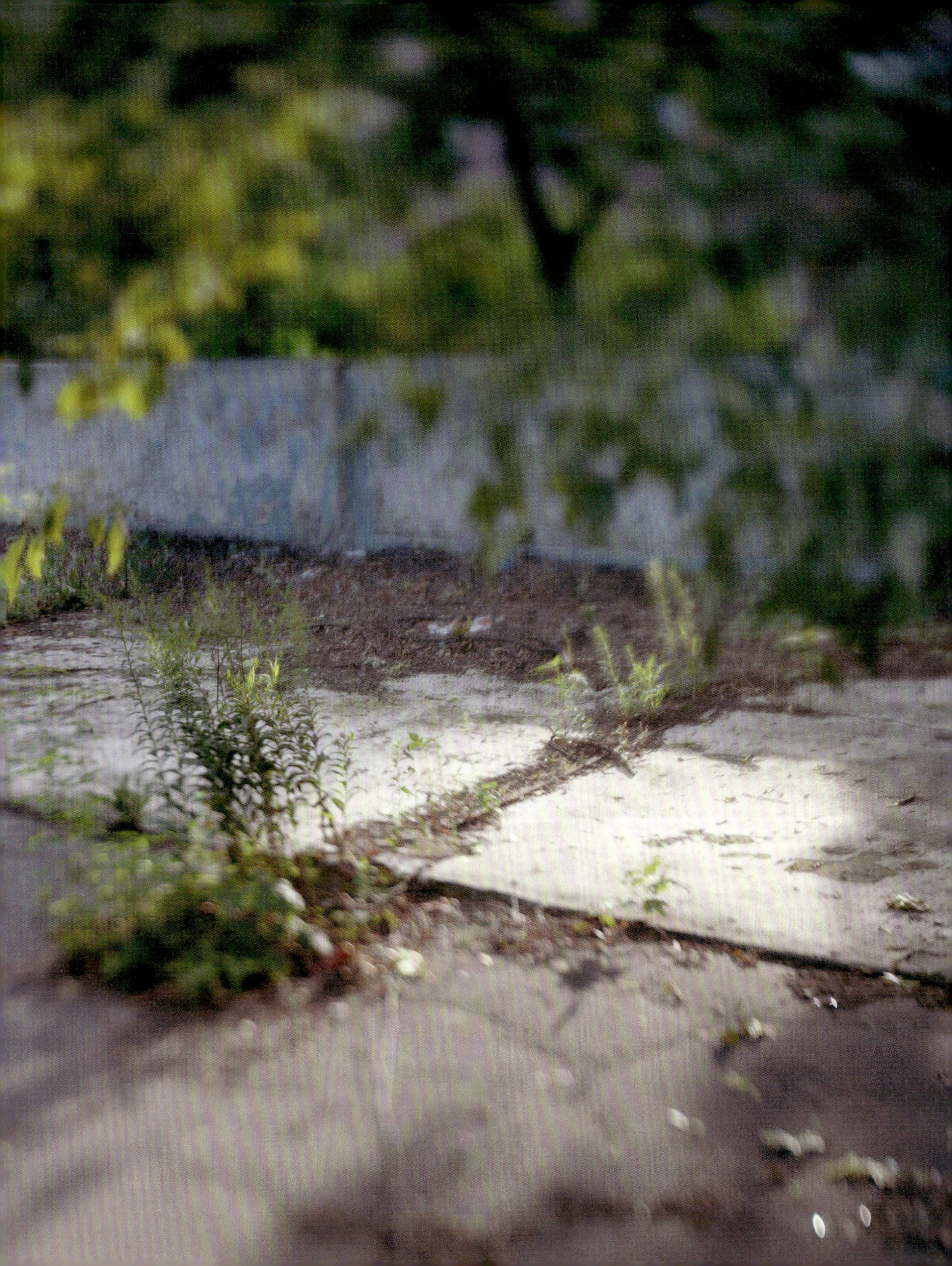

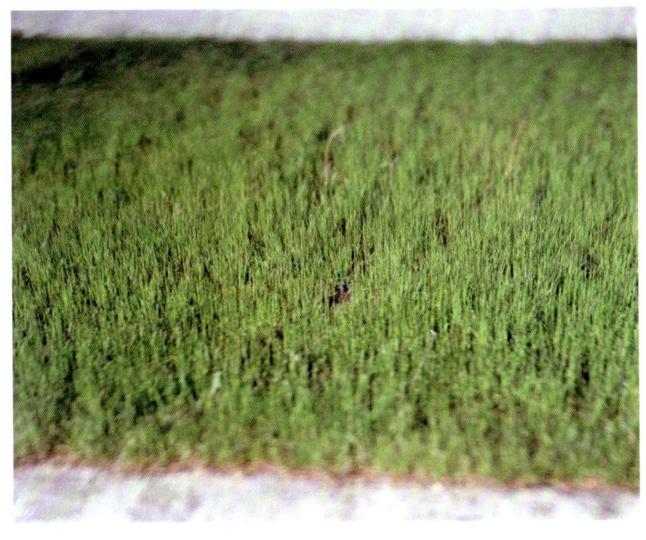
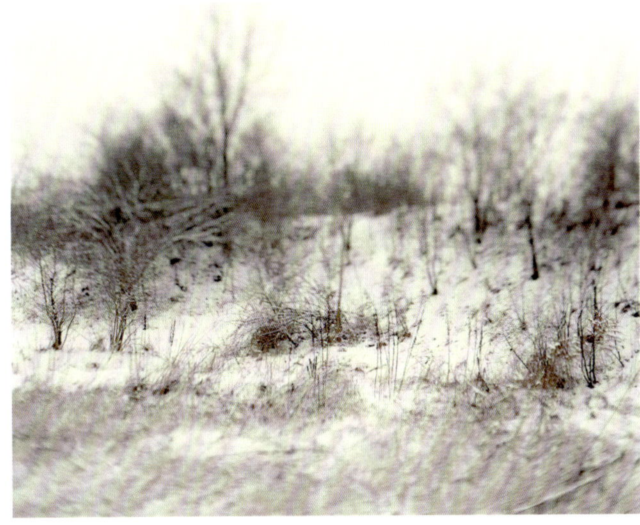
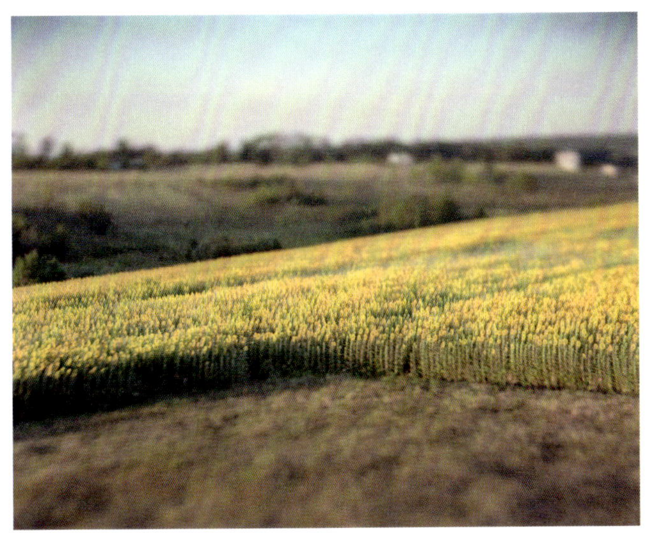
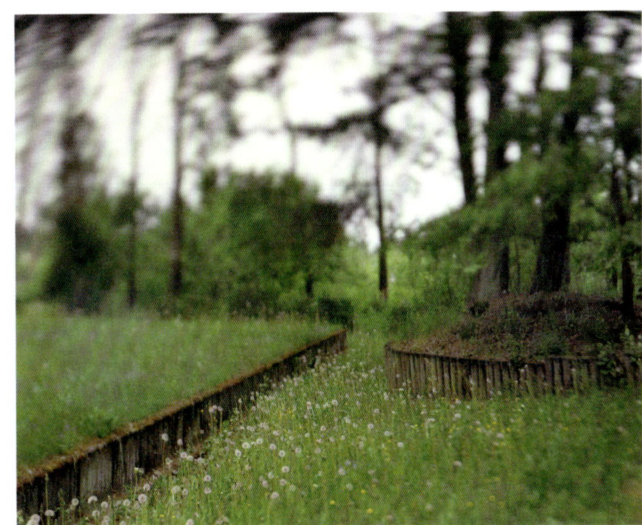
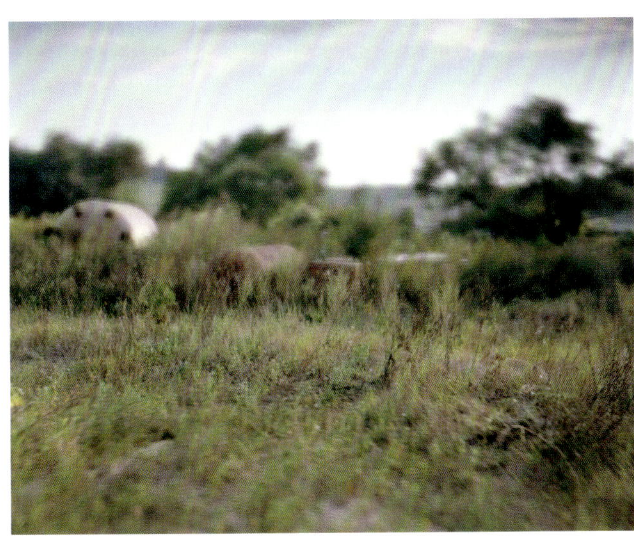
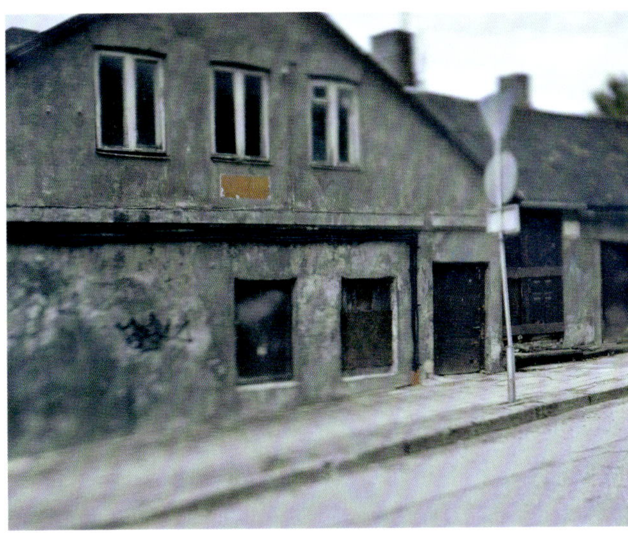

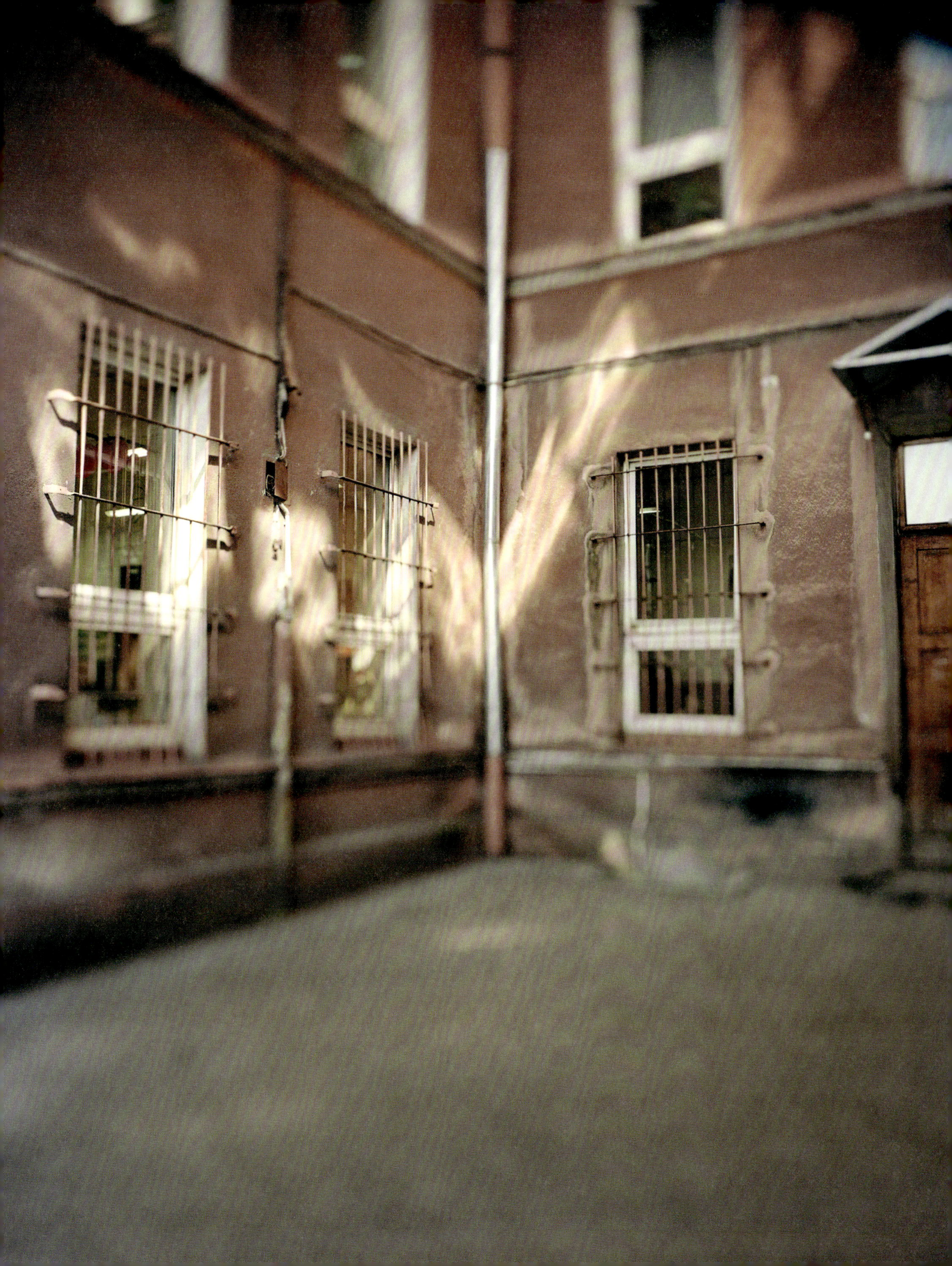

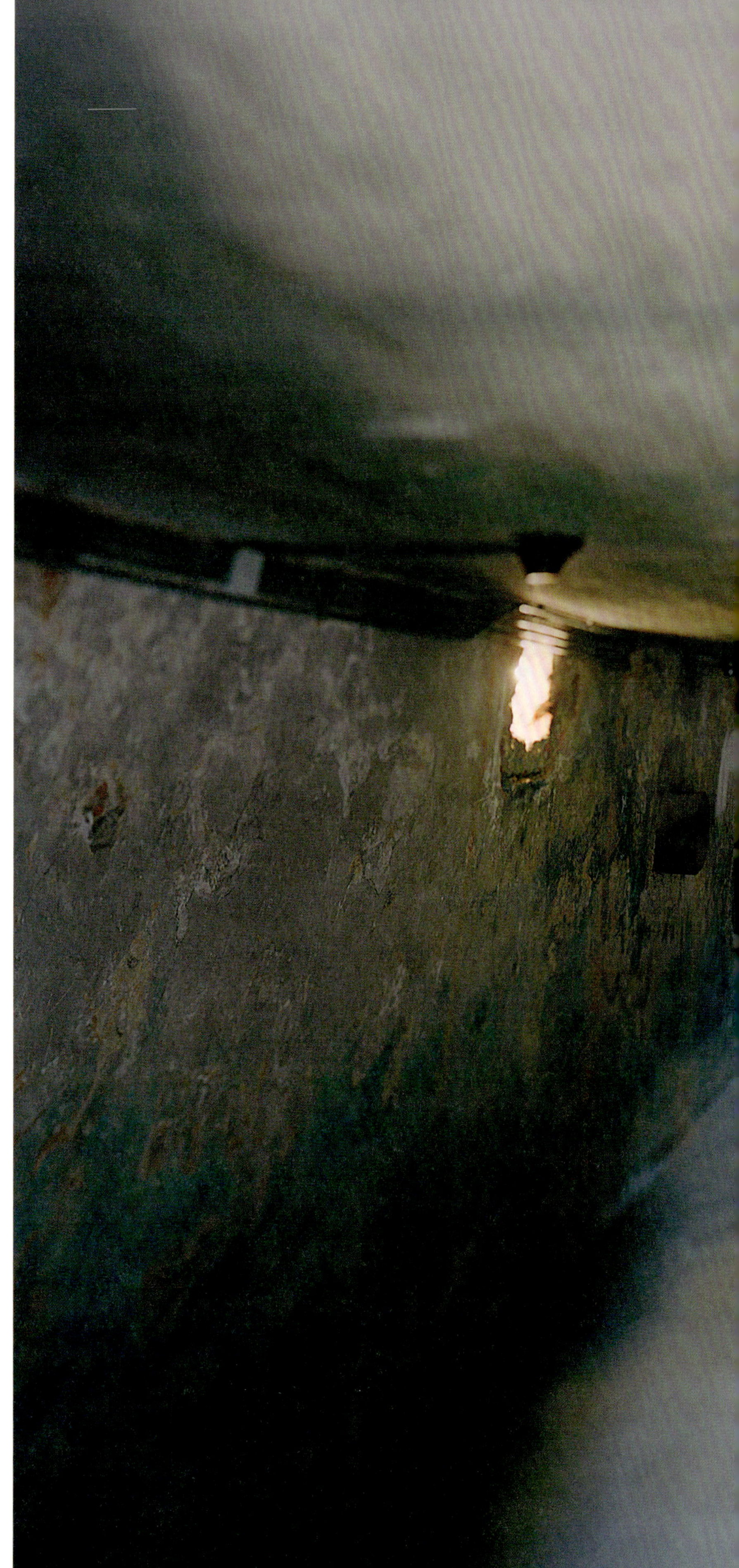

Plate 48

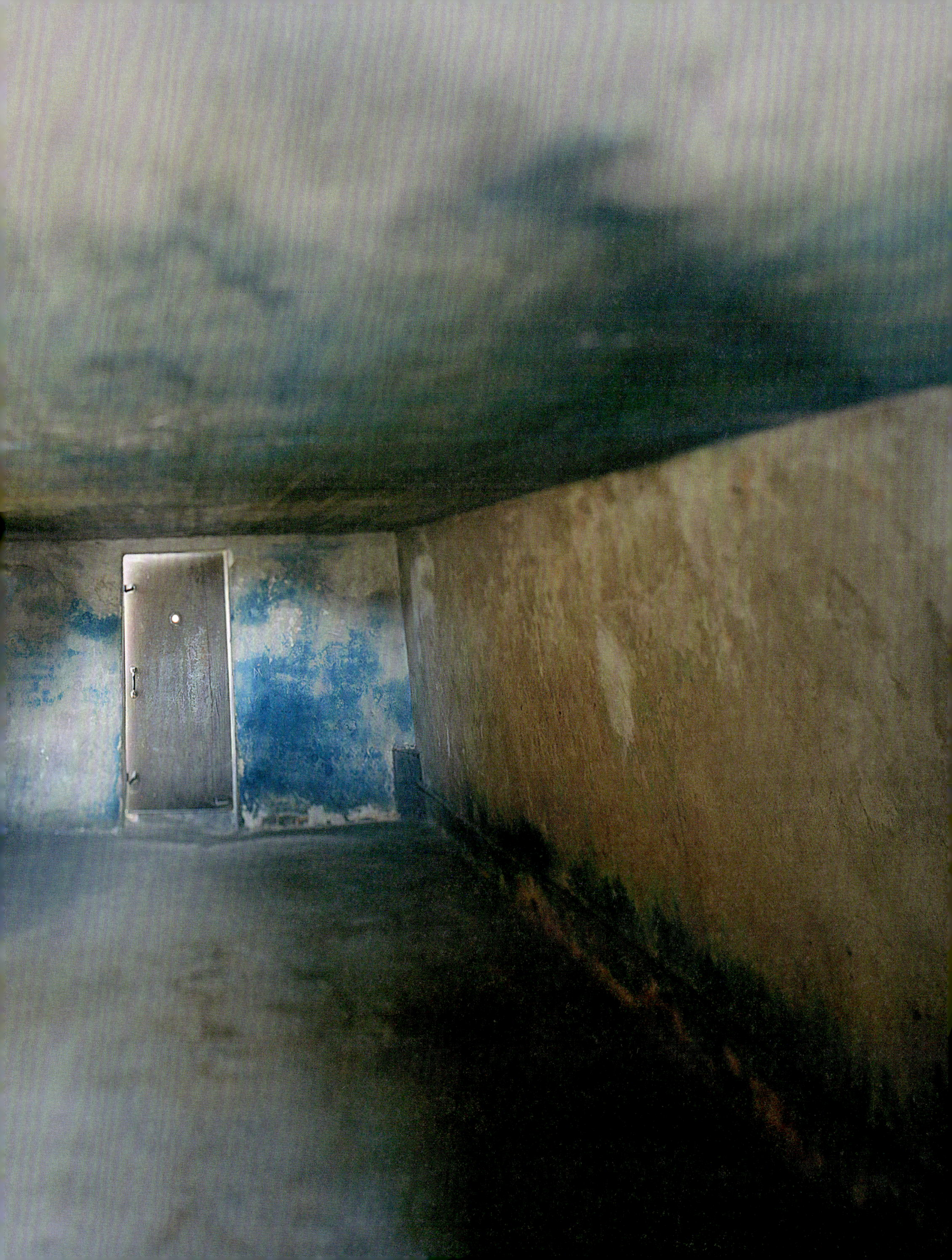

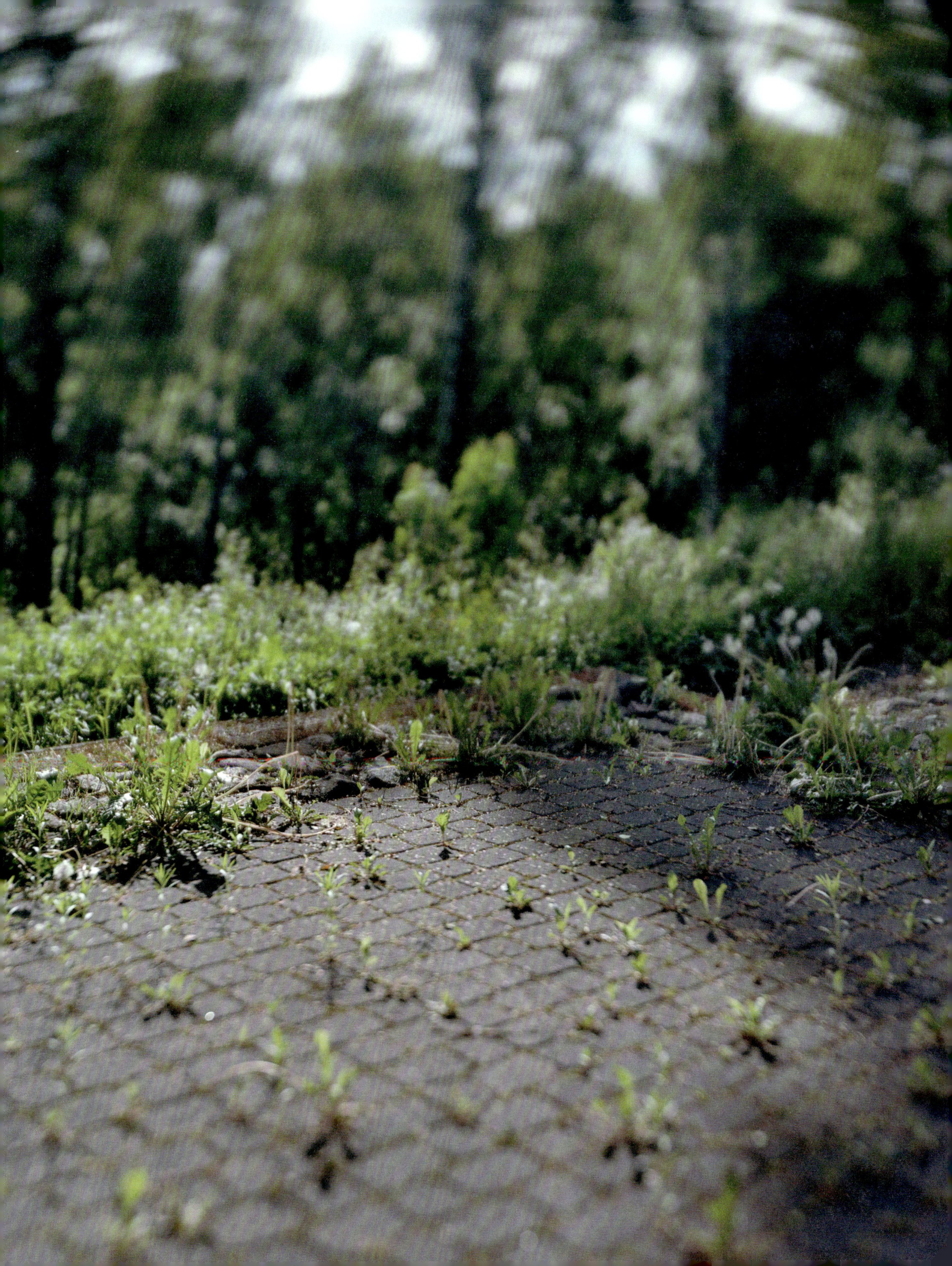

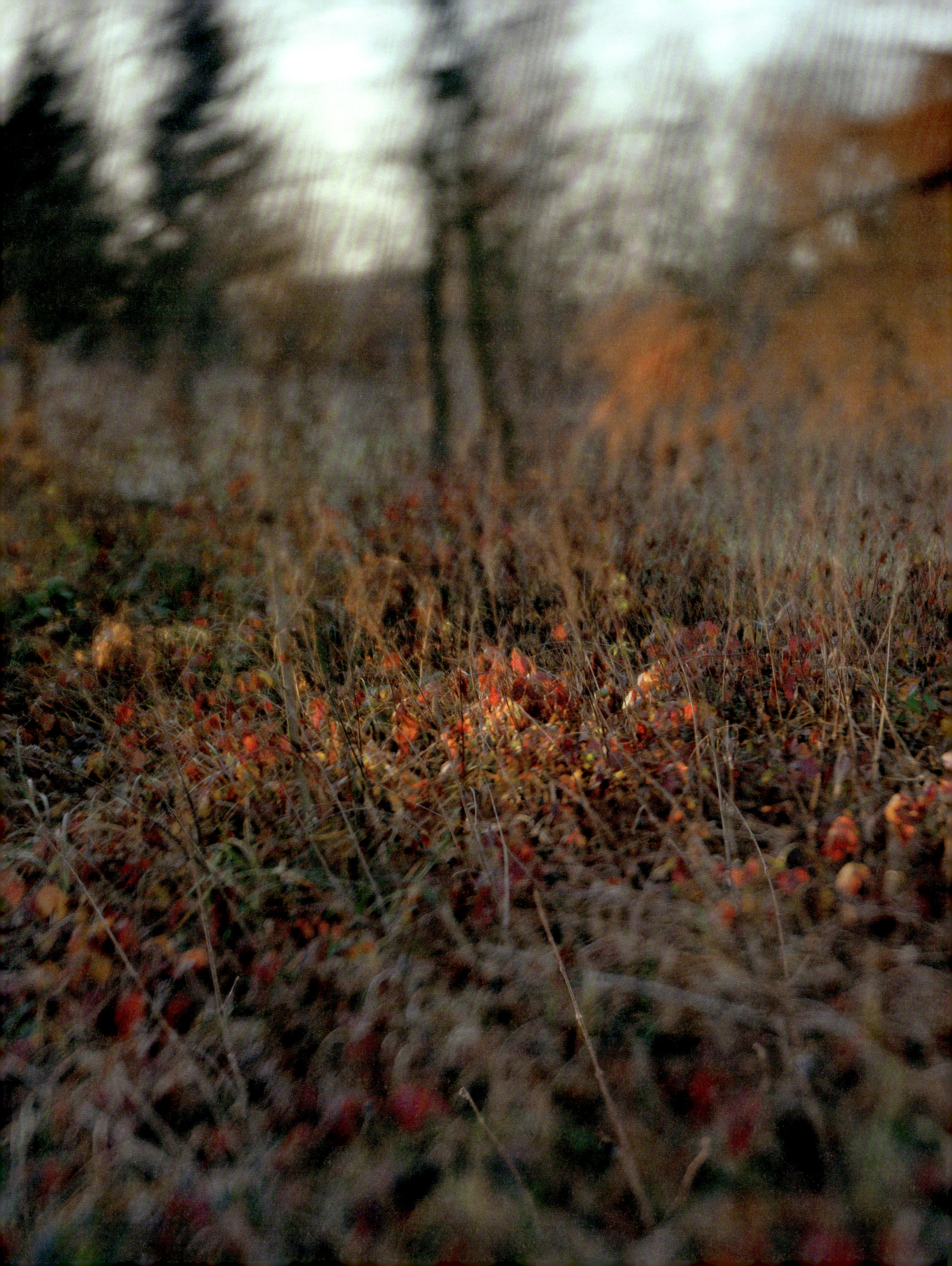

Plate 51

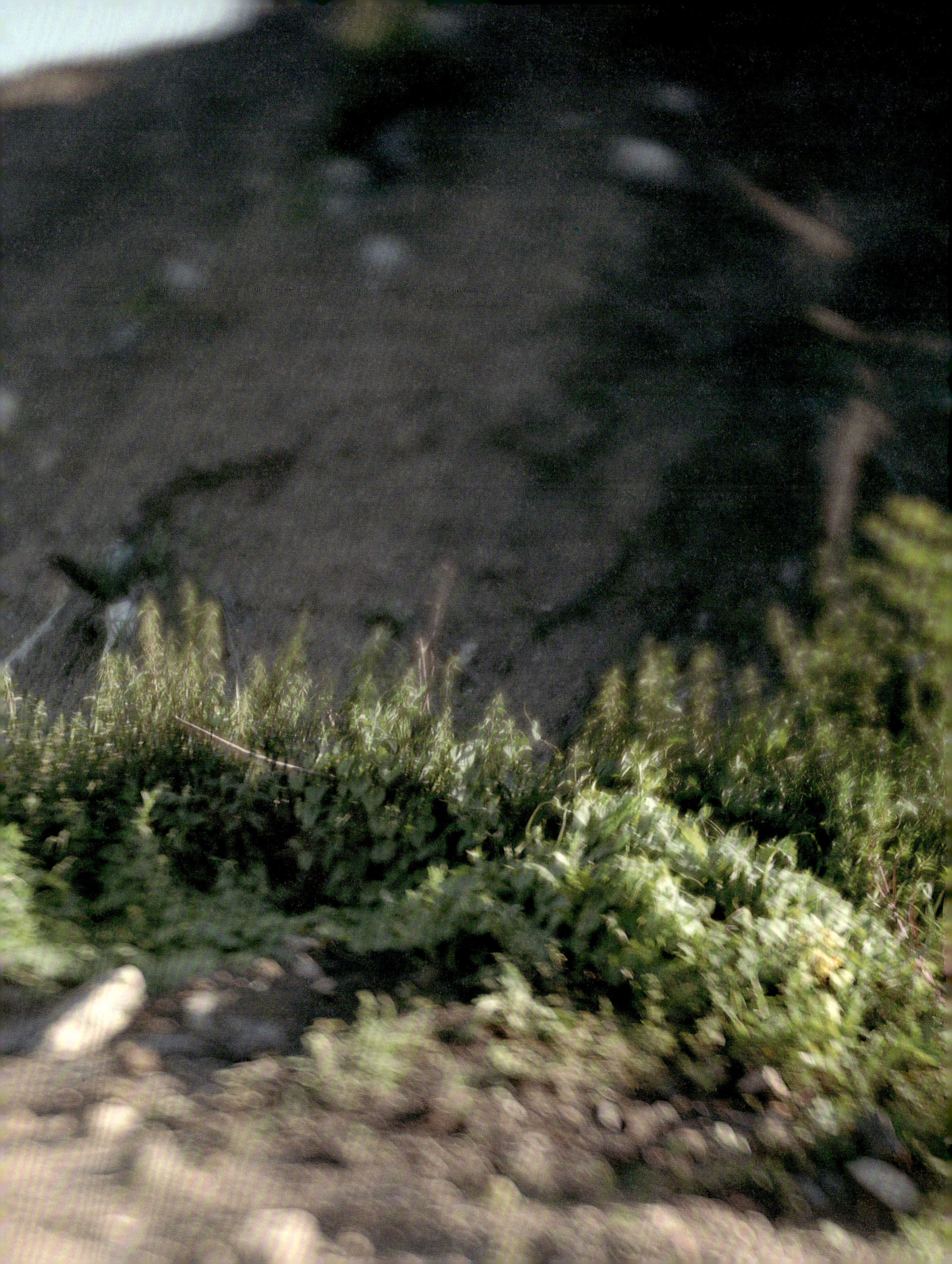

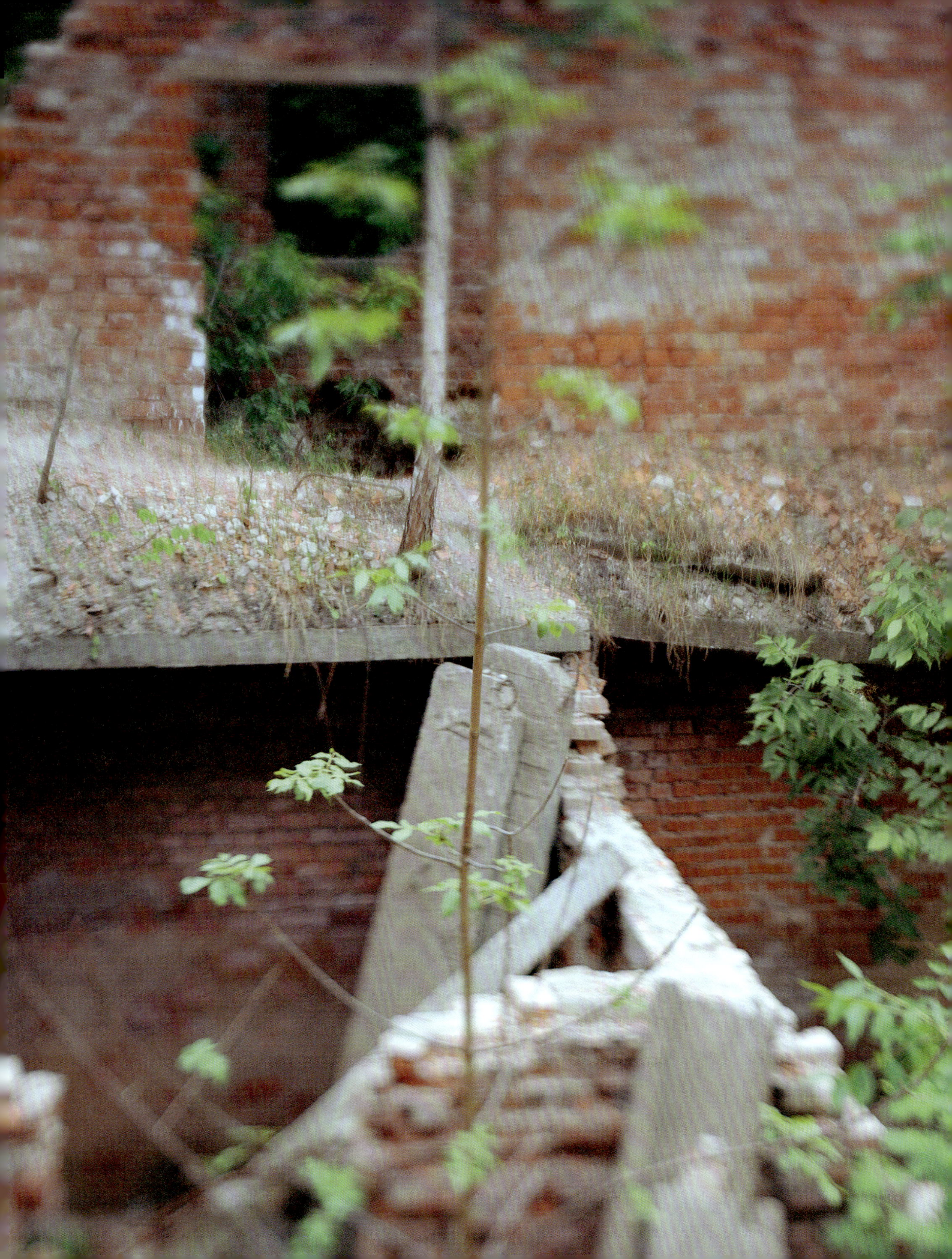

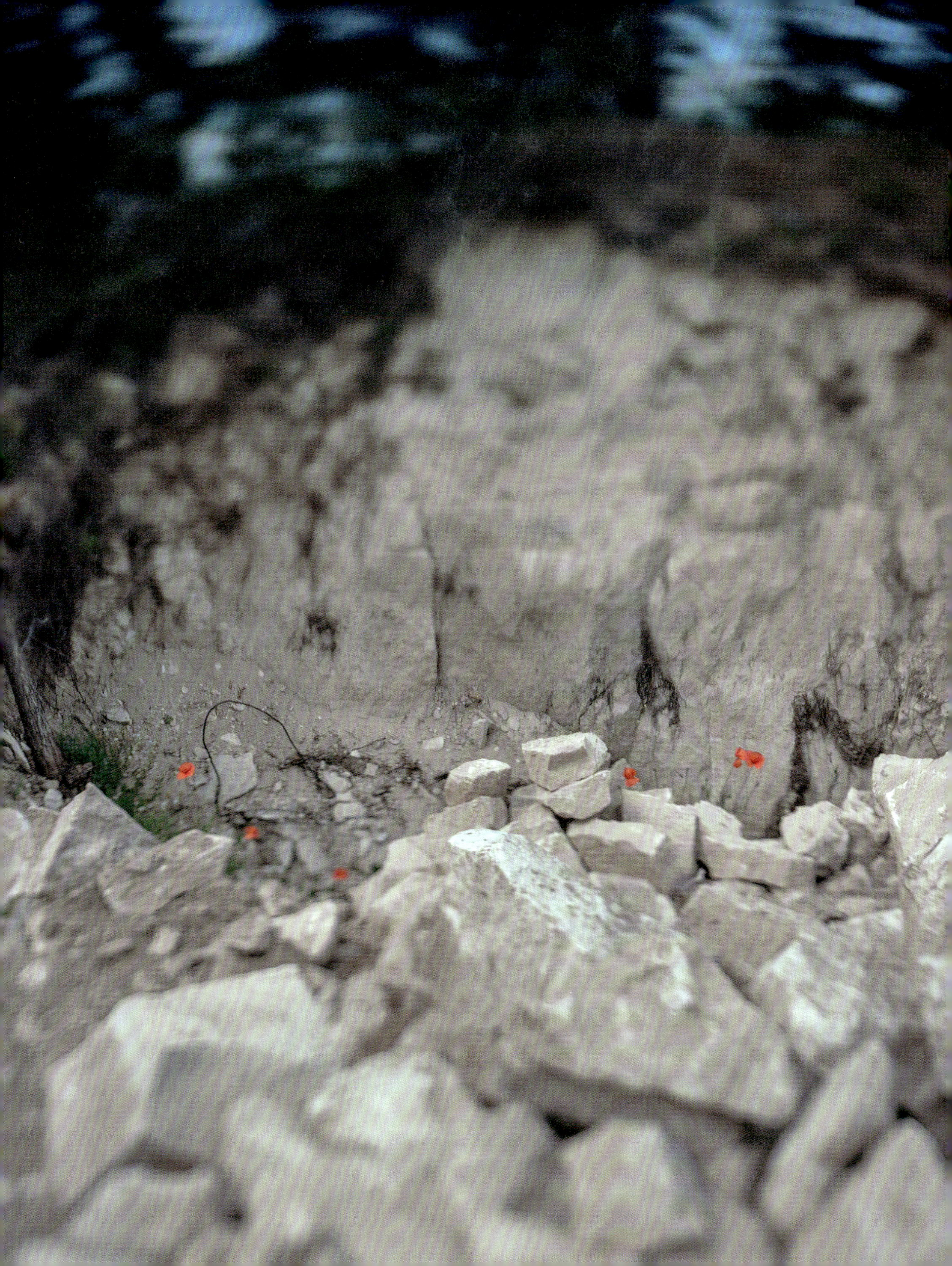

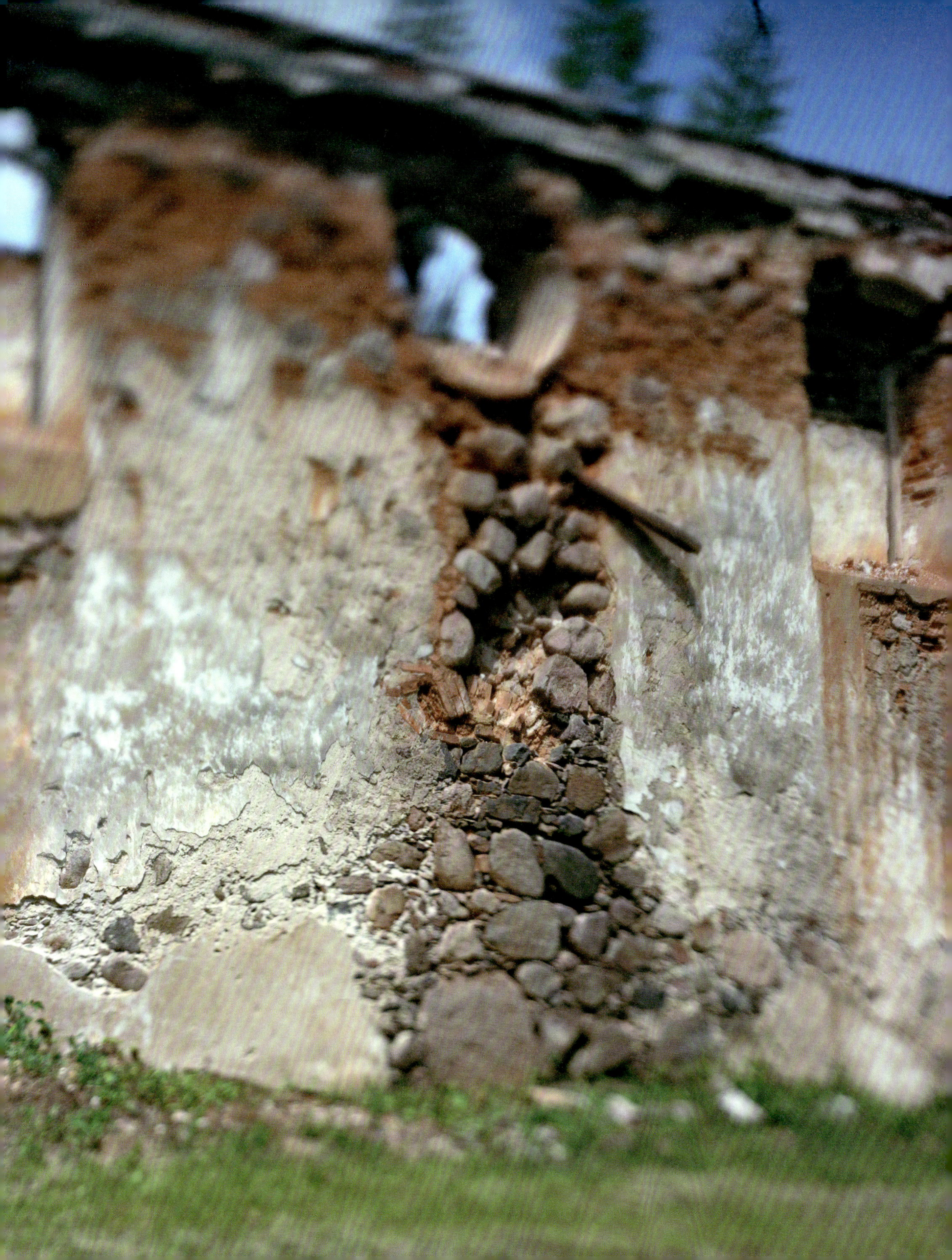

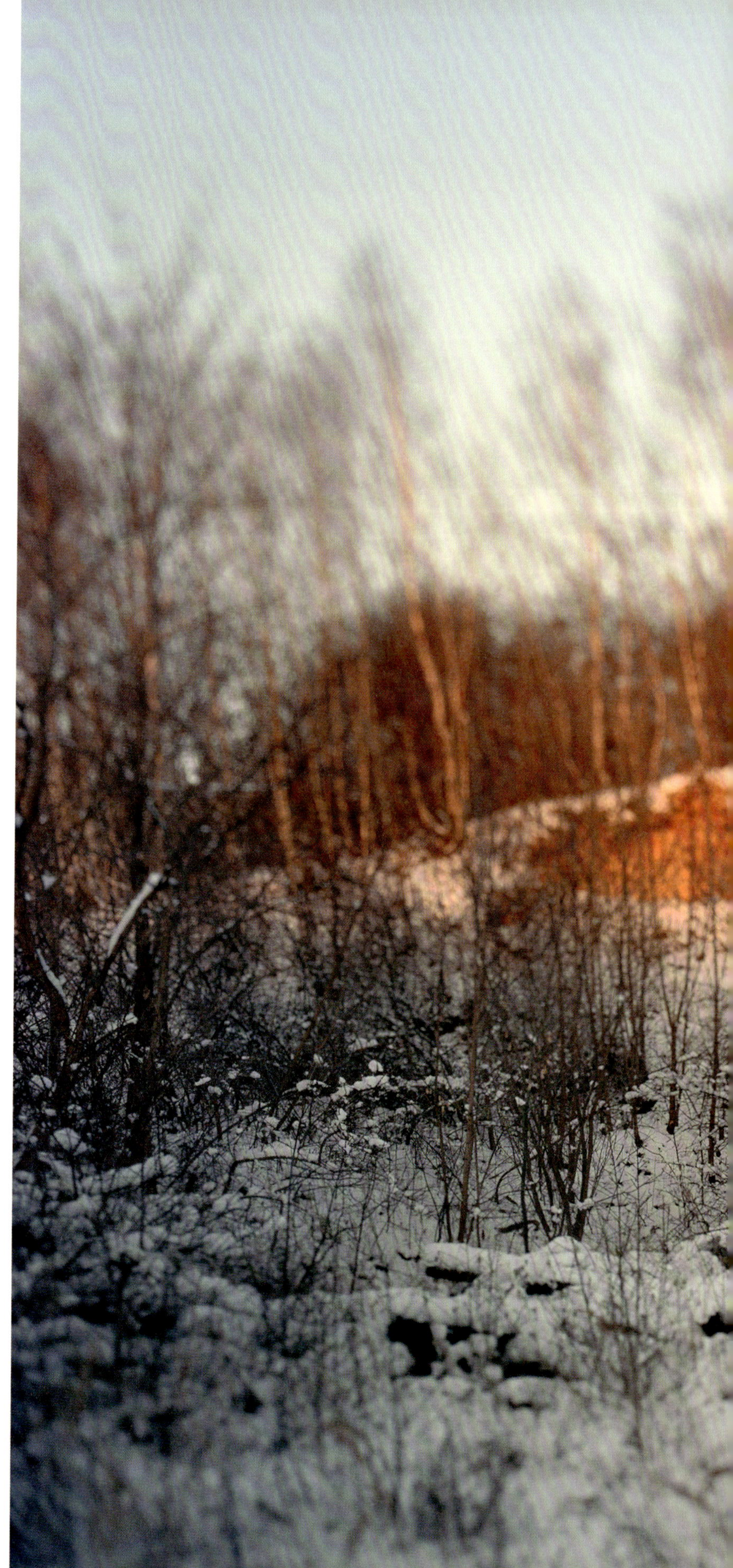

Plate 55

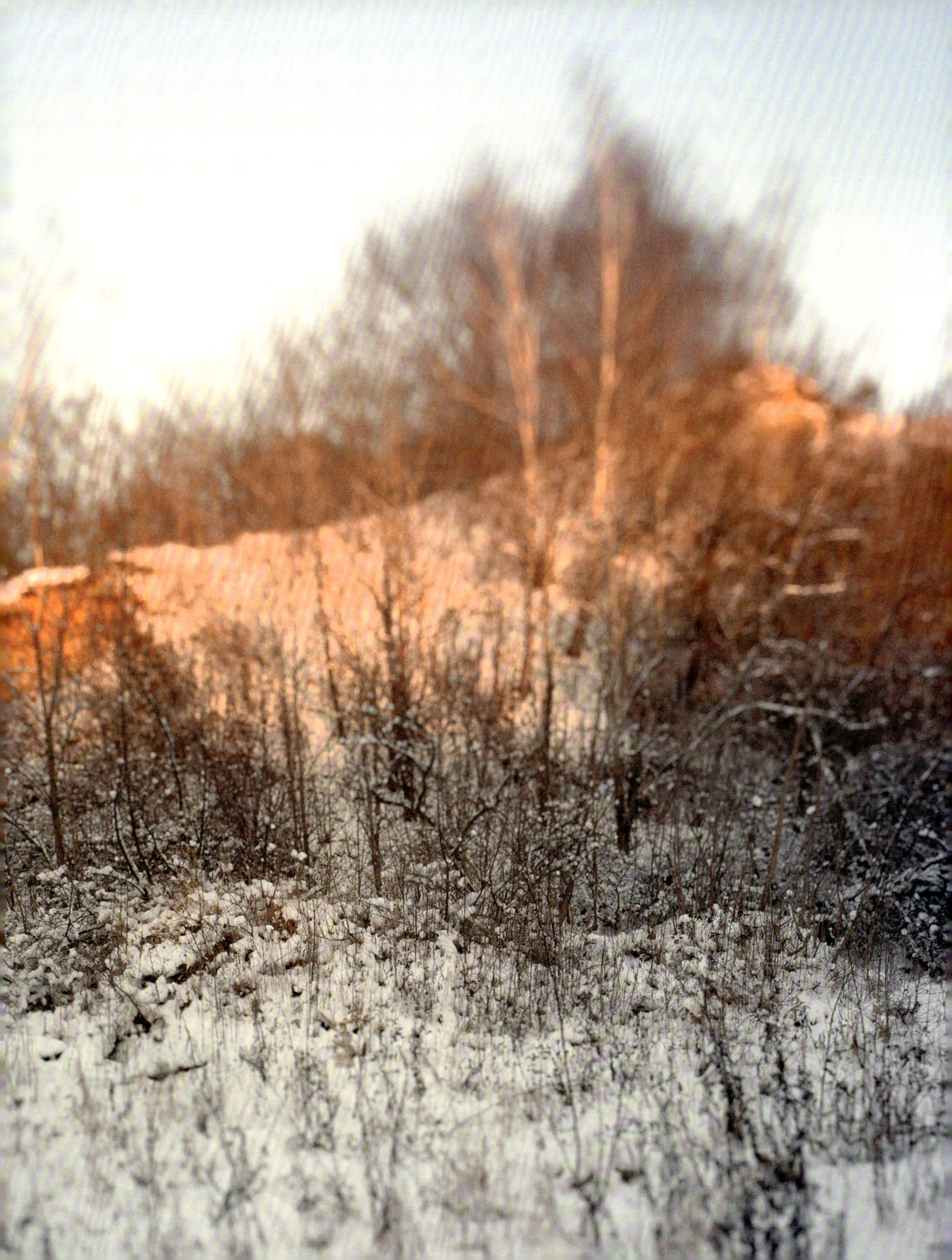

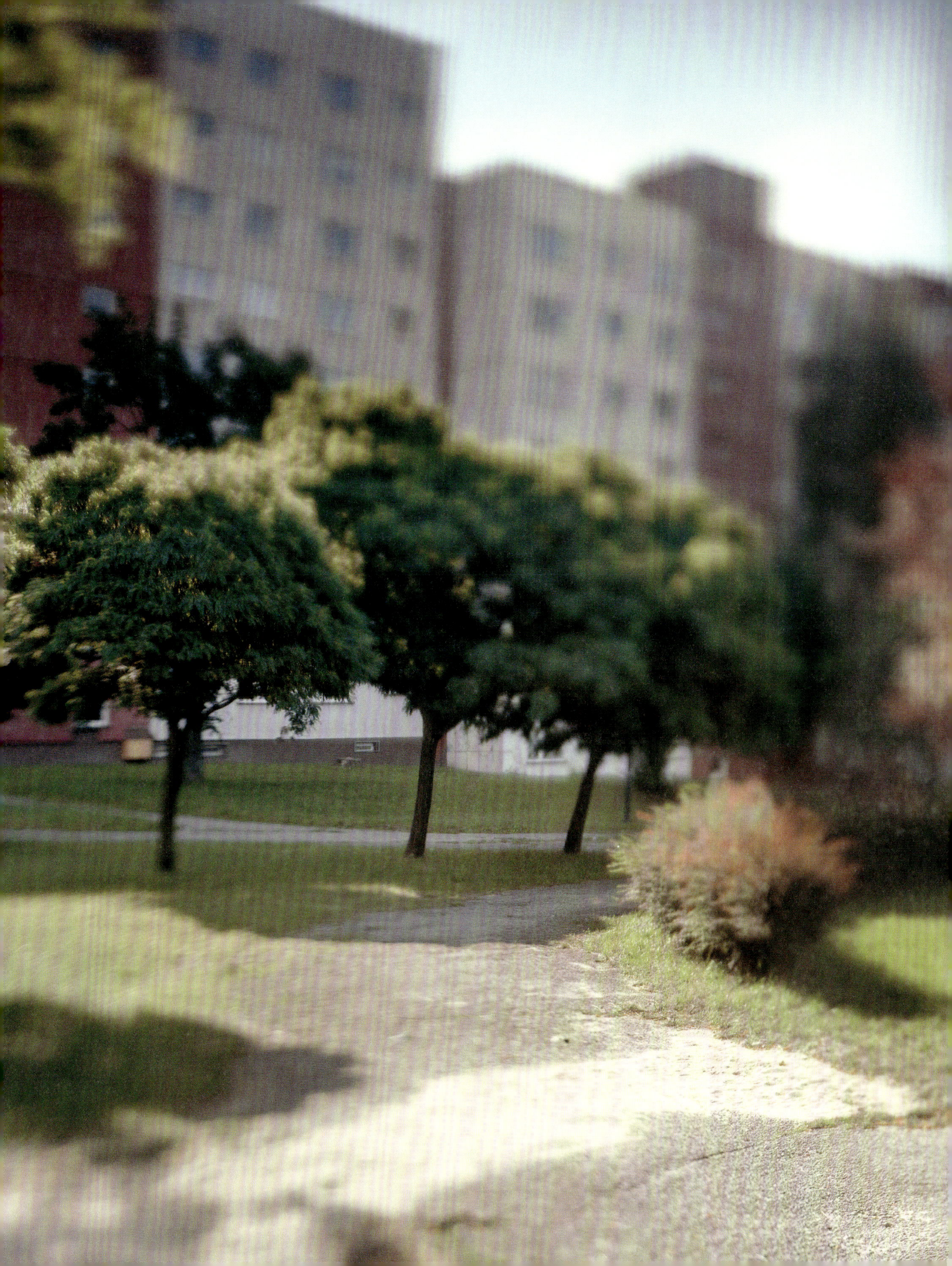

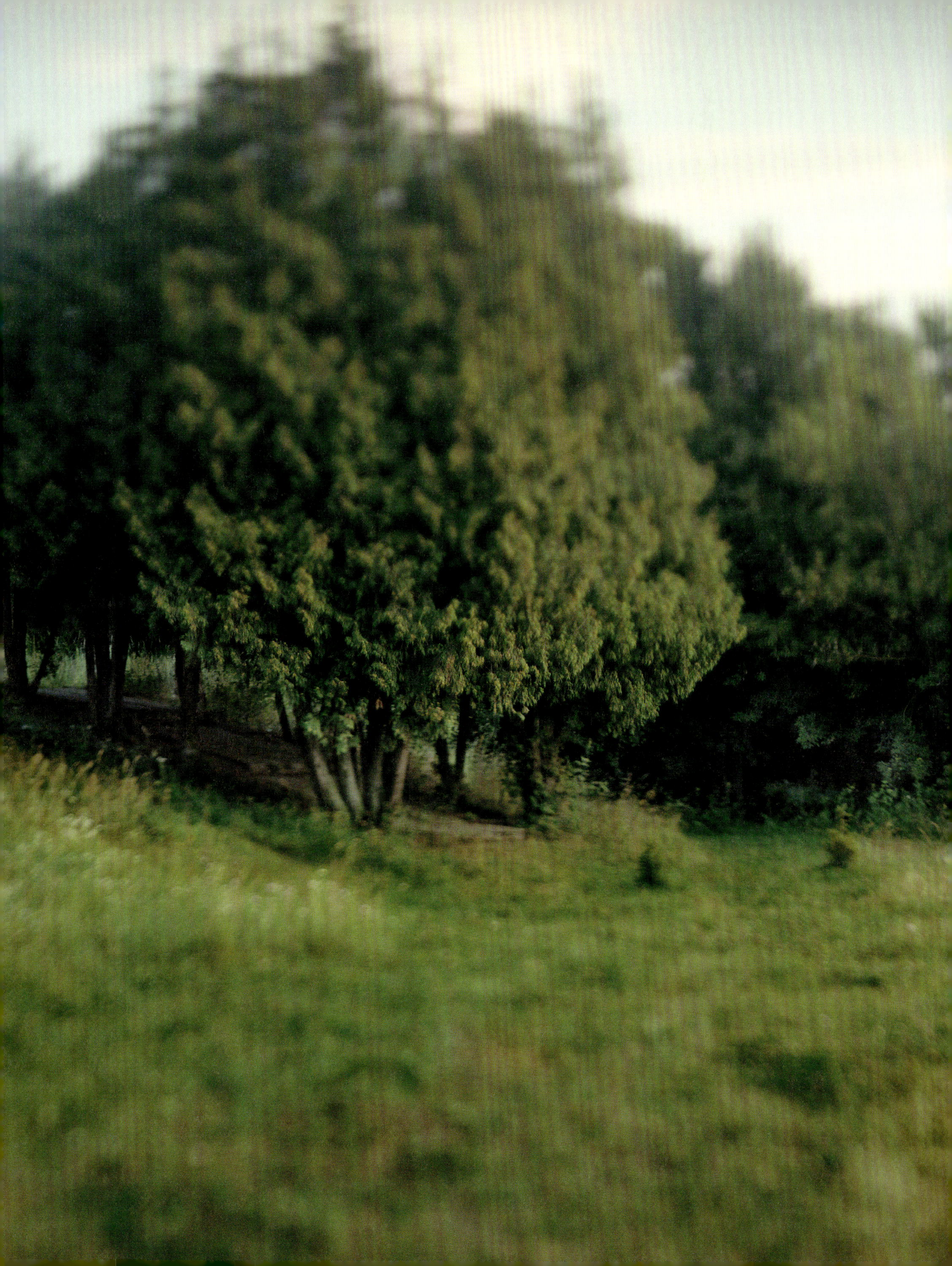

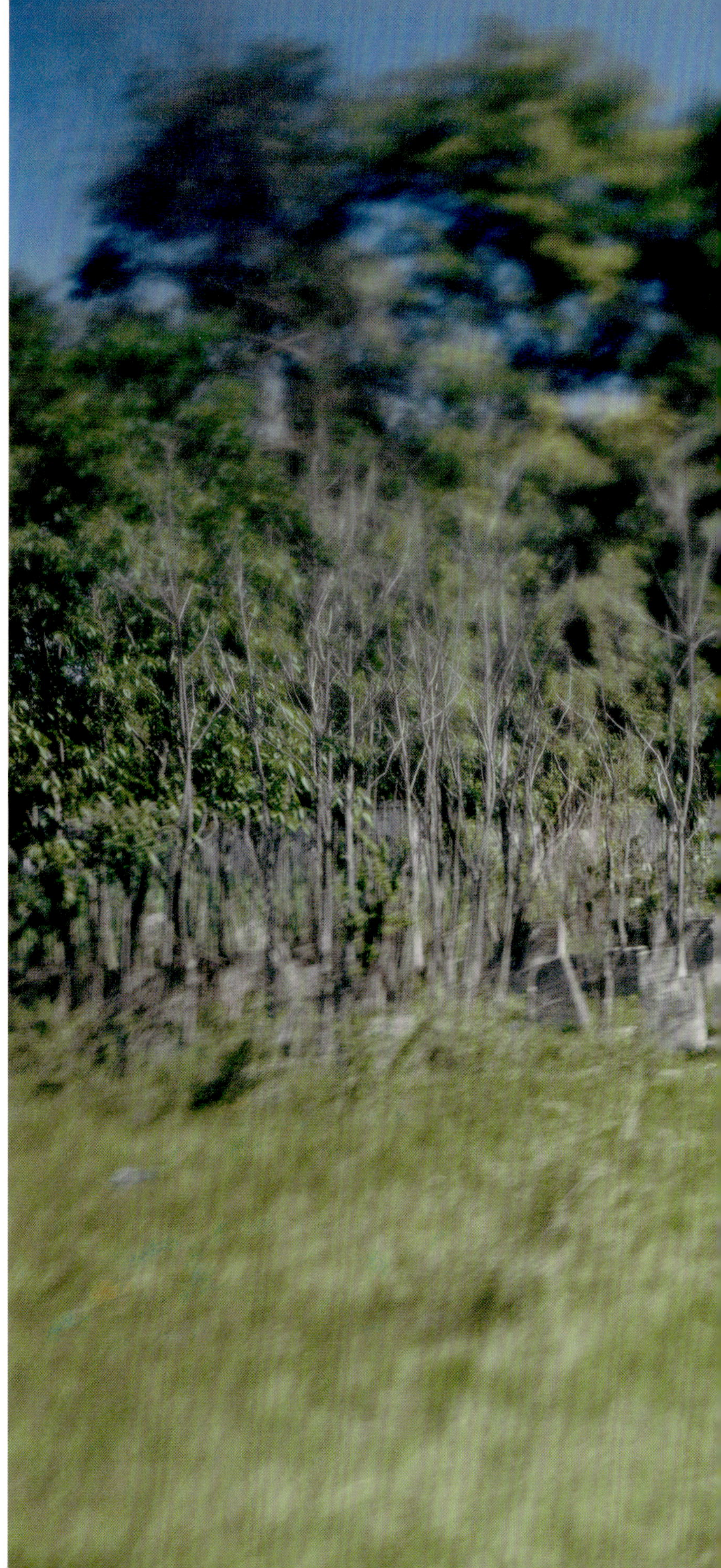

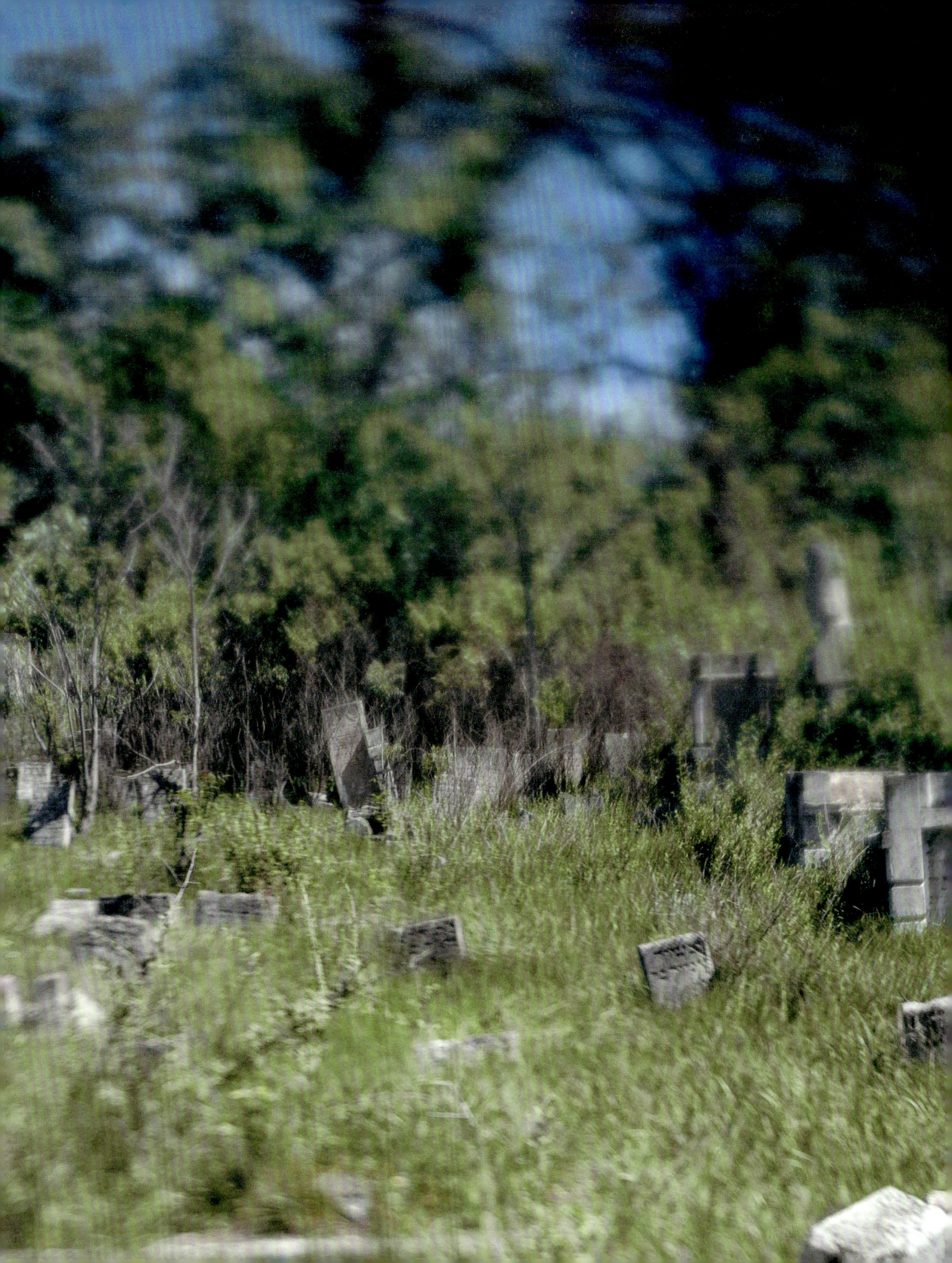

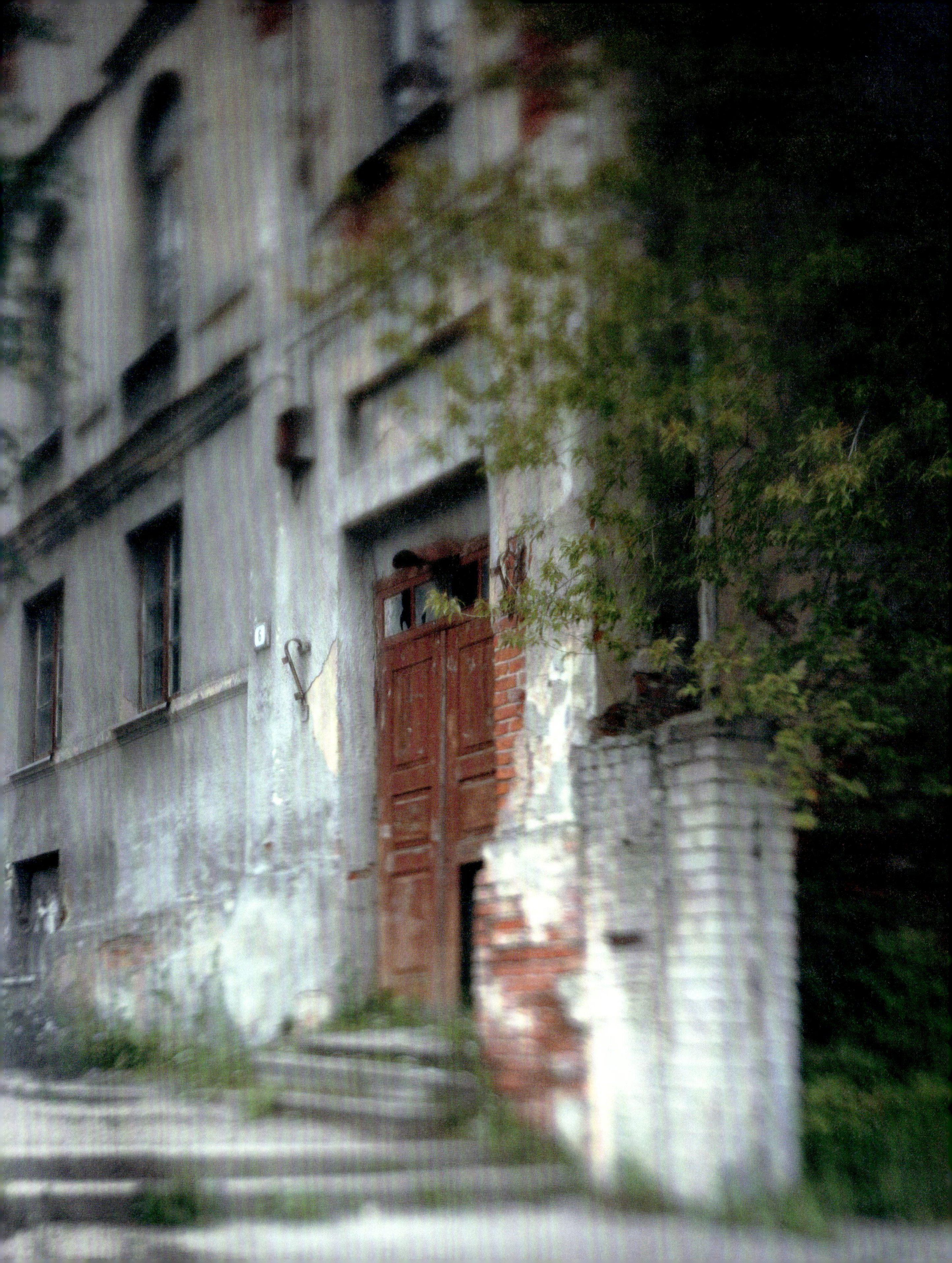

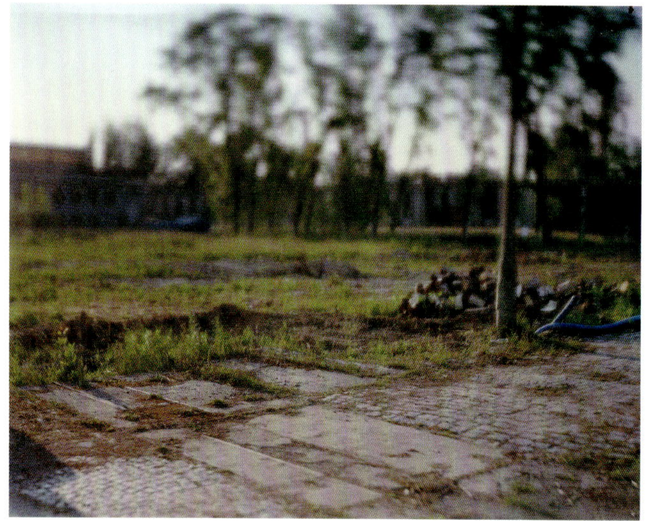
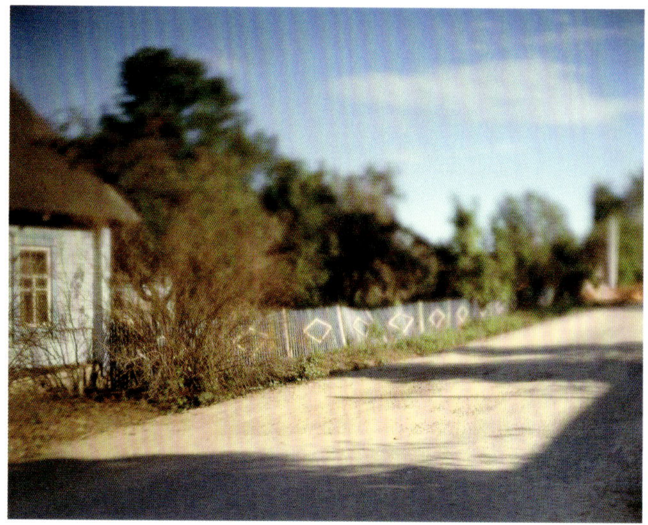
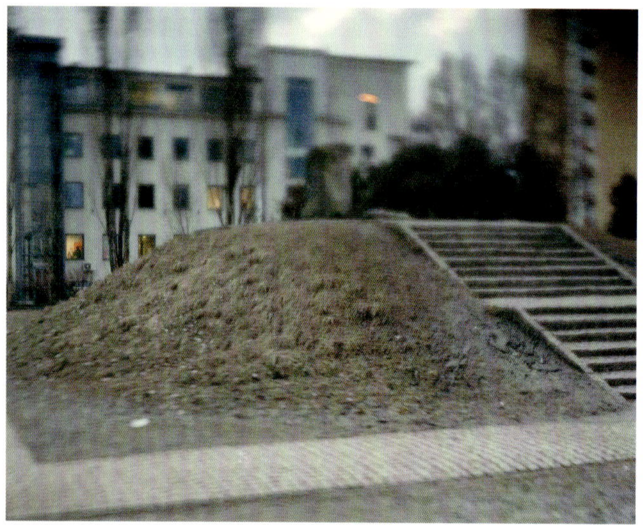
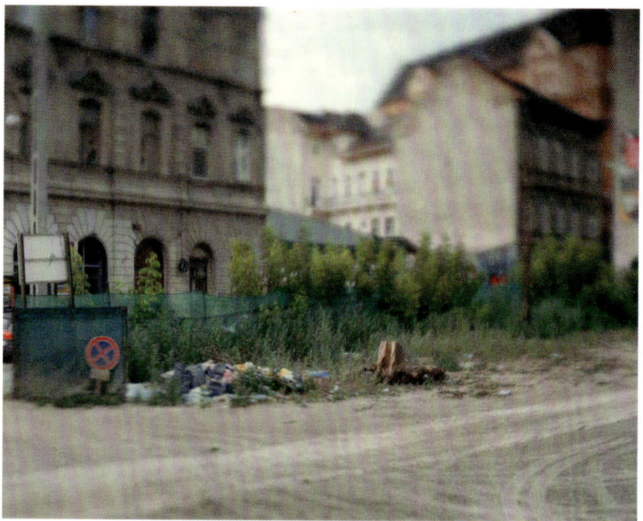
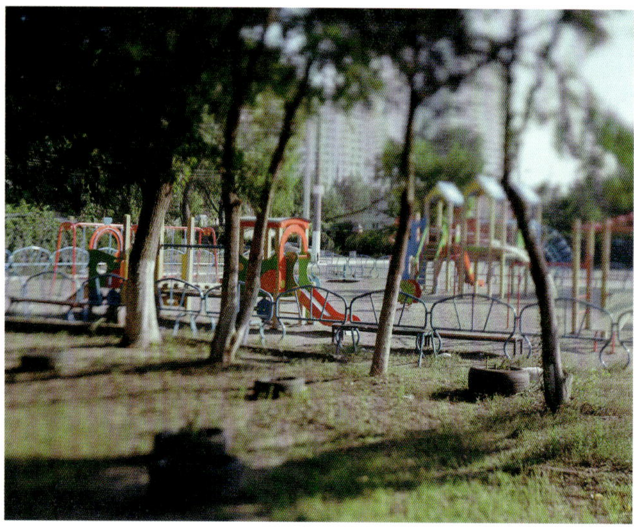
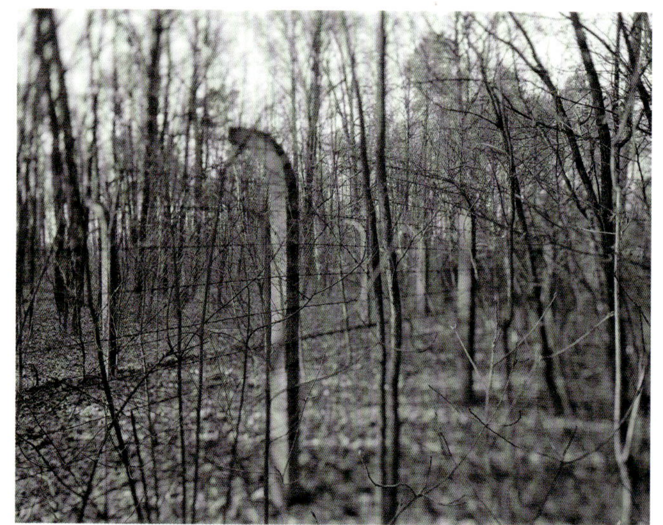

Plate 61

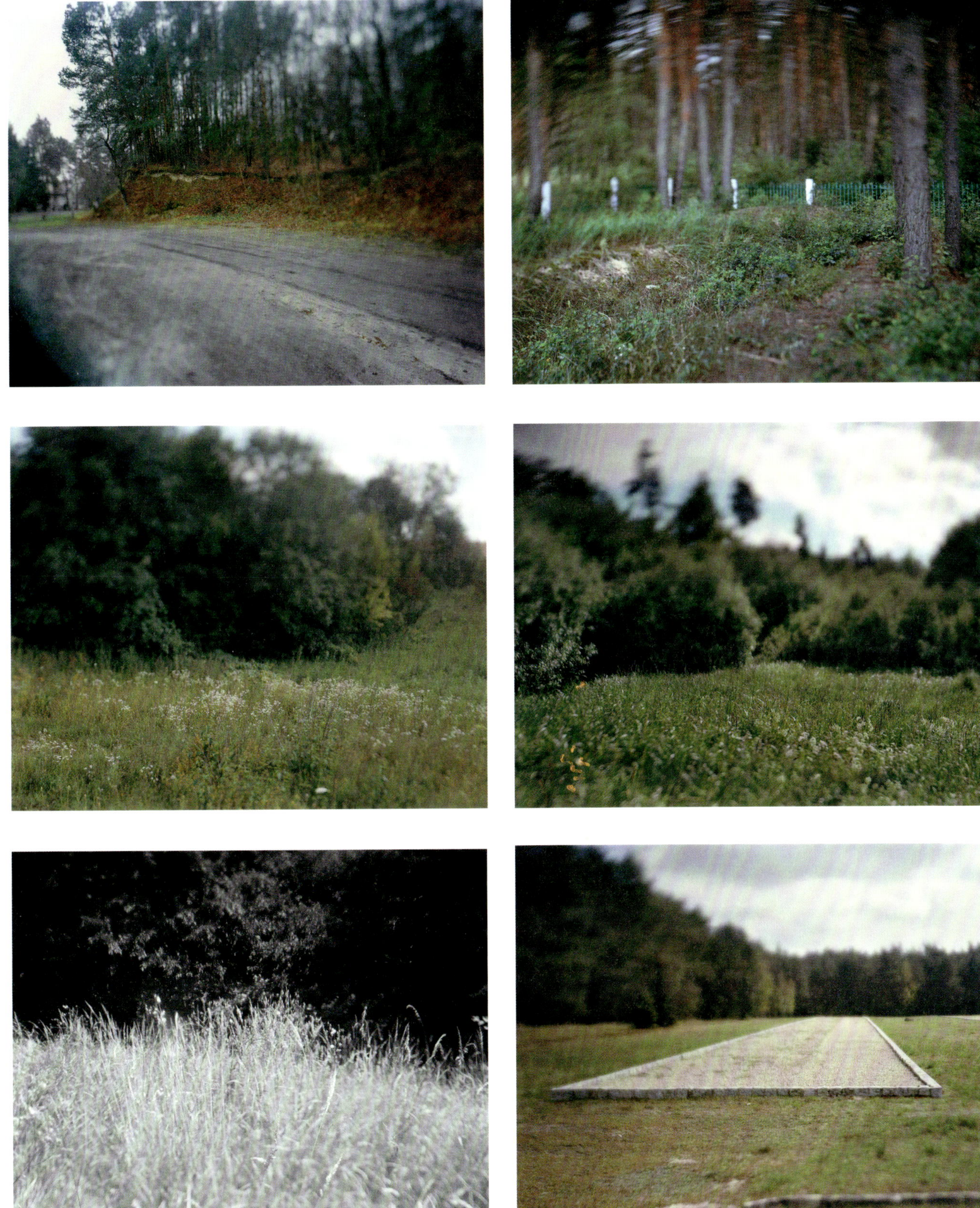

Plate 63

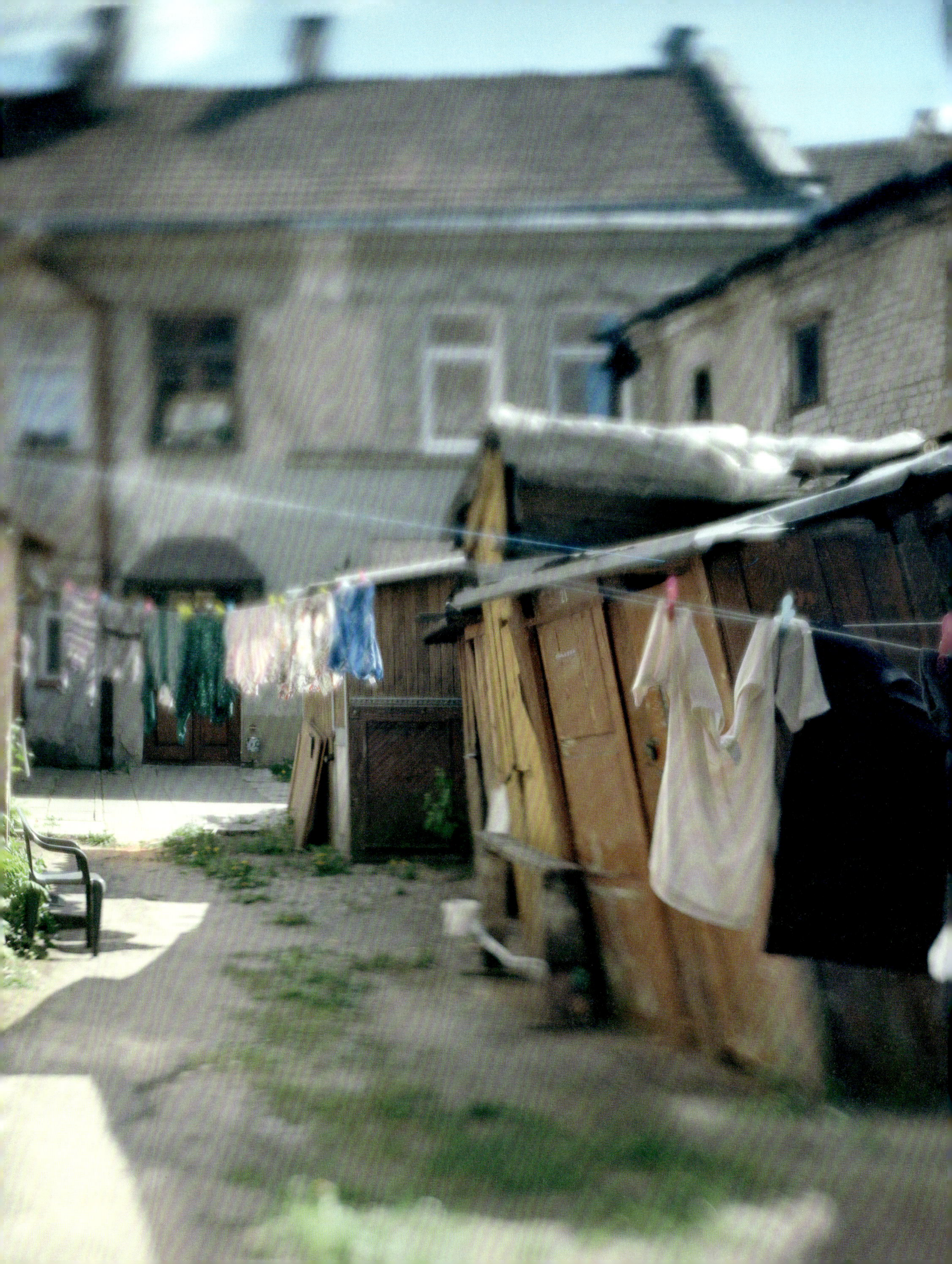

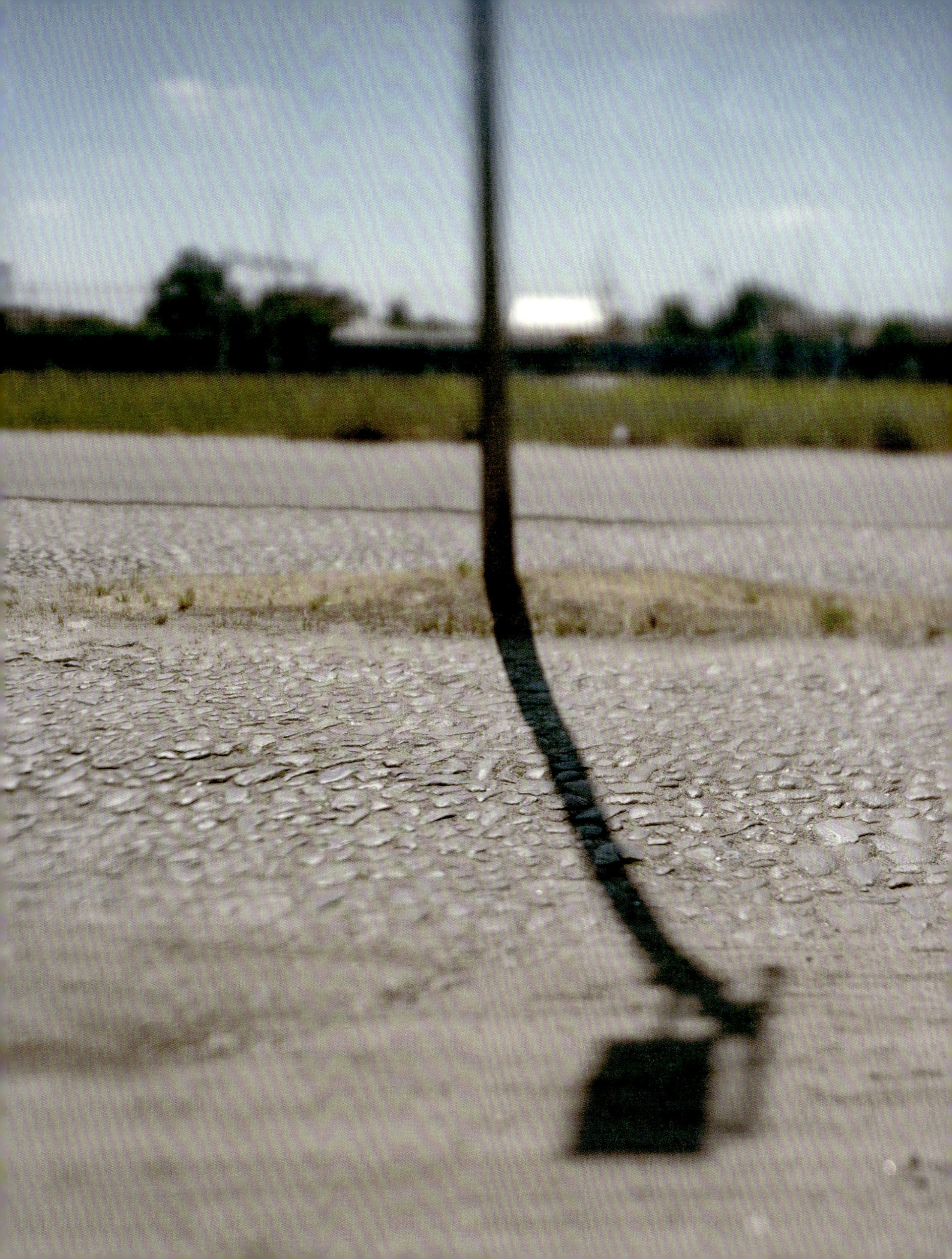

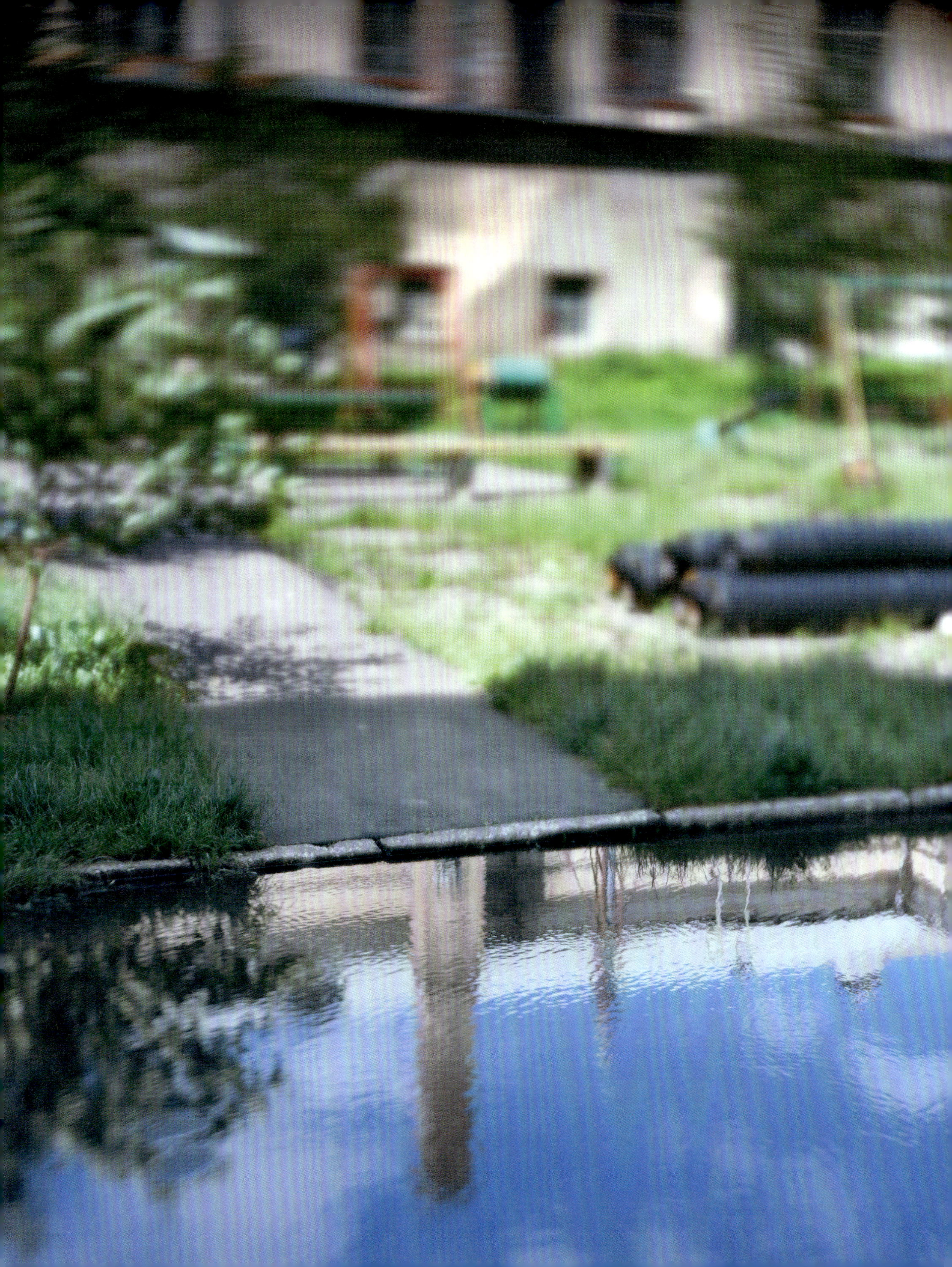

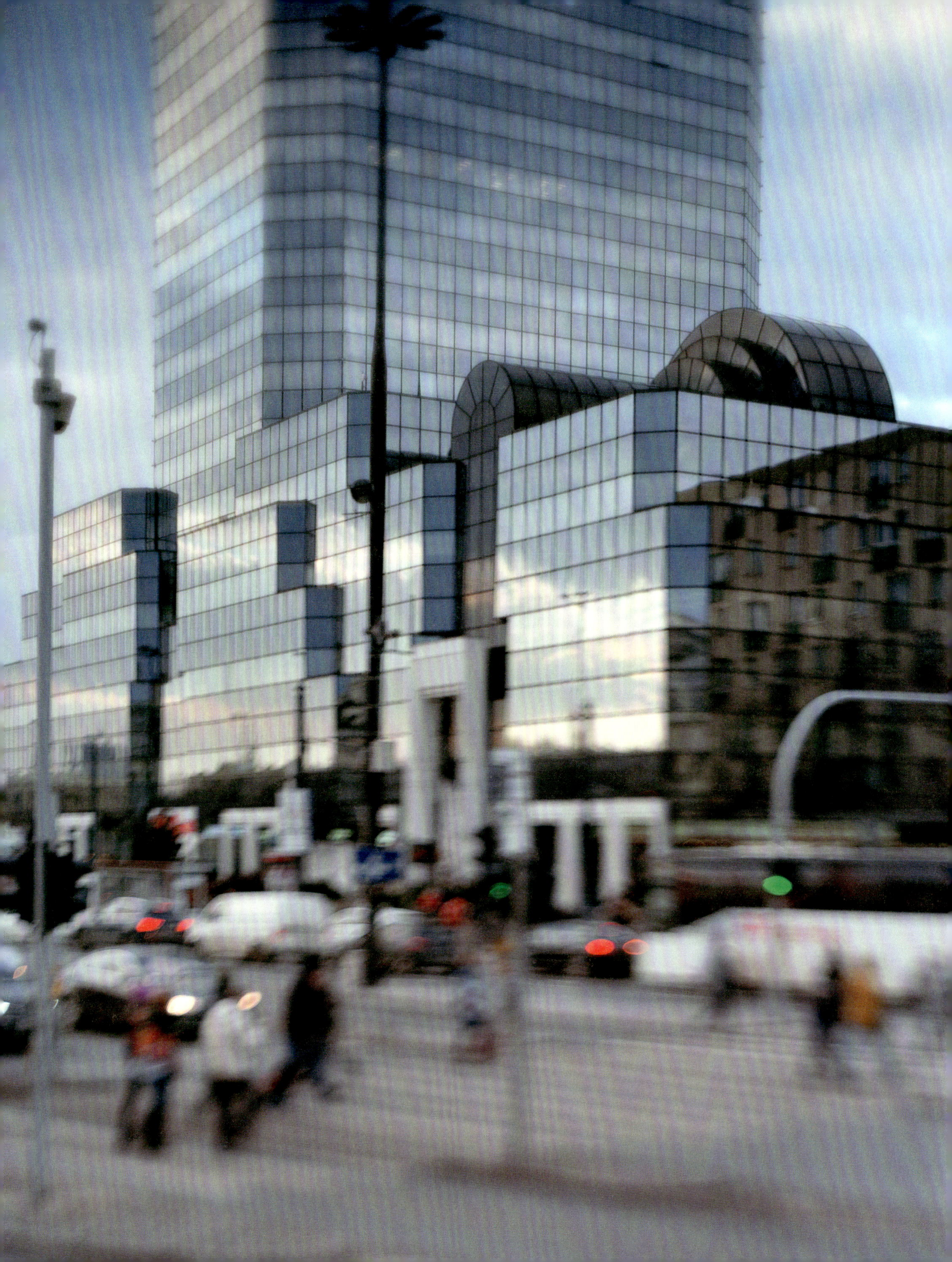

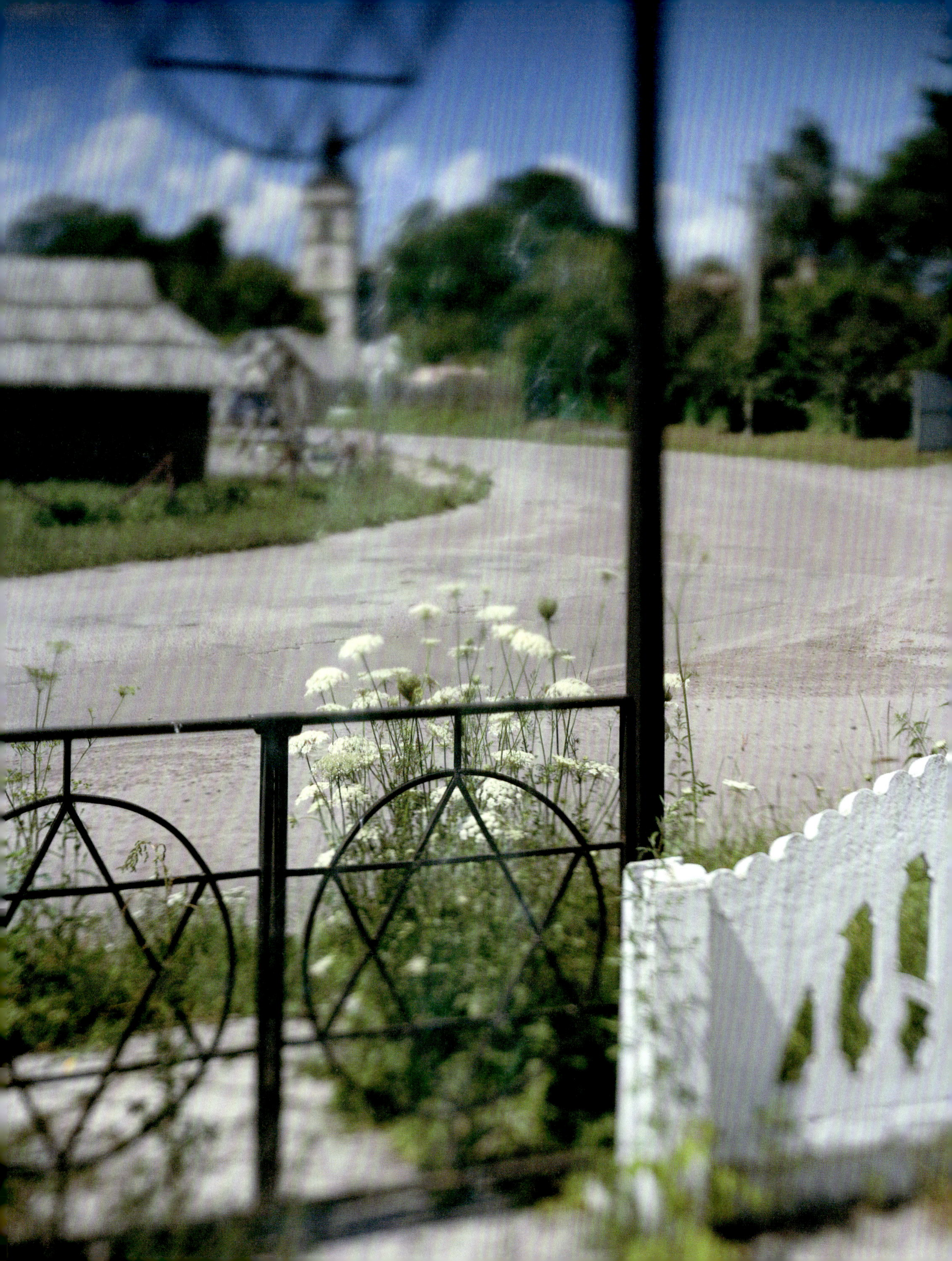

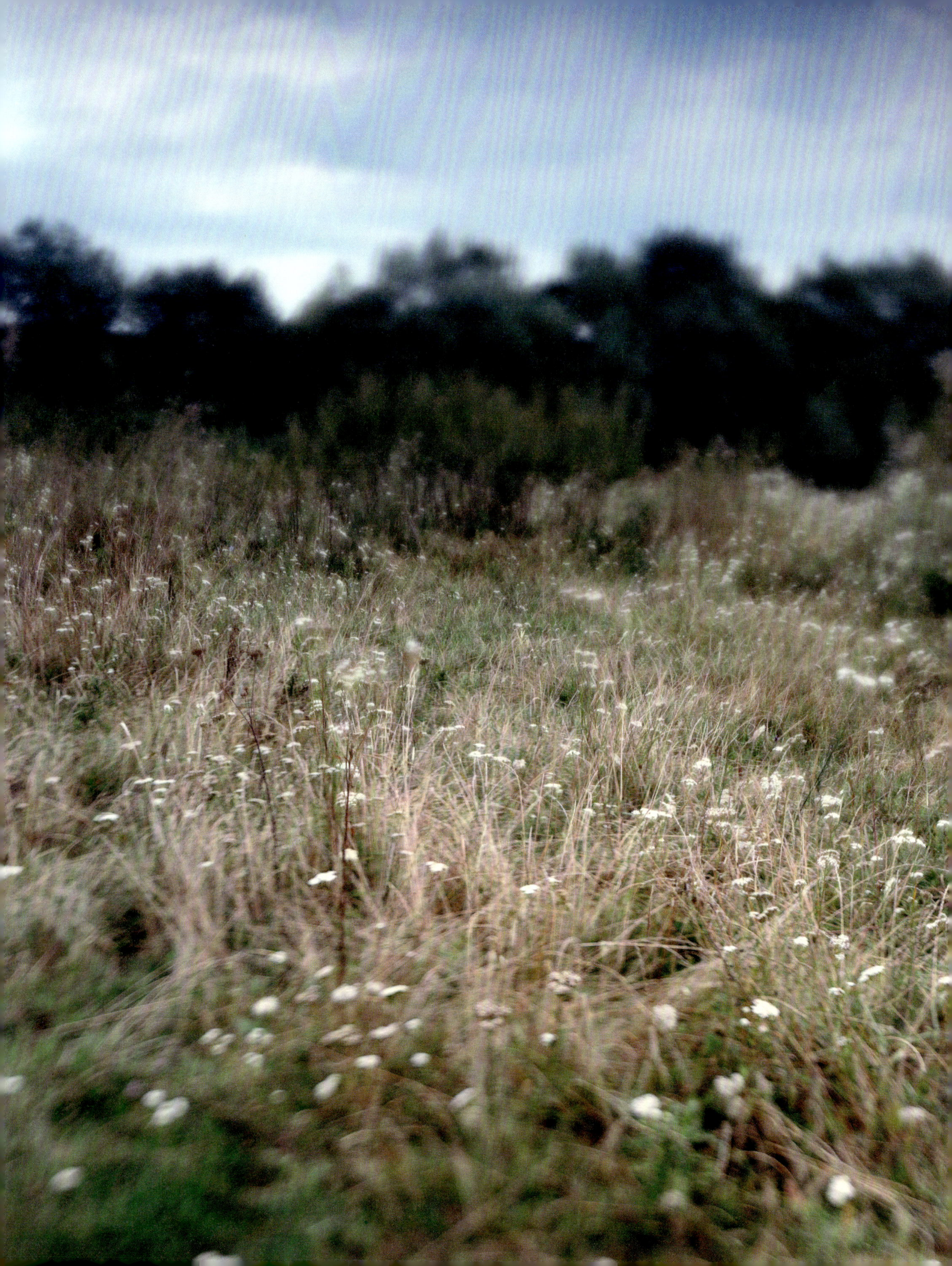

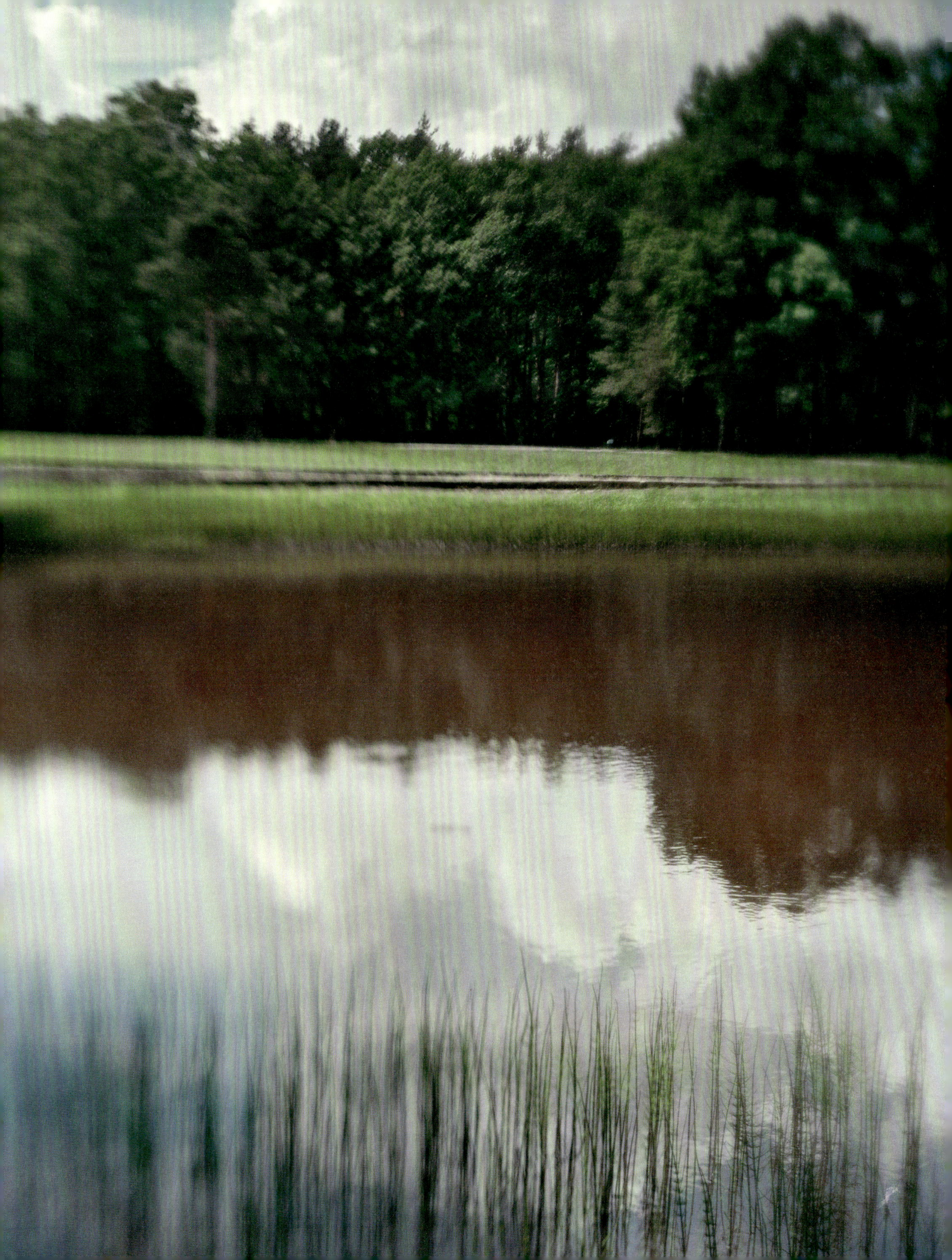

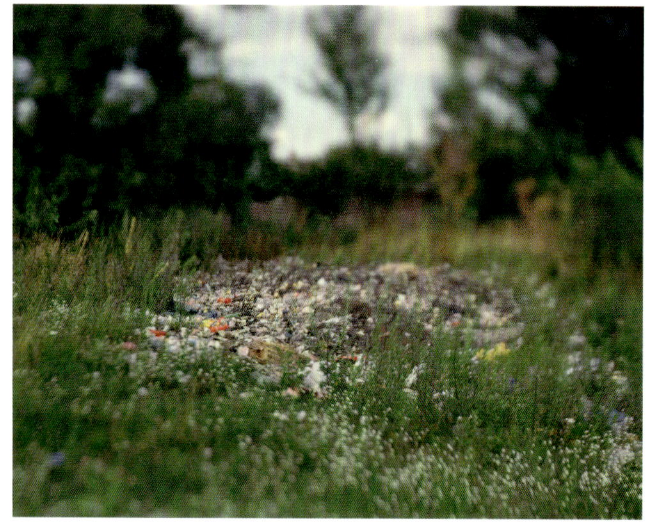
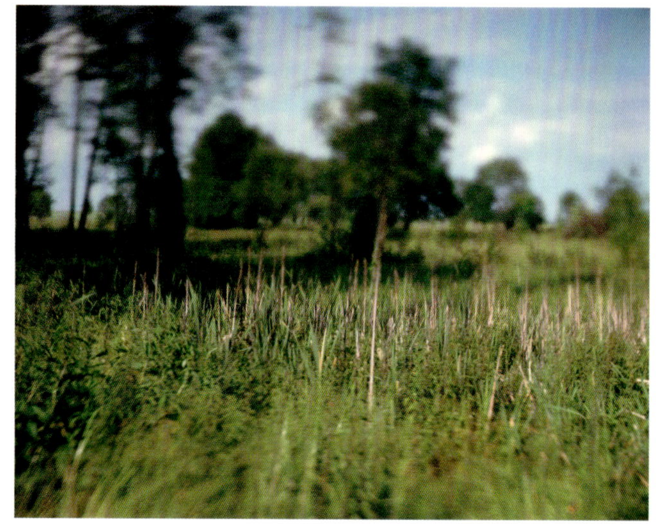
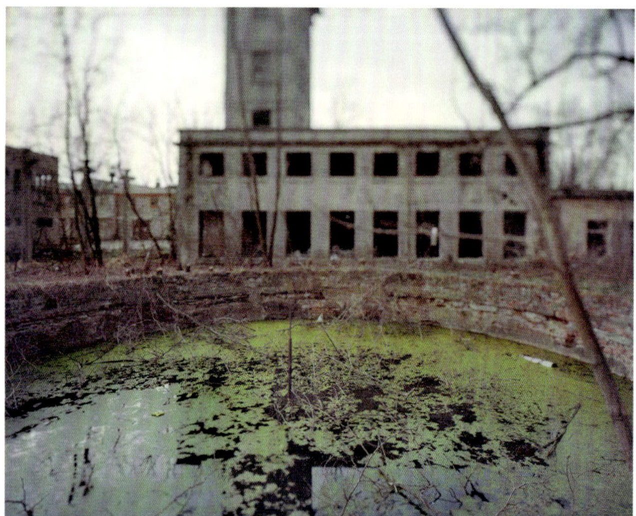
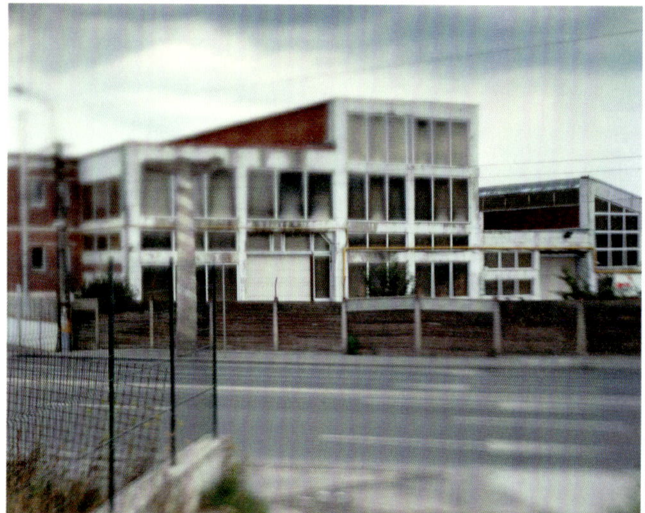
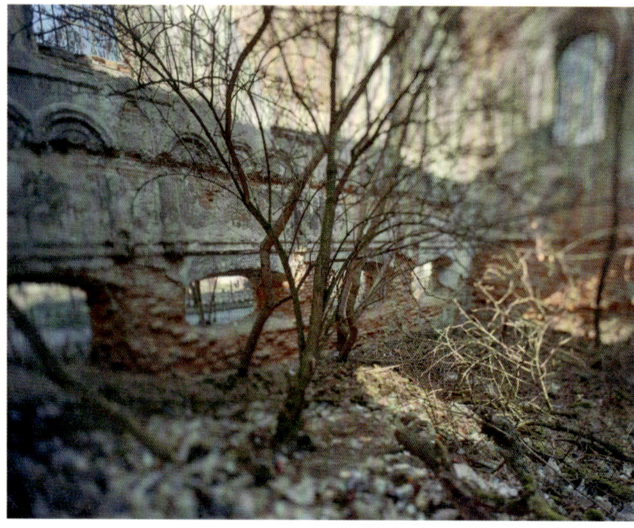
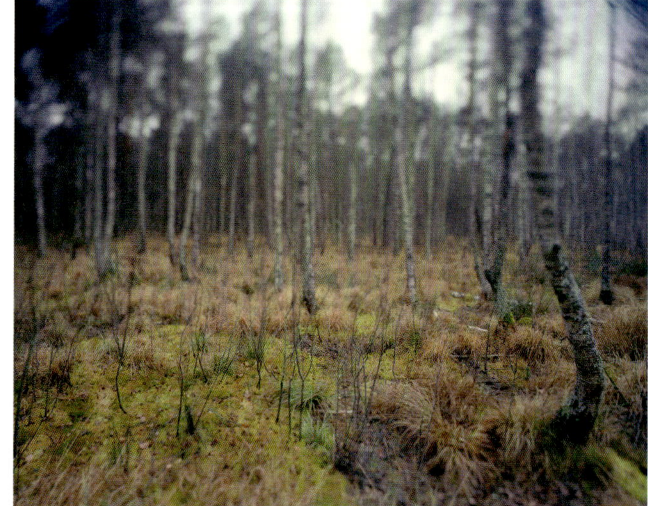

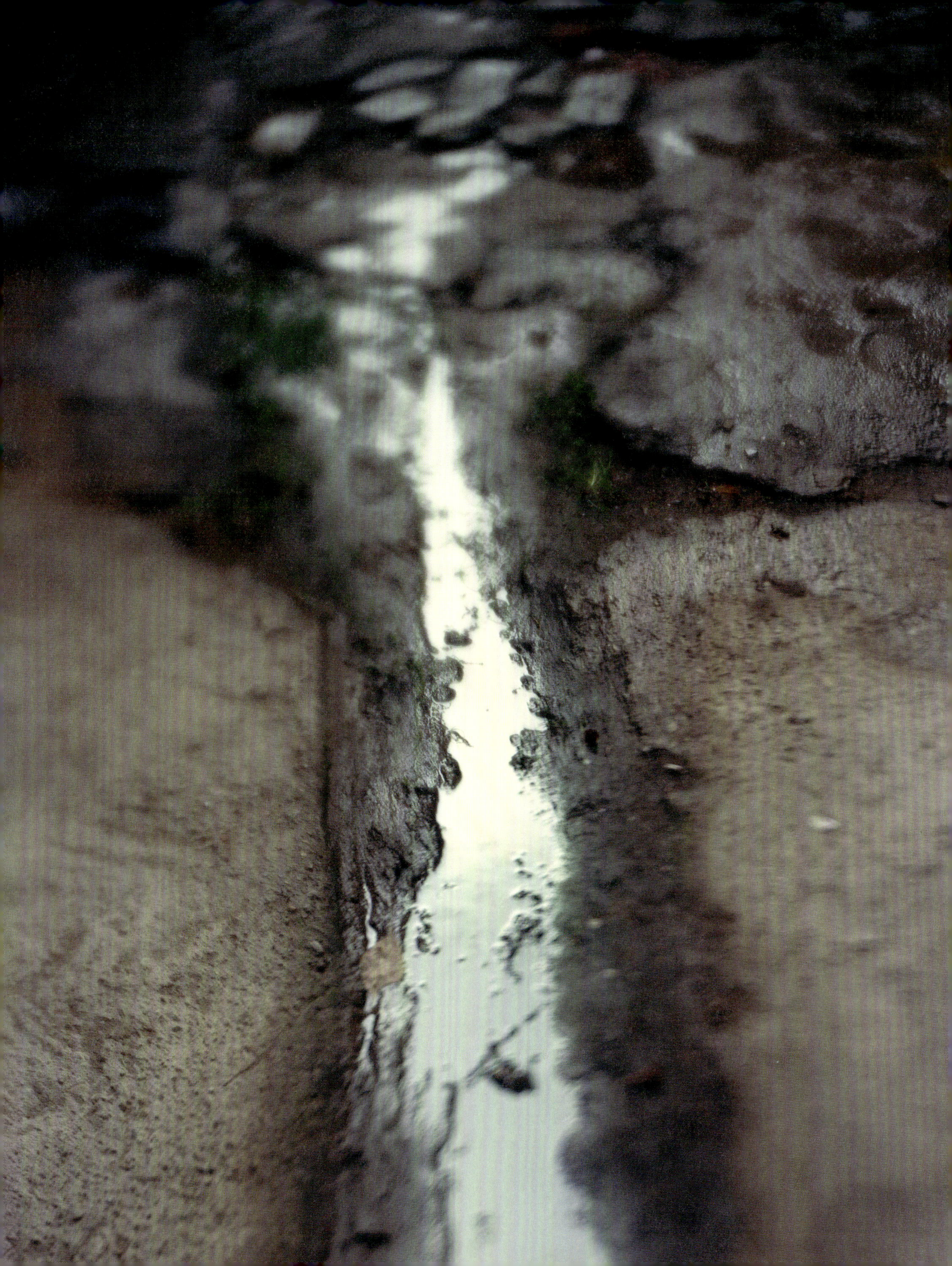

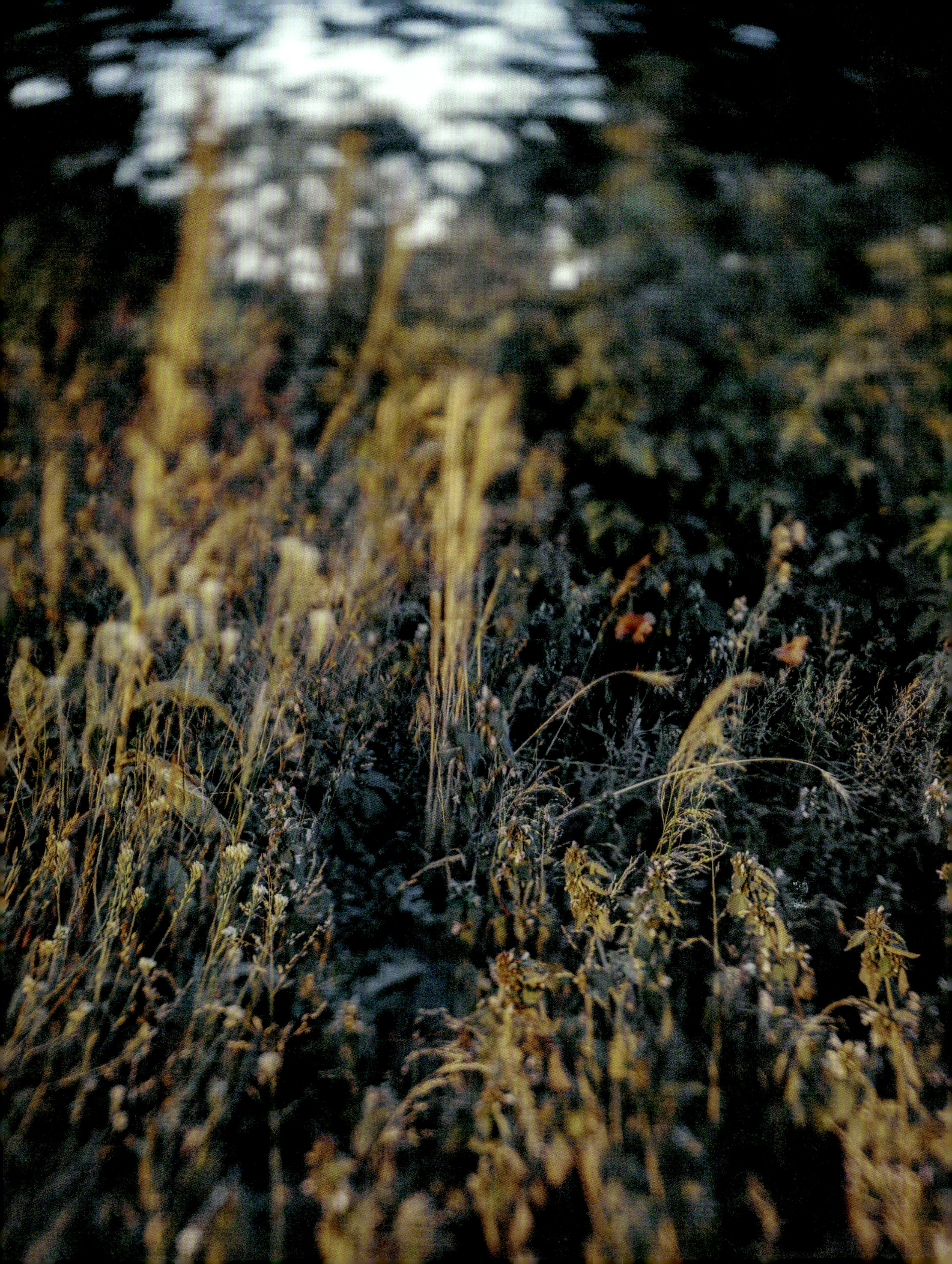

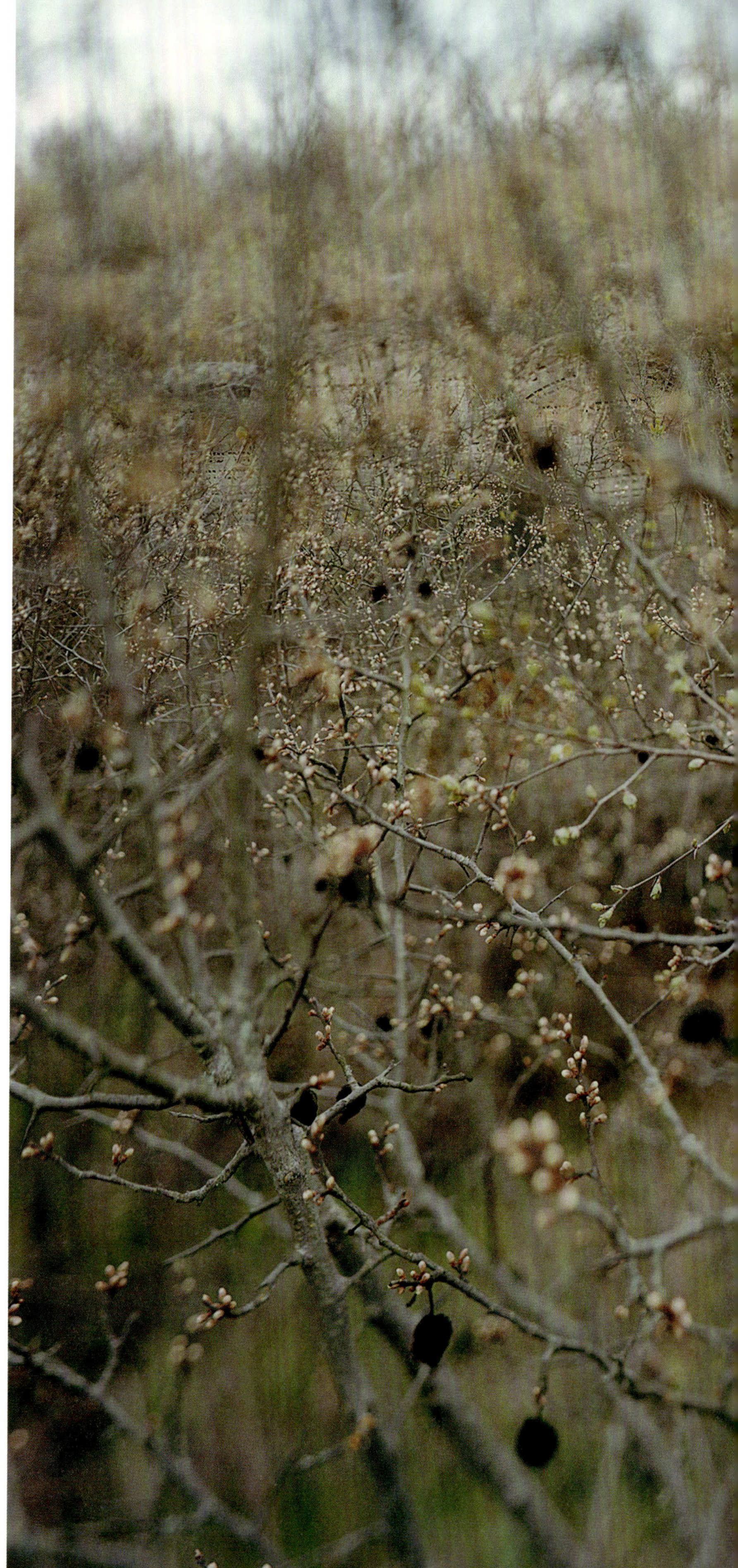

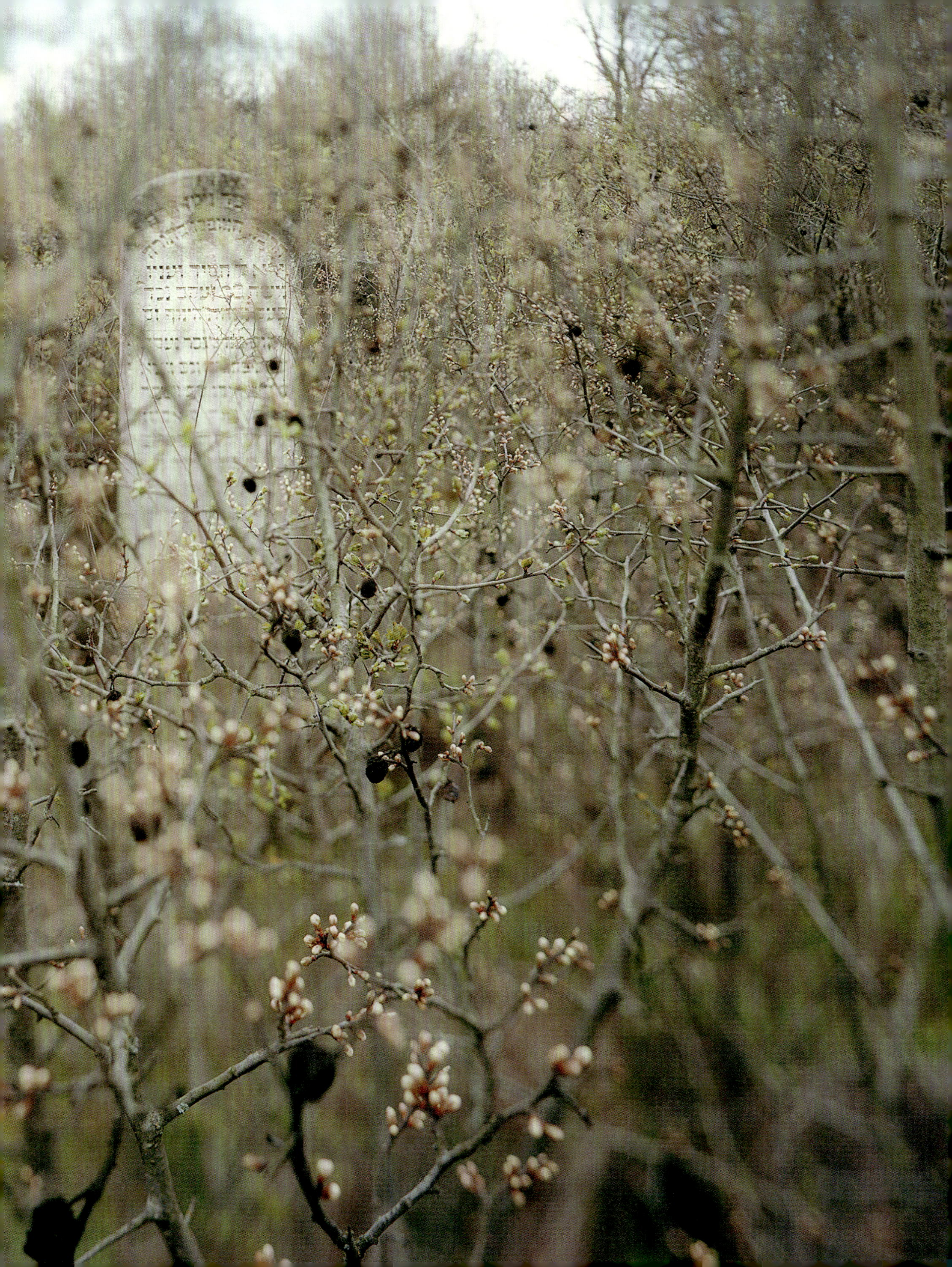

ALIVE AND DESTROYED

It is the summer of 2001 and I am living in Kyiv, the first of many spells of return to the worlds of my ancestors, in the displaced forms in which they would hardly recognize them. And not only my ancestors: for some years already I have been making a way into the fugitive dimensions of the Jewish psyche, into Jewish loss and Jewish lostness abiding within Jewish survival and Jewish memory. I have been learning my way around the Jewish nothing, to give it all a term—the Jewish as ruin, as entropy, as hidden urgency within the entropy—the Jewish as handed to me by the century preceding my birth, in which two thousand and more years of Jewish migration, assimilation, and destruction have been distilled into especially concentrated, ruthless forms. It is a given that the Jewish nothing exists mostly below the surfaces of what can be seen, touched, clearly proclaimed, and I have been learning to track its movements in travels through North America and western Europe, then Poland and the east.

It is the summer of 2001 and I go for the first time to the village of Mena, to the east of Chernihiv, where my great-grandmother was born and grew up. At age 19, or possibly age 23—the American and Russian records do not match, as so much from the archives uses the idiom of brute fact to pronounce ambiguity—she set out alone for San Francisco at the invitation of her fiancé, my great-grandfather, already there. By herself she crossed Ukraine and Russia to Japan and then over the Pacific Ocean, finally reaching the City in the summer of 1916. And in 1936, after twenty years in America had not purged from her a certain dream of return (or it could have been sheer duty), she made the journey back to Mena with my grandmother, age 17 at the time. The two of them went and came back in an epic journey of re-acquaintance and final parting, a handful of years before the catastrophe came, when no one dreamed of any such apocalypse. The story of their journey became something of a legend in the world in which I grew up—I, the third generation born in California and the first born after the war. My generation: call it the first of all future generations for whom it is not possible to speak "about" the Jewish nothing, rather for whom the Jewish must be lived out in the very terms of its nothing, by means of it. (This way of thinking came to me partly from studying Hannah Arendt, who remarks that "after Auschwitz there is no 'thinking after Auschwitz' but only 'thinking Auschwitz'" and partly from Yankev Glatshteyn, for whom poetry is "organized silence.") And the story of my great-grandmother's and grandmother's return to the place of origins formed for our family a rare imaginary meridian between the then and the now. Even though it was given only in broken outlines, the story told of a return to a world without the annihilation—as against the muteness that otherwise surrounded the old country, a world about which future generations should know as little as possible, according to those who left.

It is 2001 and I am 34 years old. It is a century after my great-grandmother's family made its home in Mena. Records, which will not appear until 2019, will say that her father was 36 in 1901, working as a kosher butcher, and his wife was a year younger. They will say that my great-grandmother was the middle of three children, with an older sister and a younger brother, information confirmed in a family photograph that has somehow survived, which she apparently carried with her to San Francisco. This photograph: a gold-toned albumen contact print from a full-plate negative, exquisitely rendered. I do not see it until 2015, when it is discovered in a forgotten box belonging to my great-uncle, never shown to anyone. I guess that this picture was made shortly before my great-grandmother left Mena for what everyone thought would be forever. In the photograph, the five of them sit as if the photograph could be a miniature "home of the world," as Jewish cemeteries were traditionally called—a place of eternity, where the dead go on living and the living rest in the ancestors' company. It is 2001 and I have not yet seen this photograph of my ancestors. I cannot say whether it would have made any difference to have known it then. I have, after all, made the trip to Mena for irrational reasons: to walk in the cemetery of my ancestors, not just to see their graves but to touch them, to touch the very graves that my great-grandmother and grandmother touched, to leave my own stones on the graves where decades before they left their stones, to continue to build old graves with new stones of remembrance. *Aftselokhes dem goyrl*, as they might have said in Yiddish: "to spite fate" I want to touch the earth of origins.

I reach Mena on a Sunday morning in midsummer and learn the location of the Jewish cemetery from a taxi driver near the bus stand. I start walking in what I think is its direction, and after a while I am joined by an old man who takes me through streets I would not think to turn down, eventually through a hole in a fence, proclaiming to me that this is the Jewish cemetery. What lies before me looks to me nothing like a cemetery, though in subsequent years it will come to look precisely like a cemetery: an open field whose boundary I cannot quite see, grass growing to knee's height, an almost silken grass, light and pale green—and no *matsevahs*, no tombstones anywhere. With a certain disbelief I wander into this field, slapped by the sudden recognition of my preconceptions. I realize I had expected to see something like the Hills of Eternity cemetery in Colma, back in California, where my great-grandmother and grandmother and all the family I ever knew were laid, where my parents will be laid and one day where my own bones may go to lay. The cemetery of my ancestors in Mena proclaims anonymity, death with no distinctions to name. It has been razed of all stone and word, gleaned even of the rubble that the smashing and extracting must have made. The cemetery offers nothing and abides in the nothing—except, I come to discover, at the far end, where there is a mass grave from the Holocaust. This grave, as if a prototype for something I would come to see in hundreds of other places in later years: a pit that the Jews of Mena dug for themselves in September 1941, my ancestors among them, a hole into which they were then shot one by one at point blank range. When all of them were dead in the pit, dirt was piled high on their bodies to form a mound, and some years later a Soviet star was installed on top of that mound, and around its contour a crude metal fence was pounded in, on which the local goats have spent lifetimes getting their horns caught. And, too, I discover beside the mass grave a few postwar matsevahs of those who apparently fled in advance of the Germans and managed to survive somewhere to the east, later to return to their town and go on with life—none of them with the names of my great-grandmother's family.

I am not prepared for any of this. Later I scold myself that I should have been prepared, but at the time I am not prepared to have striven so hard to reach the place of origins, and to have reached it, and to find there exactly no trace, which is to say traces in permanent lack of themselves. And I am hit by a profoundly desolate feeling, as if a whorl of bereftness were racing toward me from across the generations, coming at me strangely from inside myself. I wander the open cemetery field and pace back and forth, and slowly a hard-to-describe heaviness begins to press on me. I feel weak and I sit down in the grass, crumpled. I sit there for I cannot say how long, in a kind of semi-numbness, until at some point I notice a coolness of wind, and a darkening of the skies, what seems an imminent storm. I go on sitting: I see no point in standing, no difference between sitting and standing, no difference between standing and walking or walking and not walking, nowhere to walk anyway. I go on sitting in the tall grass. The skies gather clouds. And then, all at once, the clouds break and the sun bursts in—and there is a wild uplift of small butterflies whooshing into space to meet the light, uncountable thousands of them. The sound they make is a single butterfly's flight amplified into a dull unmuffled beating, and when they rise together they appear almost a hot mist of whiteness. And I realize: these small creatures were sitting with me in this place of the nothing and I had not seen them. I myself carry the genes of the ancestors, and these creatures *are* the molecules and atoms of the ancestors—now suddenly taking flight into the sky of the Jewish nothing when the sun reached down for them. And suddenly I feel myself less alone, as if liberated by the light, shown that the catastrophe has sun and cloud moving within it and comings and goings, and aliveness and doubt balancing and rebalancing in time. The mystery of this moment cannot be solved in remembering it now—but at that moment, I find a reason to stand, and I stand—and what in time becomes this book was born there in Mena, as a response to that experience, or a form of correspondence with it.

The mystery in which the book was born is the same mystery in which it has kept finding rebirth, and I can put that mystery this way: it is never certain whether it is a book made or a book found, whether I am its creator or its medium, whether it needs me or does not need me, or exactly what distinguishes a book of visual poems from a book of despair, a book of stubborn searching from a book of quixotic longing. I can see arguments for all of these to describe this book, and perhaps this is characteristic of memorial books, or a certain kind of artistic temperament, such as mine.

✳✳✳

Of the book that arrived, I struggle to speak. This is not a book of speakings and sayings, rather of pictures and images, whose task is uncommon: to reveal things that cannot be directly shown, by way of photography's special capacities to broker presence and absence. When I must speak about the Holocaust, it seems to me that I am speaking—that we speak—of two things. There is the Holocaust as history, which belongs to the past, and there is the Holocaust as culture, which belongs to the present. The present: we are currently seventy-five years from the end of the Second World War, and it has taken all of those seven decades for a plain account of the Holocaust as history to take shape. And surely the trouble of accumulating facts and data is the easier part. Facts and data, after all, do not countenance the confused temporalities by which the Holocaust arrives—the ways we receive the Holocaust simultaneously as a set of events in the flow of historical time, passing from then to now, also as an inert fact of a distinctly passed past, located in time as immobilized as eternity, and, too, as a strangely drifting, non-passing time out of time. And facts and data are helpless to solve the Holocaust's puzzles of hope and hopelessness, which grow more contradictory and difficult to learn, while the stakes of not learning grow more lethal.

I would like to be able to claim that the status the Holocaust has assumed in Western society is the right one—that it is a universal inheritance, a trauma that belongs to the whole world and not just its victims. Likewise, I would like to be able to say that social ethics forms in responsibility rather than in guilt, collective responsibility for specific catastrophes in history, including nuclear war, global warming, and genocide. And I would like to believe that compassion, once truly felt, is transitive. But such views do not prevail everywhere, for example in the places where the events that we collectively call the Holocaust occurred: in contemporary Poland, Ukraine, Belarus, Lithuania, Romania, and Moldova, where most of this book came to me between 2010 and 2019. In these places, speaking broadly, the Holocaust remains a decidedly Jewish concern, which by definition, in the post-Holocaust reality, mostly means a foreign concern.

Why? I see three main sources of resistance to the development of non-Jewish memory cultures around the Holocaust. First, there is the simple point that murder exerts claims on death. If the dead naturally grow in anonymity, for the murdered it is often the reverse: the murdered get sorted into the partisan specificities of myth, tribes, "theirs and *theirs*," "ours" and "yours," with the predictable emotional valences. For you, your murdered come forward, and ours recede. For us, our murdered eclipse your murdered—gently or violently, crudely or elaborately—you who are to us the others, the strangers. This is to say that the Holocaust is often pitched in grim memorial competition with the sufferings of other peoples under German and Soviet rule. From their perspectives, Holocaust memory does not serve recognition of other crimes against humanity; rather blocks them from recognition. Second, non-Jews suffer their own traumas from the Nazi genocide of the Jews. There is the struggle collectively to inherit the guilt of those who collaborated with the Germans in genocidal atrocities, or who murdered and exploited condemned Jews for their own purposes, under the cover of the genocide. Also there is the considerably more ambiguous situation of those (many more) who kept their heads down, looked away, and sometimes passively benefitted from Jewish mass death. Not least, there is the collective non-Jewish trauma of having witnessed—but never fully witnessing—the wholesale eradication of an ancient, integral part of their own prewar worlds. For many, the loss of the Jews was a profound cultural amputation, still unhealed, or healed poorly. Third, there are important debates about Jewish instrumentalization of the Holocaust, the uses and misuses of its memory. Of the latter, the example that comes immediately to mind is the ways that "Holocaust" in effect means "Holocaust/Israel" according to narratives of Zionism as redemption, in which eastern Europe figures as Holocaust-land, especially Poland—Poland reduced to a blood land still teeming with greedy and scheming Jew-haters, Poland essentially as the anti-Israel in an avenging logic of Jewish pain.

As a Jew and as a humanist, I do not ask whether the Holocaust "deserves" the attention it receives, a question that turns out to shelter within itself various types of anti-Jewish ugliness, expressed on a spectrum from minimization to willful ignorance to denial of what genocide was and is. That the Holocaust deserves universal recognition is not a question for me, and that it stands among—not above—a great many other crimes, none less important, is also not a question for me. My reasons for undertaking this work have nothing to do with asserting the Holocaust's primacy among historical crimes, or its place in a ranking of miseries. I do not stand with those Jews who understand the catchphrase "Never Again" to mean "Never again *to us*." Rather I am on the side of those for whom it means "Never again to anyone, anywhere, *including us*." In this connection, I do not see Poland as Amalek, and I do not see the State of Israel as salvation or refuge or homeland (rather as another country where Jews have lived, do live, will live—one corner of the diaspora for a diasporic people). Indeed, I have a particular distaste for Jewish stereotypes about non-Jews, having journeyed deeply into the worlds that the Holocaust left behind (and has not abandoned). Among Jews I find such stereotypes just as disrespectful and wrong as I find anti-Jewish stereotypes among Poles and anyone else. I hasten to add, too, that the West is not exactly a beacon of accomplishment when it comes to memorial atonement of atrocity. Essentially all non-Western anthropogenic disasters of the twentieth century fail to register as general inheritances in the would-be universalism of the West, not to mention the epochal traumas of earlier centuries inflicted by the West itself, specifically colonialism and slavery. Overall, while the concept of crimes against humanity is a fixture of international law, there is no such thing as a truly global memorial culture in which the crimes perpetrated on specific peoples are universally acknowledged as belonging to everyone.

And I spin toward a statement of my purposes. It seems obvious enough that hatred is as normalized in our world as it was in the past—in the familiar array from brutish to well-educated—and perhaps weariness is really the last word. I am not yet convinced. I am moved to turn to the Holocaust because it is at this point the world's leading example of the world-historical challenges of inheriting genocide. The Holocaust embodies the durational plight to create just remembrance of the ruination of the human. Precisely because it has been intensively studied, we are positioned to wrestle not only its historical truth, but the aftermath of its truth—both the state of knowingness it brings and the state of being at a loss—toward a deeper engagement with the experience of collective grieving by which, I think, civilization matures.

If I am to speak more specifically, it seems to me that two factors define the Holocaust's path to its pivotal position in the development of memory cultures. First, like other crimes against humanity, inheriting the Holocaust is the work not of years but of generations, decades of archival and forensic research conducted in many languages, across borders and across deep changes in political conditions. Though the Holocaust is widely accepted as the largest genocide in human history, with approximately six million victims, its details have emerged painstakingly. To take one example I consider emblematic: in 2013 the United States Holocaust Memorial Museum released the results of a thirteen-year project to produce as complete a documentary record as possible of all the ghettos, slave labor sites, concentration camps, transit camps, subcamps, forest and field and city massacre sites, and Nazi killing factories that existed in German-occupied Europe between 1939 and 1945. At its inception, the museum's team of researchers expected to find some 7,000 such locations, based on the state of knowledge at the turn of the twenty-first century. That number grew to something shockingly higher: some 42,500 genocidal sites, including 30,000 slave labor camps, 1,150 ghettos, 900 concentration camps, and thousands upon thousands of massacre sites.

And the number 42,500 is itself a reduction, depending on the granularity with which we define a location. We might take, for example, Kraków, Poland, home to one of the most famous Jewish communities in Europe, with origins extending to the first half of the eleventh century. When the Germans conducted a census of the Jewish population of the city in November 1939, two months after occupying it, they counted 70,000 Jews, who lived in many neighborhoods but most densely in the Kazimierz district. By March 1941, some 60,000 Jews had been expelled from the city, and the approximately 15,000 remaining Jews were rounded up and forced into a sealed prison-ghetto in the Podgórze district, across the Wisła river from Kazimierz. By the spring of 1942, and proceeding in a series of military actions over the next several months, most of the ghetto's inhabitants were deported east to the Bełżec death camp, where they were murdered by asphyxiation—among the approximately 435,000 Jews killed at that camp between March and December 1942, along with an undetermined number of Poles and Roma (Gypsies). Liquidation of the Kraków ghetto came in March 1943, when the Germans shot some 2,000 Jews in the streets of the ghetto, and sent approximately 3,000 to the killing center at Auschwitz-Birkenau, and another 2,000 to the nearby Płaszów labor camp. And so I ask, how many Holocaust sites in Kraków are there? Is the ghetto one site or many? Are the central square and the sites of orphanages and old age homes and the hospital and the welfare agency and Tadeusz Pankiewicz's pharmacy and the Jewish Council headquarters and the ghetto police station and the ghetto prison and the headquarters of the Jewish Fighting Organization, are these all separate locations? And each place in the ghetto where a person was killed, and each place she or he walked on the way to death, are these separate locations? And the greatest day of the militant Jewish underground's resistance, December 22, 1942, when they set off a series of simultaneous bombs in Kraków's old city, killing many Germans shopping and preparing for the upcoming Christmas holiday, and leaving flowers at the statue of Poland's national poet Adam Mickiewicz, and distributing leaflets calling for armed uprising against the Germans, is each place a leaflet fell also recruited into the geography of the genocide? And in what ways should we similarly distinguish the sites within sites within pathways to sites for each of these 42,500 places? And how should we distinguish as "places" where millions of people, each in her and his own story, abided and hid and were caught and were trapped and walked and ran and collapsed and passed through the events we call the Holocaust? Is it not the case that the question "Where did the Holocaust occur?" inevitably gives way to the question "Where did the Holocaust *not* occur?" We are left with the frustration of the Holocaust's overwhelmingness: too many places, too many numbers, too many zeroes after numbers, too much specificity and too much abstraction, too much and too many of everything.

I understand the urge to simplify, to disencumber, to reduce. I understand the logic that would distill the Holocaust to its most notorious and centrifugal locations, such as Auschwitz and the Warsaw Ghetto. I resist this tendency. I believe that the dead deserve better from us, as do those not yet born. They deserve that we frame the terms of the Holocaust's inheritance honestly, according to a straightforward principle, which I would put this way: do not say something is what it is not, and do not say something is not what it is. Do not say something is not known when it is known, or that it is known when it is not known, or that it is knowable when it is unknowable, or unknowable when it is knowable. We should not, in other words, essentialize the catastrophe either in the terms of factual or poetic thinking. And so this book begins, from one side, with the painstaking work of scholars who have laid the foundation of a decidedly de-centered approach to what we mean by the Nazi genocide of Europe's Jews. My photographs largely concern the small and often forgotten localities where the Holocaust's events occurred, understanding those locations to be placeholders for some exponentially larger cluster of locations nearby, toward what might be called a dispersive form of historical memory. From another side, this book begins from the metaphor that is commonly used to describe the start of the physical annihilation of Europe's Jews. On the night of November 9–10, 1938, Nazi paramilitary forces and civilians staged coordinated attacks against Jews and Jewish property in Germany, Austria, and the Sudetenland, in what has come to be remembered as Kristallnacht, the "Night of Broken Glass." Following this image, if we were to imagine a massive sheet of glass, so big it covered all of German-occupied Europe, and if we were to imagine the Holocaust as the smashing of that sheet of glass, the simple truth is that the shards fell everywhere, in every city and town, in villages, along the most remote roads and paths.

The second thing that defines the Holocaust's positional importance for memory cultures is its resistance to representation, the problem of remembering that which can only ever be inadequately conveyed. Genocide stems, after all, from the human appetite not just to kill but to kill off, not just to conquer but to render nonexistent—the human will to obliterate what is human because it exists at all, *and* to obliterate witness of the obliteration. Or to paraphrase the historian Mikhail Gefter, genocide is never against someone, but always against everyone. And so we turn to words like rupture, void, and incomprehension to stand for a lexicon of genocide that does not yet exist—there are no such words as "dysmeaning," "epipresence," or "abnesia," which might begin more carefully to describe what the genocide left behind, what it mutilated and keeps mutilating. Likewise, we lack concepts for the inability of memory to serve its normal function of surrogate witness and for the inability to collectively grieve. And I would argue: the liminal nature of the Holocaust is fundamental. If we say we do not know and so we will study, or we do not understand and so we will seek, we find that the more we learn, the more fractured and incomplete our knowledge. The more we grasp about the Holocaust's mechanisms and patterns and structures, the more unfathomable they become. The more, in short, we try to *say* the genocide, the further we are delivered into the predicament that whatever we say is both too little and too much. The predicament for remembrance seems impossible: the "normal" worlds of our living and suffering can only badly register worlds in which Job was not merely parable. "Who," "what," "when," "where," "how" begin meaningful questions we can ask, but the facts of the matter repel the question "why," notwithstanding our learning. To put a finger on this point: Primo Levi, in his 1947 memoir *If This Is a Man*, relates an anecdote about his imprisonment at Auschwitz—desperately thirsty, he breaks off an icicle, which a guard snatches away from him. When he asks, "Why?" he receives the terse reply,

"Hier ist kein warum" ("Here there is no why").

But for those who would remember, meaninglessness will never be memory's point of arrival, even if it is the point of departure. It seems to me that the key task in creating memory culture for historical trauma is allowing the paradoxes involved to be what they are. In remembering loss, we must somehow let loss be loss, without recuperating it falsely. Whatever lessons we derive from the Holocaust, these must be lessons in unfinished grief—grief to be renewed from generation to generation. If the Holocaust is to stir a feeling for inhumanity into the deep future, we must not make a monument of it, lest we ossify what we want to live in remembrance. If the Holocaust is to rewrite our wisdom, to keep showing us, in effect, the rainbow of sorrow just beside the rainbow of color—the one that the God character in the Torah shows Noah to mark the divine promise never again to destroy the world—our commentaries must somehow reveal sorrow as a truth about death on the side of life. That sorrow *is* on the side of life is not something obvious. For those who would remember, we are left to make meaning not only on the conventional terms of what we can attest to about the crime, but also on the terms of what we cannot discern and cannot recover—what remains lost and full of loss, defiant, discrepant, be-nothinged.

De-conventionalizing remembrance is a difficulty forever, by definition. When should that process have begun? I have no answer, except to say that it seems to me the Holocaust is already undergoing calcification in historical memory, Jewish and non-Jewish alike, already coming to resemble a dead memory object, stale information, fact without quality. I worry that this process will continue. I worry that historical memory will lose sight of what remembrance needs to succeed, namely to nurture a larger and more pressing incompleteness of understanding. I worry that the Holocaust will be flattened into platitudes and recitations, also the artifices of storytelling, as if stories were what Job demands in the plea carved into the sunken-wall memorial at today's Bełżec:

"אֶרֶץ, אַל-תְּכַסִּי דָמִי; וְאַל-יְהִי מָקוֹם, לְזַעֲקָתִי"

"Earth! Do not cover my blood, and let there be no resting place for my cry!"

I worry, in short, that the things about the genocide most essential in remembrance, its double status as learnable and incommunicable, analyzable and unthinkable, of this world and also radically apart—strangely akin to God's own apartness—are the very things most likely to be covered up in memory.

And so my task, as I receive it: through photography, to create a contemplative space within which the difficulties of remembrance can convene. Such a space would distinguish between the work of memory and remembrance, and attempt to accommodate both. Where memory is concerned with the accuracy of representations of the past, remembrance is concerned with the adequacy of the imagination for the past. Where memory is concerned with the past on its own terms, remembrance is preoccupied with the past on the terms of the present that keeps coming. For me this has meant entering the geography of the disaster directly, a geography where visible and invisible ruination live on in worlds that also go on living around them. It has meant searching that actual geography for the contradictory psycho-geography that genocide creates as an inheritance. In that psycho-geography the truths of loss are by turns constant and inconstant, and avowal is sometimes urgent, sometimes vagrant. Remembrance has no shape of its own, and memory has only the shapes we give it. This is our common problem, we who are the inheritors of the epoch of anti-humanity, unsayable and unseeable: we must find our way to the Holocaust's own terms, its own foreignness, its turbulence of non-figuration and anti-figuration inhabiting our figuring. The Holocaust itself deserves to retain agency in our remembering. It deserves somehow to address us, and to redress what we forget of the nothing. It deserves the right to impugn the uses we freight it with—even uses that better us. The Holocaust deserves the right to silence those of us who demand the restoration of tradition and continuity, likewise those of us who demand the constant rereading of the verdicts against God. The Holocaust deserves the right to silence all of us eager to contribute a word or a photograph to the book of memory. And it deserves the right to silence even those of us guarding the last page for fugacity, after everything else.

***

The poet and critic Allen Grossman speaks of two types of poems: those that are an account of an inner poetic experience the poet has had, and those that are themselves a direct transmission of poetic intensity. In the first type, the poet acts as organizer and primary thinker, and the reader is given the second-order task of interpreting whatever poetic event has happened to the poet. In the second type, the poet acts not as a mediator but a medium, with the poem itself forming—being—the poetic experience fully. The reader, in this case, is accorded the status of an "exegetical participant" no less than the poet, equally charged with the task of discerning the meaning from the inside. But are the two cases really so different? To transit a book of poems, it seems to me, is to do more than visit its pages. What poem does not invite imaginative collaboration with its hearer, and at some deep level demand it?

But for the sake of photographs, I take Grossman's point, which leads to an important distinction about how photographs signify—not so much a distinction between types of photographs as between modes in which they operate. The readiest way of saying this distinction is to counterpose the informational and poetical modalities of photographs, which in my own lexicon I call the difference between pictures and images.

The photographs in this book are pictures and images both. As pictures, they do what photographs conventionally do: represent (re-present) the visible as information, prototypically about the world beyond the picture, encoding that information in a double helix of plausible realism and reticent invention. The result delivers to us a sense of recognition and understanding, of conceptual control over the world pictured. As images, on the other hand, the photographs here are not mere illusions or replicas of real things beyond themselves. They are realnesses of their own. As images, they present—are—the primary account of whatever anyone experiences in and through them. If the most common metaphor for the photograph as picture is the term "capture," photographs as images lack a standard metaphor, but the opposite of capture seems apt enough: as images, photographs *release* things into consciousness, free the observable world from plain categories of objective and subjective, loosen easy distinctions between present and past, presence and absence. If in pictures we meet the world as it seems to be to and for itself, in images we meet the world as it is to and for us, we who stand to regard its fullness of being and its having ceased to be.

To put a finer point on it, photography as a medium seems to me a name for the *difference* between pictures and images, the interpretive tensity between them that has no better or more acute form than photographs themselves. This difference announces photographic aesthetics as primarily about alternation, a dialectic residing in photography's very etymology. Photo/light + graph/writing is not just a nineteenth-century metaphor for light behaving as a stylus, but a sharply contemporary name for a doubly sensitive surface, touched by light from one side and by language from the other. Photography is not just a way of showing what things look like, but also a visual form for the dialectic between states of language about those things: between simple names and abstractions, competing metaphors, the nuances of complementary descriptions.

My challenge, as I have given it to myself, has been to approach Holocaust remembrance through photography's own mercurial nature, its internal churn. From the beginning my method has been experimental: to search out a way for a photograph to act as a picture and an image at once, and to activate the discrepancy between seeing and saying as one kind of answer to the fraught imperative to remember. As pictures, the photographs should leverage the sense of a shared world: a world into which anyone can actually travel and actually look. But through experience I came to see that remembrance of genocide demands more from photographs than being pictures only. I came to feel a mismatch between the content of this work and conventional realist aesthetics that trade on the conceits of capture, control, clarity, access, and so forth. Why? Simply: the Holocaust itself is significantly apart from all of that. The term "capture," after all, issues from modernity's carceral urges—the broad cultural need for a visual medium that holds things captive and maintains them in pictorial captivity, that imprisons things in seeing, disciplines their appearance and interpretation, arrests time. It seems to me that the Holocaust demands something else, a supple and fallible aesthetics, a photography of dissent from the imprisoning urge, from the fictions of knowability, but also from mystification, and the hallowing of unknowability.

I have deliberately avoided the structuring contrivances of tour-guiding and travel-reenactment, also the idiom of the report, with its "findings" and "conclusions," also the exposé. Instead, rather in the way the Talmud tells us "there is no before and no after in Torah," this book offers a juxtapositional co-occurrence, a simultaneousness of visions. In this book, no site of the genocide is bigger or smaller than any other site. No site eclipses any other site in importance, explains any other site, recuperates any other site—just as no murder supersedes any other one. A bound book by definition fixes its contents into a certain order, but this book's sequence offers no order of importance, and no narrative arc. In fact I would characterize this book as anti-narrative, rejecting the inclination to emplot the spectral character of the Holocaust—the Holocaust as it flashes in and out of memory and comprehension, beyond the reach of storytelling. I venture that "the Holocaust's life as a ghost," as Zygmunt Bauman puts it, shares something with what Thomas Carlyle considers the primal hauntedness of the human psyche. The genocide blinks at the future only in brief intervals, much as we ourselves have glinted into being only for a while, later to flicker back into not-being.

The deeper answer to my artistic problem about the visual remembrance of loss is to make the photograph as image provoke the photograph as picture. The predicament of the photograph as image, as I have suggested, is the tension—the partial alignment, the incommensurability, the pulse of exchange—between what we see within the photograph and what we can say in response. We have no precise word for this tension. If I were to invent one, it would mean "the visual equivalence of silence" (why, I ask, is it only with regard to sound that we have a word for silence?). It seems plain to me as a photographer that the imagistic dimension of photographs, their status as activated silence, constantly troubles the capturing urge: with whatever subtlety, exactitude, or grace photographs describe the appearance of things, they tell exactly nothing about their meanings. And I would argue that this silence is binding, a situation of primary lack in photography that generates a powerful compensatory response—as stories, research, captions, tags, all manner of appendages in language. But this lack can also be accepted on its own terms, and directed toward a subject—the Holocaust is one example—that is itself significantly made of withdrawnness, unthinkability, dissociation from presence. And so photographs as pictures and images: where the photograph as picture will offer proof, the photograph as image will offer inference. Where the photograph as picture will proclaim presence, the photograph as image will test not-fully-intact presence against absence not altogether impalpable. Where the photograph as picture will serve as a time capsule, seeking revenge on time, the photograph as image will send a small signal from the catastrophe dislocated in time—small but enough to startle remembrance. Where the photograph as picture will serve geolocations and news, the photograph as image will make the known world go missing, riddling the earth with worldlessness. Where the photograph as picture will point beyond itself toward the world in history, the photograph as image will condense destroyedness into aliveness, and precipitate remembrance from the nothing.

It seems right to describe something of the way I made these photographs. My tool is a large format view camera, similar to designs common in the nineteenth century, which accepts cut sheets of film 4x5 inches in size. The camera is entirely manual and in one sense, simple: it has no internal mirror, no prism, no electronics, rather it is a light-tight box with a lens on one end and a ground glass on the other. The lens combines the shutter and the aperture, with glass elements mounted on either side. When the photographer opens the lens at the front, light enters the camera and throws an image onto the ground glass at the rear, and generally you have to drape a cloth over your head so that the image on the ground glass appears more clearly and brightly. The image on the ground glass is upside-down and left-to-right reversed, which is to say in the pure form that occurs when light passes through an aperture. One of the view camera's defining features is the bellows that sit between the lens and the film plane. The bellows allows a wide range of movements to be applied to both (and these movements have specific names: tilt and swing, rise and fall, side to side shift, collectively sometimes called "tilt-shift"), resulting in an extraordinary degree of plastic control over the image.

To describe these effects in brief: introducing movements to the film plane changes the drawing of the image, for example rectangles can become trapezoids and vice versa, circles can morph into ovals, isosceles triangles can be pressed into scalene triangles, and so forth (I am speaking broadly—there is no vocabulary for the changes in drawing to non-simple shapes). Introducing movements to the position of the lens changes the direction of the focal corridor, so that it can run in any orientation through space, and not just parallel to the film plane as in non-bellows cameras. And there are further variables that lend important nuance, specifically concerning the choice of lens. English has borrowed from Japanese the word bokeh to refer to the visual quality of out-of-focus things, and bokeh is an important variable that changes from aperture to aperture on a given lens, and from lens to lens depending on the number, shape, and coating of the lens elements. Older lenses have significantly different bokeh than newer ones—most of these photographs were made with antique lenses. When working with tilt-shift aesthetics, especially with wide apertures, there are many varieties of transition between the corridor of sharpness and the zone of unsharpness, depending on the precise angle of the tilt or swing—something I call the lens's "drop-off." Also there are special optical phenomena as things proceed to blackness at the edge of the image circle, the "event horizon" in my lexicon. All of this is on top of the normal variables of depth of field and differential focus, time of exposure and the predictable or unpredictable effects of motion, plus the normal variables of composition and design, and the interpretation of three-dimensional actualities into two.

The result is an intensely dynamic photographic situation. I would say that three things characterize the process of photographing with this kind of camera. First, it is cumbersome, and slow: the camera, film holders, lenses, and tripod are heavy to carry, and a full twelve-hour day of work will yield perhaps twenty negatives. Second, the process is inherently contemplative. The glowing image on the ground glass is a remarkable thing to see, captivating to the point of entrancing, and leads organically to what I can best call dwelling—dwelling in the camera's image, lingering over it. Third, the process is resistant to the common photographic practice of picture pre-visualization. To the extent that a photographer looks at the world, forms a mental image of a photograph, and uses the camera to execute that vision into existence as a more or less interesting copy, with the view camera, pre-visualization can be all but impossible, replaced by a very different kind of discovery.

In each of the photographs here, a corridor of focus runs through an inchoate visual field— cuts through it, in a sense wounds it, and through that wounding allows recognition and a certain kind of naming. What I want from each photograph is an interchange of sharpness and blur, specificity and ambiguity, contraction and release—which is likewise a vibrational interference between seeing and knowing, remembering and not comprehending, intuiting absence within presence and vice-versa. And what I want from each photograph is a place and an occasion in which this phenomenon can be felt directly, in and as itself. There is no word in English that means "a lingering response to an insoluble contradiction" or "immersive experience in the art of the lapse" or "an experience of mourning occasioned by a positive thing offsetting a negative one," or "silence given energy as vision," but Polish has a word for the consciousness that such practices induce: *tęsknota*, longing touched with grief, an aching for something *else* to be true mixed with the heartsink of what is unavoidably true. Even this word, though, is not quite right, inasmuch as it connotes nostalgia, and lacks the elements of volatility and unpredictability also at play.

Oy, so here I am, יננה, struggling to distill my artistic tasks into sentences. No: I cannot say my photographs "while standing on one foot," in the style of Hillel. But am I at liberty not to put to myself this question: "What would success in these photographs be?" And I would answer, "Simply: they should be beautiful and enigmatic. But their beauty should be averse to the beautiful, and their enigma should shun the enigmatic. In their beauty and enigma, they should be discontented in both. And it is not enough that they be beautiful and enigmatic *and* discontented. Their beauty and enigma and discontent should somehow all have equal pull, in opposing directions, so that they cancel each other out, leaving…nothing. If they accomplish that nothing, they might be successful." I answer myself further, remembering my teacher Sidney Morgenbesser: "Jason, if you do accomplish that nothing, will you still be complaining?"

***

Of the book that arrived, there is a para-book—in the form of my notebooks, written by hand and containing research and reading notes, conversations and maps, also dreams and speculations. I began to write these notebooks from the time I returned to eastern Europe in the summer of 2010 through the subsequent decade in which this book came to me. From the para-book, many separate works have spun themselves off, in different ways interrogating the contemporary geography of the Jewish past—some as photographic works, some as written essays, some as experimental texts in combinations of words and pictures, some as experimental film works, some as drawings, some as site-specific installations, some as performance works, some as activist interventions. I have understood all of these works as necessary for this book, which integrates them but does not attempt to recapitulate them. The para-book tracks the process by which I figured out what this book needed to be on its own terms.

And from the para-book I can reconstruct the journeying that this book has required of me—journeying I funded through small grants and fellowships and arrangements for leaves of absence from teaching. I am not a wealthy person, but what I lack in money I make up for in determination and resourcefulness, and my travels depended greatly on the generosity of many people I came to know. These journeys took shape essentially in two phases. From 2010 to 2015, my work grew roots in the historical province of Galicia, today divided between southeastern Poland and western Ukraine. Galicia's two main cities—Kraków on the Polish side of the border, Lviv on the Ukrainian side—became my anchors. In these years, my travels extended west to Berlin and east to Kharkiv, marking the west-east fathom of the book's geography. From 2016 to 2019, my journeys came to mark out the north-south fathom, which extends from Riga to Bucharest—and if not for the coronavirus pandemic that broke out in 2020, it would have continued to grow. Altogether, I worked in over three hundred towns and places between 2010 and 2019, many of them multiple times. A list of them is included as an appendix—a general list that does not include the often multiple locations within each location.

The map at the end of this book shows in red the extent of German-occupied Europe during the Second World War, on top of which is the overall footprint containing the sites where I worked. The territory of my work defines the Holocaust's epicenter: roughly the eastern half is the area of the so-called Holocaust by Bullets, where Jews were massacred by firing squads in or near the places where they lived, and the western half is the area of the so-called Holocaust by Gas, characterized by mass murder in industrially designed and operated death factories.

At one time I intended that I should dissolve the distinction between the book and the para-book—that the fragmentariness of the para-book should be allowed to riddle whatever refinement of insight or technique the book may attempt to display—lest the images defeat their own purpose, and substitute visual pleasure for challenge-given-visually. And though I do not subscribe to a simple antinomy between aesthetic allure and ethical seriousness, it remains very possible that the book remains in need of its para-book as a partner, not a precursor. Maybe it is even likely that the para-book in its unmanageability holds the key to the book's integrity, without which the book fails badly—and with which it possibly fails well. (Strictly speaking this book *must* fail: the question is the insight unloosened when the half-presence of history meets the half-presence of memory in images of half-ugly beauty and half-incoherent clarity.) Ultimately, however, the para-book must contract if the book itself is to exist: the book is created in the para-book's withdrawal. A handful of the para-book's entries will have to be enough.

From the para-book / 1:

in the interwar period, the 2,000 jews of krasnystaw comprised 20% of the population, a smaller proportion than in other towns in the lublin region, and with their shops lining the main square, krasnystaw's jews were nothing if not typical—a polish resident of the town remembered: "feldman had a board yard, zung—bottling plants, stucajger—a shop with leather and tailor's products, karp—a fishing tackle shop, rajchman—a shoe shop for the elites, and pinker and goldstein—bakeries, lewkowicz owned a tailor's shop, zontag—a photographer's workshop, zunger sold sweets and drinks, erenstein opened a grocery shop with alcohol, and fleszer traded in knick-knacks, a textile shop belonged to Halpern, and another photographer's workshop belonged to mandeltort, and the wealthiest were those who ran mills—szymon lejba owned a steam mill where he employed 11 workers"—but krasnystaw's greatest native son must be szmul zygielbojm, a leader of the jewish labor bund after the first world war, a member of the polish government in exile in london after 1942, and one of the most vocal advocates of allied intervention into the jewish genocide during the war—on 12 may 1943, reeling from the news of the crushed warsaw ghetto uprising, zygielbojm chose to kill himself in an act of ultimate dissent—in his suicide letter, he writes: "the responsibility for the crime of the murder of the jewish people in poland rests first of all on those who are carrying it out, but indirectly it falls also upon the whole of humanity, on the peoples of the allied nations and on their governments, who up to this day have not taken any real steps to halt this crime. by looking passively on this murder of defenseless millions of tortured children, women and men, they have become partners to the crime. i cannot continue to live and to be silent while the remnants of polish jewry, whose representative i am, are dying.... by my death, i express my most profound protest against the inaction in which the world watches and permits the destruction of the jewish people"—and of his krasnystaw today, only the shell of their plain, understated synagogue exists, to be contemplated and photographed, as i did today—

From the para-book / 2:

it is difficult to determine the number of zamość jews who survived the war—the zamość yizkor book reports the number to be 50, but other sources claim 224, 152, and 5, from a prewar population of over 10,000—what had been about half of the town—one of the survivors was hersz griner, a boy of eight years when the war began in 1939—from a highly religious family that subsisted on a modest income from the sale of wood and coal, griner lived in the historically jewish quarter near the main zamość synagogue—the one i have photographed several times—and following the german occupation of the town in september 1939, griner and his family were subjected to a kaleidoscopic series of horrors, all manner of humilia-tion, torture, hunger, and illness—his father nearly died after being violently thrown from a horse that was whipped and beaten to the point of frenzy, this in a "parade" of several such horses that the SS forcibly mounted with terrified jewish "riders"—meanwhile griner's mother became deathly sick, and in the spring of 1942, he and his family were relocated to the zamość ghetto, where his father was abruptly disappeared, and the family managed to avoid deportation through hiding, until being rounded up and forced on a death march to the camp at izbica in the fall of 1942—there, at the izbica camp, which was the camp that jan karski describes in his book story of a secret state, *thinking it was bełżec, and which karski also describes toward the end of claude lanzmann's* shoah, *in what i think is the most riveting part of that film—it was in the izbica camp that griner's mother and sister were murdered—griner spent the remaining years of the war as an orphan living by his wits in and around izbica and zamość—at one point he received assistance from another jewish orphan who provided him with false identity papers, including catholic birth and baptismal certificates, and these papers proved crucial to his survival, allowing him to navigate a way through the charity of catholic poles, notwithstanding several brushes with betrayal—at the conclusion of the war, with his family murdered, griner fully adopted his false identity, and was officially baptized, and in the late 1950s, he was ordained a priest, becoming father jakub pawłowski—but in 1970, still not reconciled to his life in postwar poland, he emigrated to israel, only to face a different confrontation with being both a catholic and a jew—in old age, he set up a holocaust memorial in izbica, in the cemetery where 4,000 jews of izbica were murdered, beside whose mass graves he prepared a grave for himself, its stone waiting for him with the words, "he returned to his people..."—*

From the para-book / 3:

the record of jewish settlement in hrubieszów dates to 1440, and by the turn of the twentieth century the jewish community formed half the town's population, and were deeply integrated into its commercial, cultural, political, and social lifeworld—during september 1939, the first month of the war, hrubieszów was occupied by the soviet army, which then yielded control to the germans, following the molotov-ribbentrop pact—and in that month, around 1,400 hru-bieszów jews went eastward into the soviet union, among them chaim zajdman, a gristmill operator—as the soviet army began its withdrawal, zajdman made the prescient decision to return to hrubieszów in order to take his wife and two young daughters into soviet ter-ritory—failing to persuade his relatives to accompany them, zajdman and his family trailed the red army with a farm cart and a horse, finally reaching kyiv after an extremely arduous journey—in kyiv, zajdman managed to secure a job in a gristmill far to the east, in agryz, tatarstan, over a thousand miles from hrubieszów, and in agryz his family survived the war—back in hrubieszów, the germans established a ghetto that swelled to 10,000 jews, including people relocated from częstochowa, mielec, kraków, and other cities—in the summer and fall of 1942, the germans emptied the ghetto in a series of massacres in the town cemetery, plus deportations to the sobibór death camp and the budzyń labor camp, leaving a rump population to work as slave laborers, who were massacred in september 1943—the red army liberated hrubieszów in july 1944, and in 1946, the zajdman family returned to poland, to find of jewish hrubieszów nothing, who can say whether the same nothing i photographed or a different nothing?—

From the para-book / 4:

the killing complex at maly trascianiec, twelve kilometers from minsk in belarus, operated from the spring of 1942 until the soviet liberation in the summer of 1944, and was the largest german camp in the former soviet union—between 60,000 and 200,000 people were murdered there, including tens of thousands from western europe, and from the minsk ghetto—most of the murders occurred by firing squad in the blahauščyna forest at the perimeter of the camp, but mobile gas chambers of the kind used at chełmno were also used, making the camp an unusual fusion of the holocaust by bullets and by gas, as if a microcosm of the whole—from late 1943, jewish slave laborers began to destroy the camp's structures, and to exhume and burn the rotting corpses, as part of the german effort to eliminate the evidence of mass mur-der—the last mass killing occurred three days before red army liberated minsk in june 1944, when 6,500 jewish slave laborers and prisoners were forced into a barn on the site, and then burned alive—since 2015, the belarusian government has created a memorial complex at the site of the camp, extending several kilometers, annotating it with the placards at various loca-tions in the campscape, which induce a conceptual relay between text and remnant, erasure and disclosure—i do not know how to describe the quality of putrid consciousness that the camp unleashes, except to say that it is impossible to "know" such a place even vaguely, which is true of all the murder sites i have spent time with, but especially the "major" sites (aus-chwitz, treblinka, bełżec, sobibór, chełmno, majdanek, maly trascianiec, janowska, płaszów, ponary, rumbala, skarżysko-kamienna, babi yar)—and whatever "sensitivity" means, it pivots on a double alienation: the site's own alienness, and our own alienation from anything like controlling knowledge—the doomed geography of maly trascianiec retains the power to burn through remembrance: the nothing it sustains keeps undoing itself from my grasp, returning me to what i can only call a sense of hereness, of being-present, though a presence chastened, incoherent to itself—

From the para-book / 5:

mass murder and genocide are related but not identical phenomena: the coordinated killing of large numbers of people may occur without the intent to destroy every last member of a group—to cause an entire people to "disappear from the face of the earth," in the words of heinrich himmler—the five million poles, russians, ukrainians, and prisoners of other nation-alities killed by nazi brutality were victims of mass murder, but not genocide—in this sense it is the smaller murderous actions that distinguish genocide, in the case of the nazis, the fanatical desire to capture and kill every jew from every hiding place—the story of leon kamm, a survivor from dąbrowa tarnowska, gives a glimpse of what the fanaticism of the nazi hunt looked like—lamm's father was in the horse-trading business, enjoying close relations with many non-jewish poles, and the family lived in a small brick house near the main synagogue— the night before the first roundup in occupied dąbrowa tarnowska in 1940, kamm's father received a tip from a polish policeman, and was able to hide with non-jewish friends he knew in neighboring villages—after returning to dąbrowa tarnowska, kamm's father worked out an arrangement with a peasant in a village just north of town, who agreed to let him build an underground bunker—on july 1942, the nazis moved to seal the ghetto in dąbrowa tarnowska, and once again the kamm family received early warning, allowing them to escape to their prepared hiding place, where they stayed until late 1942, paying the peasant family for their needs—at the end of 1942, the nazis began scouring the villages looking for hidden jews, and the kamm family decided to go to the city of tarnów, where they managed to sneak into the ghetto—in september 1943, the germans resumed deportation of jews in tarnów to the death camp at bełżec—leon and his father hid in several places, including an abandoned garret and a chicken coop, somehow evading capture, but leon's mother and sister were killed in the roundups—days later, the surviving kamms bribed a ukrainian guard to leave tarnów and made their way by night back to their village bunker, where they survived until liberation—

From the para-book / 6:

among the non-jews to whom the state of israel has awarded the medal of "righteous among the nations" for acting to save jews during the holocaust, more than 6,000 are poles, the highest count among any european country, comprising over 25% of the total number of awards—and to put this number in context: punishment of poles for aiding jews was the most draconian in all of nazi-occupied europe: immediate death to all members of a household for hiding jews, giving them lodging or a ride, feeding them or selling them food, or helping them "in any way," in the words of the nazi posters hung in every town—in a time of acute shortage and fear, the nazis incentivized polish jew-hunting with cash rewards, and it was easy for many poles to covet the property of their jewish neighbors whom they knew were marked for death, significantly heightening the risk of poles who wished to aid jews—precisely because of these complica-tions, the numbers of poles who helped their jewish neighbors are difficult to estimate—in a situation in which complete secrecy was next to impossible, the bravest and most active rescuers were cocooned by rings of others who protected them in small, quiet ways, and who knows how many hundreds of thousands of people comprised the silent guardians of the polish rescuers—i think it is fair to say that just as no jew was free from the heinous threat of betrayal by non-jews, no jew who survived did so alone, without the help of non-jews—i am thinking, for example, of a story from the town of frampol in poland, about a pole named stanisław sobczak, who saved twelve jews—sobczak hid them in the cellar of his barn, daily bringing them food and disposing of their excrement—at one point he was fingered by a neighbor with whom he had been on poor relations for years, arrested and tortured for several days, an experience that did not shake his conviction to rescue the persecuted—at another point, a squadron of germans actually quartered in his barn, directly above the hidden jews, and sobczak figured out a way to continue to visit and serve them—for over two years the jews stayed with him, until he advised them to flee at the end of the war, when the germans were burning houses and barns in their retreat—the fleeing jews had the bad luck to encounter a band of anti-jewish partisans of the polish underground resistance (the armia krajowa), who killed some and robbed all of them, and then proceeded to find and beat sobczak almost to death, and rob him of his horse, his wagon, his pigs, and whatever else they could carry—and the center of jewish frampol today is the decimated jewish cemetery, whose mass graves hold the remains of about 1,000 jews— today while photographing there neighbors told me that in 2008, american jews arrived in town to place stone markers and chains around three depressions in the cemetery earth—they went about this work aloofly, without speaking to anyone in the town, as if local poles deserved to be considered jew-hating and ignorant, and the result was that they missed what the neighbors identified as a fourth mass grave, by far the largest, whose existence was a memory they collectively kept—

From the para-book / 7:

the yizkor book of biecz, poland, tells the story of an officer of the austrian gendarmerie who came to the town in 1895—everyone assumed he was a christian, until one saturday morning, he mounted the steps to the rabbi's apartment above the synagogue and knocked on the door, and asked to join shabbat prayers, and from that point he became a regular guest of the rabbi at his home—not long after his arrival, a peasant uprising erupted in the region, fueled the anti-jewish political right, and it became known that a mob would arrive in biecz on a tuesday—the market day—and for days in advance there was little travel, because the roads were considered dangerous, and the community's telegraphs for help went unanswered—on monday evening a polish mob of about 3,000 could be seen gathering on the hills outside town, armed with spades, pitchforks and axes—at dawn on tuesday, as the jews hid in their cellars and the town braced for violence, the jewish policeman went out alone to face the throng, having told no one in advance—standing before them, he removed his gun and began firing into the air, and assuming that he was the vanguard of a police crackdown, the crowd became terrified and completely dispersed—as it turned out, the army had in fact planned to intervene, although deliberately late so as to be seen as "saviors" from the already-begun looting and violence—foiling both the mob's and the army's plans, the jewish policeman's courage and initiative cost him his career—he was rapidly dismissed from service—all of which presages what did not happen thirty five years later, at the time of the german occupation, when no elijah appeared, and all but a handful of the 1,300 jews in biecz were murdered in massacres in the town, and deportations to work camps, and at the death camp at bełżec—a handful made their way back to town in the months after liberation, and again no elijah appeared to intervene in the postwar fear, chaos, and volatility, which tipped at one point into an anti-jewish riot in which a polish mob targeted three of the last jews of biecz, and murdered them—

From the para-book / 8:

a dream: i am in a forest making my way to a mass grave, which i understand to be the one in the dąbry forest near rzepiennik strzyżewski in southern poland—i am walking through the forest with a local who is teaching me the way to the grave, and his instruction is to follow a particular dirt track until you reach the first shovel nailed to a tree, which then shows a path marked by other shovels nailed to trees—and this image i am certain derives from something i saw the first time i went there, an actual rusted shovel head nailed to a tree at the height of a human head, likely the very steel used to dig the mass grave, uncovered at some point by a local person—and in the dream we follow the trail of shovels hung on trees until we reach the mass grave—in the dream, as in life, a concrete slab covers the grave, coarsely mixed and roughly set, now chipped and stained and partly moss-covered—and in the dream, as in life, the local people who made the slab pressed small stones into the concrete before it dried, to form the number "364," the number of victims, this is what they knew, perhaps all they knew— and the dream is of this number, whose stones acquire a kind of pulse and physical dilation, and i feel myself to be in the presence of some great insight—i woke up and scribbled some words into my notebook, words the dream gave me—and today i find them strange and almost indecipherable: "oneness minus one"—i cannot quite retrieve the dream that would explain them, but i can partially reconstruct the logic of the dream: the number 364 is the number for a complete year minus one of its days, the whole kept from completeness, the whole punctured and drained to gone, oneness minus one—

From the para-book / 9:

the town of șimleu silvaniei in romania was known in hungarian as szilágysomlyó, and its jews arrived only in the mid-eighteenth century, by 1940 becoming a modest community of 1,500 people, about 15% of the population—and the story was similar in surrounding sălaj county, whose small jewish communities together came to about 14,000 people—and like other jewish communities in wartime hungary, the jews of șimleu silvaniei and the region managed mostly to survive until the german occupation of the country in march 1944—in april 1944, about 8,000 jews were confined to a ghetto created in a brickyard in the village of cehei (in hungarian, somlyócsehi), about five kilometers from șimleu silvaniei—the ghetto was designed to exist for a handful of weeks, to starve and torture its prisoners while keeping them barely alive, in advance of their deportation to auschwitz-birkenau—and this is precisely what happened: three transports left the cehei ghetto for auschwitz between 31 may and 6 june 1944, carrying a total of 7,851 people, who were among the 145 trainloads carrying 435,000 hungarian jews that summer to german death camps, mostly auschwitz, where 80% of them were gassed on arrival—surely the darkest months in the eighteen centuries of jewish life in hungary—and it has taken me the better part of a day to find the place of the short-lived ghetto at cehei, beginning at the northern transylvania holocaust memorial museum, located in the synagogue of șimleu silvaniei, which is closed when i arrive there, but i manage to get hold of its care-taker through calling the numbers written on the door, and he comes especially for me and opens the building, which recalls for me positively repurposed synagogues across lithuania and poland except that this one has been stabilized but not renovated, and its non-renovation is like a muscle exercising me through time, the sheer force of its color-absorptive browns and ochres in its high-ceilinged light makes my body nearly sway—i study the displays carefully and i re-photograph the coarse blow-ups of snapshots of school groups doing commemorative work in the area in previous years, one of them showing a group of children at the entrance to the cehei site—the caretaker can only approximately describe to me where it is located, and when i reach the place he has directed me to, i go in loops and circles, finding no signs or markers at all—the site is near a local train station, which is closed and empty, and i stand around for some time in directionless waiting—when a truck drives by, i jump to hail it, and me—a foreigner who does not know romanian, speaking in a mashed potato of french and spanish, i must be about the last person the driver expects to meet—he struggles to grasp my purposes until i show him the snapshot of the children from the museum, which he studies before walking me a kilometer or so to a particular location, where the sign in the snapshot marking the ghetto's location no longer exists, but he points out the angle of the dirt road and of the hillsides in the picture, and indeed these are a precise match for what we can see where we stand—i spend a few hours kicking through the site, which is a storage area for piping and tubing and industrial building supplies, also doubling as a dump for rusting machinery not yet gone to scrap, all of it unreconcilable to whatever exists under the rind of appearances— this is the familiar dissociative state of the geography of genocide—and the cehei before me joins eventually with inner visions from the other end of the train line, a particular corner of auschwitz-birkenau: at the edge of the camp, among stands of birch trees almost from the landscape of life, small ponds jump with frogs and twitch with mosquitoes, touched by spirits in sad flight—in the summer of 1944 and in the remaining six months of the camp's operation, the killing rate was so furious that its four crematoria could not handle the volume of bodies to be incinerated, and victims were burned in massive open-air pyres among the birch trees, their ashes then dumped in these ponds, those ashes almost discernible in the pulver-thickness of the way the water moves in wind and the twitching of frogs—and cehei's rusty engines dock with the ash-lagoons to make a particular countersign of the nothing—

From the para-book / 10:

a dream: i am walking through the countryside in volyn in western ukraine with A., some-where in the vicinity of the mass grave outside liuboml—she is walking ahead of me, quickly and impatiently, and doubts it can be found, and i am going slowly and deliberately, certain it can be—suddenly her impatience turns to eagerness and she disappears over a hill, and my deliberateness turns downcast—i feel the futility of a search for a place of futility, and the strangeness of my preoccupations flashes forward—then a large and wild blackberry bush appears, full of fruit and thorns, a growth of blackberries unlike any i have ever seen—its size is a function of my own proximity to it: each step i take toward it makes it grow bigger and thicker, and each step away shrinks it—when finally i am standing next to it, it dwarfs my own body, and as i step into its jungle, i see the marker for the mass grave appear, coiled in blackberry vines—i step toward the marker, and suddenly A. stops me from behind—as if it were not obvious, i ask her whether this is the massacre site, and she says it is well known that blackberry bushes grow on top of massacre pits—i ask her how she knows this, and she looks hard into my eyes and says, "for the sake of god's truth i have to tell you the earth's truth"—and puts a blackberry into my mouth—

From the para-book / 11:

a dream: i see myself after my death, me in the realm where my afterbody soul must cope with my choices, my actions during this lifetime—i am standing on the bridge that crosses the river near sławków, where the germans ambushed a caravan of jews trying to return home in the early days of the war, shooting them into the river below—i am on that bridge with the big camera, not knowing where to find the picture, on the side with the view in the direction of the river's current or against it—when i come out from under the dark cloth there is a procession approaching me, and suddenly it is not for me to photograph—i am greeting them one by one, they are the souls from all the mass graves and the murder sites i've stood before—for every kaddish i've said, i meet the dead of that place, each one, each approaches slowly and i spend eons in greeting, and the tears are tears of reunion, the tears of grief i'm not capable of now—

From the para-book / 12:

in a dream, i am at a jewish gathering i do not understand—ultra-religious jews doing things i do not understand—reciting texts, meditating, reading aloud, sitting in circles, prostrating afterwards—an older white-haired man with a friendly face tells me a secret technique of remembering, as if an ancient insight, a confession to me, something widely practiced in his religious community, a jewish wisdom technique i should know—he tells me that the way to complete remembrance is to begin to write descriptive thoughts, as they come, in whatever sentences or fragments arise in the mind, and then to note the pauses, the gaps, where the sentences end and break off—because, he says, these gaps are just as important a part of the remembering as the named somethings—and he says that i should write these pauses or ends with a dash, in a column beside the sentences, a dash for every time a pause happens in the act of recollection, and a dash for every completed statement before the next one arises—and if i do this, i will be left with two columns, two tablets, one of words and one of dashes, and these together are memory—and he tells me about a friend who has recently died, a writer, and we begin the exercise with his friend in his mind—he gives me paper and a pen, though i myself never knew his friend—but it turns out that he has never actually done any of this before, that he's just an admirer of it, maybe an admirer from a distance—and he confesses its extreme difficulty as he takes back the pen and tries to demonstrate it for me—and he does not actually demonstrate it—rather he sits before the empty paper—

From the para-book / 13:

with A. i have returned to sharhorod for the first time since 2001, and immediately i want to find out about klara kurman, who i met and photographed that year—she was 71 that summer, had lived in sharhorod all her life, had survived the holocaust in the sharhorod ghetto—and i can still see her sitting on her front steps, peeling garlic, among the last jews still living in a town whose population had been three-quarters jewish for two hundred years before the war, and a quarter jewish even at the end of the soviet period—A. and i start asking about her, and learn that she has been dead for some years already, one person said five, another eight—and when we reach her house, it is obviously abandoned, closed up and the garden overgrown—with some trepidation we walk up the front steps and pull open her front door, to find the interior completely decimated—thieves have taken everything, down to the floorboards, and it is as if it were the same story as the cemetery of my ancestors in mena or romny or orhei or chişinău or the hundreds of raped jewish cemeteries i have since visited in other towns and cities of yiddish-land—what am i to do with the returning feeling of loss compounding loss, of klara's own heaviness of spirit now sedimented in the dirt and emptiness that remains of her home— klara: you survived the genocide and lived to an old age, after which the consequences of the genocide savaged the evidence of your life—what photographs can i make that combine blind premonition with uncomprehending aftermath?—

From the para-book / 14:

i first learned about liepāja from the photographs: lines of jews on the sands of the baltic sea, standing posed before crowds of people, standing above the pits into which they would fall, facing the camera, facing away from the camera, corpses piling up in the pits, riflemen stepping through the mounds of bodies delivering final bullets to those who fell without quite dying— which is to say each step in the process, the victims before, during, and after execution—i know of no other perpetrator-made visual document so replete, even as it is also partial, for example the perpetrators who appear are latvian collaborators, not germans, and we do not see either the regimen of the killers' actions, or their drinking and camaraderie—but in contrast to places where the murdering was concealed, emblematically i think of sobibór, the fact of such open photographing on the sands of šķēde beach indicates a public event or at least semi-public, perhaps not in the initial massacres there in the summer of 1941, but most likely so by the time of the largest massacres in mid-december 1941, when some 3,000 people were murdered in three days—the world sees these photographs because of a liepāja jew by the name of david zivcon, an electrician who while making a repair at the liepāja german security police headquarters, discovered the negatives by accident and stole them, had a jewish photographer by the name of meir stein print them, and hid the prints in a tin box behind a brick in the wall of the security police horse stables—the next year zivcon was given hiding along with eleven other jews in the home of two righteous latvian gentiles, robert and johanna seduls, who constructed a basement bunker with bricks from the destroyed liepāja synagogue—zivcon survived and retrieved the photographs, which were part of the evidence entered at nuremberg—it is the pictures that moved me to travel to liepāja, and when i reach the beach it is late afternoon on a day of clear skies, unlike the ashen skies of the photographs, and what reaches forward to grab me is what the photographs all but conceal: the nearness of the sea, the littoral position of the nothing in this place, the nothing as if on the cusp of the infinitude that the ocean stands for—unlike the other places intensified in loss, where loss (paradoxically) accumulates, at liepāja the nothing faces the infinity horizon—and a detail from the accounts of the massacres returns to me: the victims stood on the ocean side of the pits and did not face their executioners, which is to say that it was this ocean they saw at the moment of death, this ocean or dissolution—

From the para-book / 15:

there has been unusual activity at the lontskoho prison at the corner of kopernika and bandery streets in lviv—the prison: an abject place, originally constructed in the late nineteenth century for the austrian gendarmerie, it was a place of repression, torture, and murder first for the (reestablished) polish state of the interwar period, then the soviets from 1939 to 1941, then the germans from 1941 to 1944, then the soviets again from 1944 to 1991, and continuing into the period of independent ukraine from 1991 until it was closed in 1996—in 2009, it opened as the "national memorial museum prison on lontskoho street," essentially a political shrine to ukrainian nationalists imprisoned by the soviet secret police, which is to say a museum of highly tendentious historical memory—in particular, the museum trades on a compromise of silence over the holocaust: there is no mention whatsoever that ukrainian nationalists were key participants in the huge pogrom that the german orchestrated upon entering the city in june 1941— to carry out the holocaust in occupied poland and ukraine, the germans relied heavily on ukrainian nationalist militias, which hoped their cooperation would earn them german support for ukrainian independence—and so while ukrainian and polish mobs robbed, raped, beat, and tortured jews in the streets of lviv in a carnival-like atmosphere, ukrainian nationalist militias forced abducted jews to exhume the bodies of some 4,000 soviet political prisoners murdered by the retreating soviets at the city's prisons, including at lontskoho—following the exhumations, ukrainian militias shot these jews into pits in the prison's central yard—they were among the 4,000 to 7,000 jews murdered across the city in the pogrom—the activity in the prison yard is a forensic dig, and i go to see it, returning each day for a week: by the end of the first day, two large holes have been created with bulldozers, and by the next day, one hole has already been filled in and the second expanded, and the next day the second hole has been filled in and a third begun, and so on in a rapid opening-up and packing-back-down of the earth—it is not an archaeological dig by any professional protocol: no systematic measurements are taken, and no geo-location system is in use—but a great quantity of human remains are uncovered, intact skeletons emerge, which are photographed before being pulled apart and thrown into unmarked bags and bins, as if human remains were like any other artifacts found in the pits, including for example boots still clinging to the skeletons' feet—after a few days, television cameras arrive, and the authorities hold press conferences, asserting in grave tones that the bones belong to ukrainian victims of soviet repression, that they are martyrs of the ukrainian national cause—and i understand why they say this: it is useful and timely to convert the earth of the prison yard into nationalist soil, given the current war between ukraine and russia following russia's illegal 2014 annexation of crimea, a war of attrition that has all but crippled the already weak ukrainian economy—but as an outsider and a jew i cannot see the lontskoho dig this way: though i side with the ukrainians in the current conflict, i cannot launder the ukrainian nationalist movement's participation in the holocaust, or the brutal history of its anti-polish ethnic cleansing—the forensic dig has pulled piles of bones out of the prison yard, but there is no evidence whose bones they are: they might be the bones of ukrainian nationalists but they might just as well be the bones of jews those nationalists murdered, or poles the soviets murdered, or soviet prisoners of war—i revolt: no, there is no "national" earth, no—all bones belong to the collective body of the human disfigured by license after license to kill—and at a certain point it is all too much, being there is too much, and my back is gripped by spasms so strong i can hardly stand, and then me: sinking into the turned-over execution dirt, clenched and bent over, weeping at human remains dumped decades ago like garbage, bagged up now for a new politics of enmity—and an image forms in my mind's eye: it was a broken compass that led me here, with a quivering bone shard for a dial, erratically pointing toward each of the cardinal directions of genocide: the known everyone and the anonymous everyone and the targeted everyone and the implicated everyone—

From the para-book / 16:

in a dream, i am in a forest in lithuania—i am tripping over roots in midsummer, the sky heavy in clouds, the tree canopy thick, a dampness in the air—when i reach the holocaust mass grave, it is marked by a memorial stone half hidden in yellow-green moss, strangely lucent, the long grave bed covered in the same moss-glow—i did not see them before, but when i reach the mass grave, i see paths from east and west, crisscrossing from various directions toward this place—until i see no paths, rather balls which i understand to be the paths baled up and put at the base of the trees to mark the site of the mass grave—and in that place my trial begins, i stand accused of a memory crime having to do with my camera, and a secret desire to make hell beautiful—for this crime my sentence is "to be with no further path"—my father appears, wearing his yarmulke and raging, he has been stalking me—he knows to appear when i am psychically cornered—i have been found guilty and my father spews more and more rage at me, and wants me dead—as always i cannot comply, cannot die thoroughly enough, can never be dead enough for him—he rages until we are standing by the mossed-over monument face-to-face, and he produces a gun, points it, shoots me point blank between the eyes—my murder startles me awake—

From the para-book / 17:

i keep returning to the simple point that the "it" changes according to the way we say it: it means one thing to say that the holocaust was the murder of six million people, and something else to say that the holocaust was the murder of one person over and over again, six million times—my attentions keep turning to the smaller and more particular forms of saying—today, again, i followed the incident of 11 June 1942 in olszanica, in which two members of the gestapo, leo homeniuk and johan bäcker, together with a contingent of ukrainian police, marched a group of jews from the town hall to a place beneath a railway bridge just outside of town—the jews had been rounded up from the surrounding hamlets of bóbrka, myczkowce, orelec, rudenka, stefkowa, and wańkowa, and from olszanica itself—the ukrainian brigade had already dug a pit for them—after nightfall, the two gestapo men murdered each victim with a bullet to the head, 132 men, women, and children, one by one—apparently the precise location of the mass grave is lost—the first time i went there, i photographed the bridge, and the next time a local told me that a small marker sits near the site—i looked from afternoon into nightfall, and failed to find that marker—

From the para-book / 18:

from babruysk: to search—after the century of horrors without recompense, to search without catharsis, to search without the delusion called god, who does not listen to the jewish night as you do—to search, to envision your humanity migrating beyond the empirical you, to point the dead toward an in-gathering of their own choosing, perhaps that they should enter new lives facing future, and if so—to search for the name in that day-to-come, though it is better to speak with different pronouns and different metonyms, perhaps those the torah uses, to search for your own heart, your own soul, your own strength—to search, to follow god past the idea of god, past anyone's idea but especially your most trusted teacher's idea, to follow the way of god past someone else's sincerely holy life, in pursuit of your own psyche, where you find: sadness expanding limitlessly, behaving like a universe, and bent toward itself, hanging like a pearl of consolation in a still more mysterious void—to search, to point your own sudden appearance at the gates of the nothing and the aliveness of your curiosity—to search, to accept that the disin-herited self has already been too intensively inherited, and that the discovering self will always be a guest in the house of the disinherited—to search, not to confuse what might console the dead with what might console the unborn, and what might console you, who are in between—to search, to stand against those who answer harshness with harshness except, you discover, in letters secretly written, also in photographs shyly glued into albums—to search, to doze under stars that quiet the road, to sing the kaddish to the sound of a bell falling—to search, to scatter your glances in the chamber of the book, to know a summer treetop in its shimmering, to remember the daytime moon in winter, to give back to god the signs of the still-unreached past and the future without tragedy—to search—

AFTERWORD

Holocaust photography is not like other sorts of photography. The rules, you might say, are different, because the roles are different. How the photographs are viewed, understood, appreciated is in every way nonstandard. Whether or not it's acknowledged, whether or not it's even welcome, there is necessarily a moral-historical dimension to the image, an extra-visual significance. The photographs are markers of memory, are called upon to bear witness (or to serve as a reminder for us to bear witness), are added to the pile labeled "never forget." They are inescapably didactic. The tragedy overwhelms the image, mutes the image—you see what's there but feel, or are supposed to feel, what's not. The photographs are thus on some level functional, instrumental, art in the service of memory and thus maybe less art than a kind of cataloging (or, less generously, a kind of tourism). It is something like memory journalism. (Though the flip side is a built-in vitality, a historical sheen, an imperviousness to most varieties of aesthetic criticism.) What's essential, really, is the caption. The photographs can of course be effective. A pretty picture of an unspeakably horrific place, or rather a pretty picture of a pretty place where an unspeakably horrific act happened, installed above a sober caption—you will feel something, certainly. But what you are feeling might rightly be called an associative horror: the photograph is an arrow, a reminder, a visual injunction to mourn. A postcard of a particularly macabre sort.

Alive and Destroyed is of a different order entirely. This is a transcendental work. The photographs are not merely documents of destruction, and their artfulness is not instrumentalized, is not used to put the tragedy in relief; rather they present an argument-in-images, a startling confrontation of the mandate, burden, and limitations of Holocaust memory.

The photographs are of Holocaust sites but these are not photographs of ruins (though there is ruin) and cannot be reduced to elegies (though there is great sorrow). The subject is the disharmony of the site, the tension between what's there and not there. It is an attempt, as Francisco writes, to "broker presence and absence." Memory is invisible but it has a weight, a shadow, it's dark matter: it cannot be described but perhaps its effects—on the space, on you—can be. The result is disorienting—wide swaths of the photographs are out of focus, the use of tilt-shift confuses your sense of scale—as it must be, our sense-making apparatuses (eyes, intellect, soul) are insufficient. It is our world but warped. It is spectral, it is a memoryscape. The sort of praise an artist dealing with the Holocaust usually receives—communing with what's gone, conveying invisible tragedy, perceiving ghosts, capturing the spillage of horrific past onto placid present, etc.; in short, an ability to unerase time—would be inadequate here. This is not, or is at least not only, a work of memorialization; it's more involved, more demanding. You are implicated: these photographs do not let you off the hook, do not allow you to drily observe. Remembering is not a passive exercise, is not synonymous with "being reminded." These are no postcards and there are no captions. You must struggle to see the unseeable. You will never succeed, but you must struggle nonetheless.

The experience of viewing these photographs approximates to a degree I wouldn't have thought possible the sensation of actually being there, at a not yet memorialized site of atrocity. (Where there's a memorial the memory-language has been established, fixed, and you don't really have a choice but to respond, though ignoring is a type of response.) You cannot see anything but a blank field or a nondescript house or stately forest, and you lean close to hear the whispers, but it is silent, still, and yet you feel it, perhaps; you then wonder if what you feel is in fact the sense of obligation to feel; you breathe, you walk, you admire the beauty; you feel guilty about admiring the beauty; you remind yourself, not for the first time, that beauty is not antagonistic to tragedy; you daydream, you forget for a minute where you are, and then remember, and remind yourself, not for the first time, how easy it was to forget; and you see anew.

The title of this book is *Alive and Destroyed* but the larger project is hardly contained herein and is far more extensive than these 118 photographs. Over the course of almost a decade, Francisco visited more than three hundred locations—nearly all of which have multiple sites—and produced more than three thousand photographs for *Alive and Destroyed*. I don't mean only to give you a sense of the immense curatorial achievement this book represents, but to convey the staggering scope, ambition, and significance of the project as a whole. Here is the construction of a comprehensive memoryscape, one that is meticulous and granular, that maps 1:1 to history, that is vast and hyperlocal, sweeping and particular. Such a project is, of course, impossible, Borgesian, could not be completed in a lifetime, or even several lifetimes—the United States Holocaust Memorial Museum has counted nearly 50,000 sites of atrocity, and is nowhere near done counting. But the unfinishable nature of the project is not accidental, is its essence, for it is a response—an almost unbearably poignant response—to the endlessness of the tragedy.

Lastly, a word about the artist. To conceive, undertake, and commit to such a project demands an extraordinarily rare combination of talent, wisdom, patience, and humility. I consider myself outrageously lucky to have traveled with Jason in Poland and Lithuania, to see up close as he made some of these photographs, as he sought out, inhabited, intuited, captured the space. It is a remarkable thing to behold. The photograph is but the culmination of a process that might take hours or even days; maybe there's a map but maybe not, and even if there is it only takes you so far. You have to find the spot and then the spot within the spot. This work is a testament to Jason's dedication and persistence but really to his instinct, which is without parallel. It's as if the man can smell history, can hear echoes that have long since faded away. Once he has found what he's looking for, he opens his wooden tripod and attaches his antique camera and plants himself where he must, traffic and onlookers be damned. He will stay as long as necessary, schedules be damned. What he's waiting for is something I can't articulate, because it's in a language I don't speak, but few sights have inspired me more, have driven home the responsibility and burden and power of the artist as Jason crouched beneath his floral-print cloth, finger on the cable release, waiting, seeing, being.

—Menachem Kaiser

LOCATIONS

Below is a list of locations where I made photographs for *Alive and Destroyed* between 2010 and 2019, a small fraction of the over 42,500 known sites of the Holocaust. The photographs in this book plus hundreds more not published here comprise the complete project.

Those locations that appear in this book are identified by plate numbers in the list itself. Photographs in the six-way grids are numbered clockwise beginning at the top left. In the list, years indicate separate visits during which I made photographs. Most of these locations contain several sublocations not independently designated.

Toponyms are given in the official languages where places currently exist, except in a handful of cases in which English has its own fixed version (such as Warsaw for Warszawa). For Romanization of Ukrainian, Belarusian, and Russian toponyms, I have followed the standard governmental recommendations of those countries. Thus, I use Lviv, the Ukrainian name for the city, rather than the Polish Lwów, the Russian Lvov, the German Lemberg, or the Yiddish Lemberik. Likewise, I use Moldova, though when my ancestors lived there in the time of the Russian Empire, they knew it as Bessarabia—a name my family in San Francisco never managed to stop using.

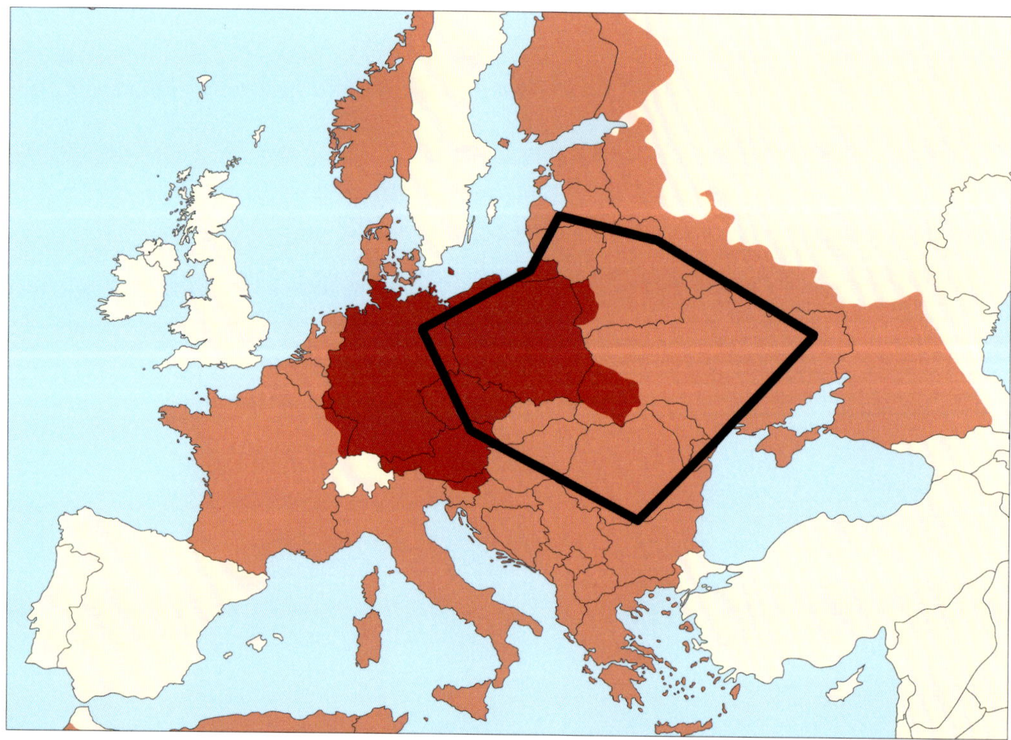

This map shows the extent of German-occupied Europe during the Second World War, on top of which is the overall footprint containing the sites where I worked between 2010 and 2019 for *Alive and Destroyed*. This region was the Holocaust's epicenter. Roughly the eastern half of this zone was the area of the so-called Holocaust by Bullets, and the western half was the area of the so-called Holocaust by Gas.

ACKNOWLEDGMENTS

Over the years that this project took shape, I have had the blessing of the support and generosity, reflection and conversation, experience and expertise of many people. All of them have been integral to the process, each in their own way. It is a separate book to describe their contributions justly. Here I offer my gratitude.

In Poland: Jakub Nowakowski, Tomasz Strug, Piotr Słomian, Larysa Michalska, Edyta Gawron, Roma Sendyka, Erica Lehrer, Tomasz Rzeźwicki, Rafał Sagan z"l, Magda Rubenfeld Koralewska, Michael Rubenfeld, Adam Schorin, Natalia Czarkowska, Uwe von Seltmann, Gabi von Seltmann, Jonathan Webber, Connie Webber, Anna Wencel, Bartosz Wencel, Ruth Ellen Gruber, David Clark, Rachel Lichtenstein, Paul Schneller, Michał Wiśniewski, Wojciech Wilczyk, Jessica Rosenberg, Jonathan Ornstein, Ellen Shapiro, Józef Klimczak, Leszek Allerhand z"l.

Also in Poland: Menachem Kaiser, Maia Ipp, Dara Bramson, Lynn Suh, Krzysztof Czyżewski.

In Ukraine: Vasyl Yuzishin, Renata Kulchytska, Valeriya Solovyeva, Sofia Dyak, Vladyslava Moskalets, Tomasz Jankowski, Anya Chebotariova, Alexander Nazar, Boris Dorfman, Mikhailo Vorobets, Marla Raucher Osborn, Jay Osborn, Yaroslav Hrytsak, Galina Fruman, Vadim Golub.

In Germany: Klaus Illi, Bettina Bürkle, Christian Herrmann, Jennifer Allen, Stefan Kliesch.

In Lithuania: Ugnius Zasimauskas, Audra Čepkauskaitė, Andrew Miksys, Sarah Mitrikė, Edita Gliožerienė.

In Belarus: Asya Gefter, Alexander Litin.

In the United States: Craig Weiss, W. Keith McManus, Mary Catherine Johnson, Faith McClure, Alexander Nemerov, Anna Grimshaw, Eric Goldstein, Matthew Brittingham, Michael David Murphy, Jeff Fort, Susette Min, Jonathan Greenberg, Joel Leivick, William Van Loo, Arthur Kiron, Laurence Salzmann, William Boling, Paul Mueller, Lukas Felzmann, Joel Silverman, Elena Sergeeva, Angelika Bammer, Deborah Lipstadt, Kevin Karnes, Gary Fessenden, Anthony Dominiczak, Frances Flannery, Carlton Mackey, Julia van Helmond, Oskar Czendze, Matthew Bernstein, Michelle Ores, Hope Cohn, Sheila Ruen, Miriam Francisco, Janis Francisco, Michael Francisco.

Also in the United States: The Tam Institute for Jewish Studies at Emory University, the Emory University Research Council, the College Office of Emory College of Arts and Sciences, the Laney Graduate School of Emory University, the Howard Foundation, the Fulbright Scholar Program.

Also in the United States: Michael Itkoff, Ursula Damm, Gabrielle Fastman, and the team at Daylight Books.

And above all, everywhere and in all corners of this work: Asia Fruman.